THE HOUSING BOOM
and BUST

THE HOUSING BOOM

and BUST

Revised Edition

THOMAS SOWELL

BASIC
BOOKS

A Member of the Perseus Books Group
New York

Copyright © 2009 by Thomas Sowell
First published in 2009 by Basic Books,
A Member of the Perseus Books Group
Revised edition published in 2010 by Basic Books

Books published by Basic Books are available at special discounts for
bulk purchases in the United States by corporations, institutions, and
other organizations. For more information, please contact the Special
Markets Department at the Perseus Books Group, 2300 Chestnut Street,
Suite 200, Philadelphia, PA 19103, or call (800) 810-4145, ext. 5000,
or e-mail special.markets@perseusbooks.com.

A CIP catalog record for this book is available
from the Library of Congress.
LCCN: 2009925585
ISBN: 978-0-465-01880-2
Revised Edition ISBN: 978-0-465-01986-1

10 9 8 7 6 5 4 3 2 1

CONTENTS

+ 1ry govt + lack of affordable housing.

121-37 Mkt vr. Govt,

Preface to the Revised Edition

Two financial writers for the *New York Times* summarized the current situation in housing and in the economy this way:

> Real estate, which has traditionally brought the economy out of recession, seems increasingly likely this time to hold it back. The housing market's epic boom early this decade has turned into an epic bust whose effects may take years to shake off.

How we got into this predicament, and whether what is currently being done in Washington is likely to make things better or worse, is the subject of this book.

Usually a revised edition of a book is an occasion for correcting some of the things that were said in the first edition. In this case, however, both the analyses and the inferences in the first edition have since turned out to be painfully accurate, so this new edition will primarily update the economic situation, bringing out new facts that have become available since the first edition last year, and analyzing misguided new policies, promoted by politicians of both parties. Perhaps, instead of a revised edition, this might more aptly be called a "reinforced" edition.

The finger-pointing that almost invariably follows in the wake of any disaster— economic or otherwise— has generated much political rhetoric and spin, much of it repeated in the media and some of it in academia. What is crucial is to separate the facts from the rhetoric, so as to understand what got us where we are. Otherwise, we may needlessly extend or even repeat a national trauma that is hard enough to get through just one time.

How complicated is the problem? The economics of the housing boom and bust are pretty straightforward. The politics of it include a lot of misleading statements, but these can be broken down with the help of facts— and the more facts we look at, the more the rhetoric clears away, like fog evaporating in the sunlight. We may sometimes become disgusted at what we learn when we look at facts, but at least we are no longer confused by political spin.

The great Supreme Court Justice Oliver Wendell Holmes deplored "phrases that serve as an excuse for not thinking" and said, "think things not words." This book will look at things, and try to cut through the words that obscure them.

Thomas Sowell
Hoover Institution
Stanford University

Preface to the First Edition

Scary headlines and scarier statistics tell the story of a financial crisis on a scale not seen in decades— certainly not within the lifetime of most Americans. Moreover, this is a worldwide financial crisis. Financial institutions on both sides of the Atlantic have either collapsed or have been saved from collapse by government bailouts, as a result of buying securities based on American housing values that eroded or evaporated.

This financial tsunami has been followed by a political flood of rhetoric, accompanied by finger-pointing in all directions. Who was really responsible? What set this off?

There was no single, dramatic event that set this off, the way the assassination of the Archduke Ferdinand set off the chain of events that led to the First World War or the way the arrest of political operatives committing burglary at the Watergate Hotel led to the resignation of President Richard Nixon. A whole series of very questionable decisions by many people, in many places, over a period of years, built up the pressures that led to a sudden collapse of the housing market and of financial institutions that began to fall like dominoes as a result of investing in securities based on housing prices.

This book is designed to unravel the tangled threads of that story. It also attempts to determine whether what is being done to deal with the problem is more likely to make things better or worse.

Thomas Sowell
Hoover Institution
Stanford University

ACKNOWLEDGMENTS

As with many of my other books, this book owes much to my two dedicated research assistants, Na Liu and Elizabeth Costa. In addition to their ferreting out and sifting through vast amounts of reading material to find the things that were relevant to this study, Ms. Costa has done the copy-editing and fact-checking, while Ms. Liu has converted my ancient WordPerfect 5.1 word-processing files into the much more complex Quark files from which this book has been directly printed. I am grateful to them both and to the Hoover Institution, whose generosity has made possible the work that we all do. Thanks are also due to Dr. Gerald P. O'Driscoll, a Senior Fellow at the Cato Institute, whose critique of a draft of this book clarified some issues for me and therefore ultimately for the reader. Helpful communications from scholars Peter J. Wallison and Alex J. Pollock of the American Enterprise Institute, and from Professor Lawrence J. White of New York University, clarified some of the puzzling history of securities-rating agencies and the Securities and Exchange Commission's regulation of those agencies, while Peter Schweizer of the Hoover Institution clarified some of the mysteries of federal regulations. Any interpretations or errors can only be my responsibility.

Chapter 1

The Economics of the Housing Boom

Staid *was the last thing you could call mortgage lending during the housing boom.* **Frenzied** *might be a better term; and as the boom became a bubble,* **out of control** *would be even more appropriate.*

Mark Zandi

Few markets have had such a skyrocketing rise, followed immediately by an equally steep plummet to new depths, as the housing market has had in the early years of the twenty-first century. From 2000 to 2005, the median sales price of American single-family homes rose by more than 50 percent, from $143,600 to $219,600. In some places, the rise was even sharper. Over those same years, the median home price in New York rose 79 percent, in Los Angeles 110 percent and in San Diego 127 percent. In coastal California, the rise was especially sharp— and so was the later fall.

Who or what caused the housing boom and bust?

There was no single cause of the housing crisis, and there is certainly plenty of blame to go around, especially among Washington politicians of both parties, who have been strenuously looking for villains outside of Washington. During the housing boom there were some voices of sanity that warned against the risky way things were being done, both in Washington and in Wall Street. However, during that boom, warnings were brushed aside with clever phrases or with pious statements about the benefits of increased home ownership.

When trying to get at the causes of any major social phenomenon, we are likely to find that these causes range across a wide spectrum. The causes of the housing boom and bust have been as general as the flaws and shortcomings of human beings and as specific as the effects of Federal Reserve System policy on interest rates or a change in mortgage loan eligibility standards by the Federal National Mortgage Association ("Fannie Mae") or the Federal Home Loan Mortgage Corporation ("Freddie Mac"). The housing market is greatly affected by interest rates and credit eligibility rules, but there is much more to the story than that.

The record-breaking housing price rises that preceded the record-breaking housing market collapse were not evenly spread across the United States but were heavily concentrated in a relatively few places. Much confusion between local trends and national trends in housing markets contributed to counterproductive government policies. We need to understand what led to both kinds of home price trends during the boom before examining the causes and consequences of the housing bust— and the repercussions that spread, not only across the nation but internationally.

THE CAST OF CHARACTERS

In order to follow the story of the housing boom and bust more easily, it may be worth pausing to briefly note the main cast of characters in the housing markets. While the individual home buyer may deal solely with a bank that provides the money to buy the house, in exchange for a mortgage to be paid off in monthly installments, behind that bank and over that bank are all sorts of other institutions, whose actions affect or control the housing markets.

Among the government agencies regulating various aspects of banking is the *Federal Reserve System*, which also has powers to take actions which affect interest rates and the money supply. Given the great importance of the level of interest rates in the home mortgage markets, the Federal Reserve is a major player in that market, even though that is just one of the markets in which its influence is felt.

The Federal National Mortgage Association (*Fannie Mae*) and the Federal Home Loan Mortgage Corporation (*Freddie Mac*) are two government-created, but privately owned, profit-making enterprises that buy mortgages from banks. By selling these mortgages, banks get money from a 30-year mortgage without having to wait 30 years for monthly payments from home buyers to pay off their debts. With the proceeds from these sales to Fannie Mae or Freddie Mac, or to other financial institutions, the banks then have money to lend again to create more mortgages from which to profit.

More than two-thirds of the mortgages made in 2004, for example, were resold to some other financial institution, including Fannie Mae and Freddie Mac. These two government-sponsored enterprises bought more than one-third of all the mortgages in the nation that were resold by the original lenders. In order to qualify to sell their mortgages to Fannie Mae or Freddie Mac, banks must conform to the rules and standards prescribed by these mortgage market giants, including rules and standards that banks must in turn apply to people who seek loans to buy houses. One of the consequences, however, of reselling mortgages on a large scale is that the initial lender has fewer incentives to be meticulous about the financial qualifications of the people to whom mortgage loans are made.

The U.S. Department of Housing and Urban Development (*HUD*) is another major institution in the housing market. HUD exercises authority over Fannie Mae and Freddie Mac, and therefore indirectly over banks and home buyers, as well as directly influencing mortgage lending practices.

Other important players— and relatively new players in recent years— are Wall Street firms which buy mortgages, bundle thousands of them together and issue securities based on the value of the anticipated income from monthly mortgage payments. Wall Street firms have sold these bundles to investors across the country and around the world.

These and other organizations affecting the housing market are very different from one another and are responsible to very different constituencies. The Department of Housing and Urban Development (HUD) is a Cabinet-level agency directly responsible to whatever administration is in power in Washington. Although the Federal Reserve System is also a government agency, it is led by a board whose members' staggered terms in office overlap different administrations, in order to make them independent of any particular administration.

Fannie Mae and Freddie Mac are responsible to their stockholders, as Wall Street firms are. But Fannie Mae and Freddie Mac are also what are called "government-sponsored enterprises"— meaning that they were created by the federal government, which has some continuing involvement in their policies. More important, that government involvement leads other financial institutions to lend to these two hybrid institutions at lower interest rates than they would to completely private enterprises, because of the implicit assumption that, in the event of a crisis, the federal government would not let Fannie Mae and Freddie Mac fail.

Investors also buy securities issued by these two government-sponsored enterprises with the same reliance on a federal guarantee that is nowhere explicit but is widely assumed to exist de facto anyway. Therefore, when Fannie Mae and Freddie Mac take bigger risks in pursuit of bigger profits, the market may continue to buy their securities because the federal treasury seems likely to make up losses that might result from these risks. As the *Wall Street Journal* put it: "Their profit is privatized but their risk is socialized."

What all this means is that, with such very different organizations having a major influence on the housing markets, there is no inherent reason to expect them to coordinate their actions, so as to produce some consistent policy in those markets. They each have their own incentives, their own agendas and their own constituencies.

Other organizations of various sorts can also play a role in the housing markets, including in some cases the U.S. Department of

Justice, as we shall see in Chapter 4. But, for now, the organizations just described can be considered the main players.

THE COST OF HOUSING

Housing is special in a number of ways. It is special to homeowners, for most of whom their house is their largest financial asset and, at the same time, their greatest financial liability. Census data show that home equity— the value of the home, over and above what is owed on the mortgage— is by far the largest single asset in the average household, accounting for 42 percent of the household's total net worth. Meanwhile, a study by the Federal Reserve System found that mortgage debt was 82 percent of the total debt of homeowners.

Whether people are buying or renting, monthly housing costs are often also the largest single item in their current budgets. In some places with especially high housing prices, such as parts of coastal California, either rent or monthly mortgage payments have taken one-half of the average person's income. An extreme example is Salinas, California, where the monthly mortgage payment on a median priced house has taken 60 percent of new home buyers' median income. That of course severely limits what kind of standard of living home buyers can afford with what is left.

Interest Rates

Housing is also special because a house is something that can seldom be bought and paid for immediately in cash. Because borrowed money is what usually pays for houses, the interest rate on that borrowed money is crucial— and that interest rate varies greatly with circumstances in the economy as a whole, in addition to varying considerably over time and from one borrower to another. While some factors affect housing prices in local areas, other factors operate nationwide. Interest rates are set nationwide by the Federal Reserve

System, through the interest rate it charges to lenders, who in turn lend to the general public, including people buying homes.

The interest rate on a conventional 30-year mortgage was about 8 percent in 1973, 18 percent in 1981 and 6 percent in 2005. At any given time, the interest rate also varies from person to person, depending on the financial condition and credit record of each individual. Those individuals whose credit ratings are below par may be denied loans at the prevailing interest rates, but granted "subprime" loans, which charge higher interest rates to offset the greater risk of lending to people who have lower incomes or a history of credit problems.

In general, not only are people with lower credit scores charged higher interest rates for mortgage loans, people charged higher interest have higher rates of late payments, defaults or foreclosures, suggesting that the market has accurately assessed the risks. All this means that the cost of buying a given house can vary greatly with the times, with the individual and with the various "creative"— and risky— ways of trying to make the monthly mortgage payments affordable, especially in markets with high home prices.

Just a difference of a percentage point or two can significantly change the cost of buying a home. When buying a house by taking out a 30-year mortgage for $400,000, the monthly payment will be less than $2,200 when the interest rate is 5 percent, but more than $2,600 when the interest rate is 7 percent. That is a difference of more than $5,000 a year.

Another way of saying the same thing is that a monthly mortgage payment that would cover the cost of a 30-year mortgage for $400,000 when the interest rate is 7 percent would cover a 30-year mortgage of nearly $500,000 when the interest rate is 5 percent. In short, declining interest rates not only enable more people to be able to afford to buy a house, they enable the same person to buy a more expensive house without a higher monthly mortgage payment. In both cases, lower interest rates increase the demand for housing and thereby drive up home prices.

During the early years of the twenty-first century, the interest rates that the Federal Reserve System charged financial institutions were brought down to extremely low levels. Between the beginning of 2001 and the spring of 2003, the Federal Reserve System brought down its interest rate from 6.5 percent to one percent. Moreover, these rates were not only lower than they had been in decades, they remained at these low rates for years. Competition among financial institutions in turn brought down the interest rates they charged, including interest rates on mortgage loans. Mortgage interest rates fell to their lowest level in decades. Not surprisingly, housing prices rose to record high levels. This helped set the stage for the housing boom.

Down Payments

One of the biggest hurdles to becoming a homeowner has been the traditional substantial down payment required— often 20 percent of the price of a home. That has been an especially large hurdle where home prices are highest. People who already have a home can often sell that home, even if it is not yet paid for, paying off the mortgage from the sale price and using the money left over— their equity in the house— as a down payment for a new house. That has usually been the primary source of a down payment for California homeowners buying another home, their savings usually being secondary. But, after the housing boom turned to bust, savings became the primary source of down payments in California, as homes no longer sold as fast or for as much money as before.

People who are buying a home for the first time, however, have had to come up with the hard cash, which many found difficult or impossible— again, especially in places with very expensive housing. While first-time home buyers were about half of all home buyers in California in the mid-1990s, that proportion fell to about a third during the housing boom in the early years of the twenty-first century. Down payments from first-time buyers in California were much less than down payments from repeat buyers— less than $30,000 compared to more than $100,000 for repeat buyers in 2008, for example.

Lenders are, of course, well aware that requiring substantial down payments limits the number of people who can afford mortgage loans— and therefore limits the total amount of business they can do and the profit to be made from making mortgage loans. Obviously, there must be some offsetting advantage to having such a requirement for it to continue, despite its restriction on the number of business transactions to be made. That advantage is reducing the risk of default. A home buyer with a substantial investment in the home from the outset is less likely to someday simply walk away from the mortgage and the house, leaving the lender in the lurch.

In exceptionally expensive housing markets, first-time buyers have had to pay an especially high proportion of their incomes for monthly mortgage payments, since they have often made the minimum down payment possible. First-time buyers have also more often than others resorted to various "creative"— and risky— methods of financing the purchase of a home.

EXPENSIVE HOUSING MARKETS

Although the financial repercussions of the housing boom and bust have been national and even international in their scope, many of the problems that provided the impetus for these economic disasters were local in origin. The national and even international market for local mortgages has meant that the repercussions of housing crises in various localities can spread far beyond those localities. Moreover, a confusion between the local and the nationwide availability of "affordable housing" has contributed to government policies that led to the boom and bust. To understand all this, we need to start at square one, the scattered localities around the country where housing prices have been some multiple of the national average, and were rising much faster than the national average, during the housing boom.

California— and especially coastal California— has been the largest of these exceptionally expensive housing markets. It has also been the most expensive and with the fastest rising home prices. At the height of the housing boom in 2005, the top ten areas with the biggest home price increases over the previous five years were all in California. Yet California home prices were once very similar to home prices in the rest of the nation. It was only after the decade of the 1970s that home prices in much of coastal California became far higher than home prices in the country as a whole.

In the San Francisco Bay Area, for example, the median-priced home in 2005 cost more than three times the national average. In the city of San Francisco, the median home sales price that year was $765,000. In March of the same year, home prices in San Mateo County (adjacent to San Francisco) rose at a rate of $2,000 *a day* and later peaked at just over one million dollars in 2007. This price was paid for homes averaging less than 2,000 square feet.

San Mateo was by no means unique among California communities in having modest-sized houses that were selling for what would be charged for large luxury homes elsewhere. For the state as a whole, including its interior valleys where housing prices were lower, the median sales price of homes peaked at $561,000 in 2006, when the median size of the houses sold was 1,600 square feet. Most Californians were not living in mansions, but many were paying what would be mansion prices, in some other places, for modest middle class homes.

Although the housing boom and bust is a national problem in terms of its repercussions, its origins tended to be concentrated in particular places with unusually high housing prices and unusually volatile changes in those prices. For example, while home prices rose 13 percent nationwide in a single year, from 2004 to 2005, the range was from a 4 percent rise in Michigan to a 35 percent rise in Arizona.

As already noted, California housing prices have long been some multiple of prices in the country as a whole.

What is different about such places?

Certainly the cost of building a house does not vary anywhere nearly as drastically as the prices of houses in different places. Nor does the quality of the houses vary that much between the high-priced states and the lower-priced states. Although San Francisco has some of the highest home prices and apartment rents in the country, the houses are often rather modest and built close together. As for apartments, the *San Francisco Chronicle* reported a graduate student looking for a place to rent in San Francisco, who was "visiting one exorbitantly priced hovel after another."

Conceivably, rising incomes or rising populations might explain why some places have higher or faster rising housing prices than others. But, in fact, incomes were rising *less* in California than in the rest of the country during the decade of the 1970s, when California housing prices became a multiple of the national average. Nor have population increases usually been what has driven home prices up in some places so much faster than the national average. Population increase on the San Francisco peninsula during the 1970s was virtually identical with population increases nationally— 11.9 percent versus 11.5 percent, respectively. Housing prices in Palo Alto, California (near Stanford University), nearly quadrupled during the decade of the 1970s, when that community's population actually declined by 8 percent.

What then does distinguish the places with skyrocketing housing prices from other places?

Studies of housing prices across the country show that what varies drastically from one place to another is the price of the *land* on which houses are built. Economists at the National Bureau of Economic Research estimated that the cost of a quarter-acre lot added about $140,000 to the price of a house in Chicago, over and above the cost of constructing the house itself. In San Diego, a quarter-acre lot added about $285,000 to the cost of the house itself, in New York

City the same size lot added about $350,000, and in San Francisco nearly $700,000. The extraordinary cost of the land in San Francisco helps explain why modest but very expensive homes in that city are often jammed close together.*

While great variations in the price of land from one place to another help answer some questions, these variations raise other questions. Why are there such great variations in the price of land from one place to another, in the first place? Moreover, why did the price of housing suddenly become radically more expensive in California in the 1970s, when it was not before? Surely the amount of land in California did not change radically during that decade.

In a sense it did. It changed politically.

The decade of the 1970s saw a rapid spread of laws and policies in California severely restricting the use of land.** Often these laws and policies forbade the building of anything on vast areas of land, in the name of preserving "open space," "saving farmland," "protecting the environment," "historical preservation" and other politically attractive slogans. Moreover, these restrictions were extended to more and more land over the years.

The normal transfer of land from one use to another over time was often stopped by such laws and policies, so that a farmer who quit farming was not allowed to sell the land to someone who might build

---

* For a graphic example, see the photograph on page 58 of the article titled "Is This House Worth $1.2 Million?" in the October 28, 2002 issue of *Fortune* magazine.
** Amazingly, some supposedly sophisticated people apparently believe that there is an actual physical shortage of land in places with high housing prices: "Those areas already are crowded," a *Wall Street Journal* reporter said, even though more than half of San Mateo County, California, for example, consists of open space and similar land use restrictions are common in other communities with extremely high housing prices. The comment is from James R. Hagerty, "After Big Run-Up in Real Estate, Some on Coasts Are Cashing Out," *Wall Street Journal*, September 22, 2004, pp. A1 ff. Equally amazing is an assertion by Professor Richard A. Posner, in his book *A Failure of Capitalism*, that "land for home building was plentiful" in California during the housing boom (p. 119). There is certainly plenty of vacant land in California on which it is physically possible to build homes. But that very plentifulness of vacant land is due to severe legal restrictions on building anything. What is economically salient for the housing market is the amount of land on which housing is legally permitted to be built.

houses on the site. Instead, the former farmland could be forced to become "open space" by various restrictions placed on its use. In this and other ways, large and growing amounts of land in many coastal California communities became "open space"— more than half of all the land in San Mateo County, for example. This artificial scarcity of land of course drove up the price of the remaining land in the county, creating the conditions in which modest-sized homes became literally million-dollar homes in that county.

While California was different from most of the rest of the country in the extent and severity of its land use restrictions, it was not unique. The same kinds of land-use restrictions which spread through many coastal California communities during the 1970s spread through various other places around the country, either during that decade or in other years. But, in whatever years building restrictions were tightened in various localities, those were usually the same years in which housing prices skyrocketed.

A study of the dates that marked the takeoff of home prices in various communities across the country found that those times "in which housing markets became unaffordable closely followed the approval of state growth-management laws or restrictive local plans." An international study of urban areas with "severely unaffordable" housing likewise found that 23 out of 26 such areas around the world had strong "smart-growth" policies. The consequences contrast painfully with the self-congratulatory phrase. As a former governor of the Reserve Bank of New Zealand put it, in another international study of home prices, "the affordability of housing is overwhelmingly a function of just one thing, the extent to which governments place artificial restrictions on the supply of residential land."

In addition to prohibitions on building, land use restrictions in some places have also taken the form of requiring that each home be built on a lot no smaller than an acre, or several acres, in contrast to the usual middle-class home on a quarter-acre lot. Loudoun County, Virginia, for example, enacted laws in 2001 which restricted the building of homes to one house per 10 acres in some places, 20 acres in others and 50 acres in still others. Fayette County, Kentucky, has set minimum lot sizes at forty acres.

Minimum lot-size laws ensure that the land costs of building a house will be vastly greater than otherwise, and housing costs correspondingly beyond the reach of most Americans. It is a way of surrounding upscale communities with a wide buffer zone, keeping less affluent people at bay. The resulting high costs of housing do not adversely affect homeowners already living in the upscale community. Most of these existing homeowners either have mortgages negotiated before the land use restrictions were enacted or else own their homes outright. In either case, the values of their homes shoot up after the restrictions, so that they gain financially as well as by keeping out less affluent people and thereby preserving the character of the community as they like it.

Because these were usually local laws and policies restricting building, such restrictions have not been uniform across the country. Instead, there have been extremely expensive enclaves here and there with extremely restrictive land use laws, with most of the rest of the country having much more modest housing prices. A study of housing prices across the nation concluded:

> Today, a family in an American city without growth-management planning can buy a very nice "middle-manager's" home, with about 2,200 square feet, four bedrooms, two-and-one-half baths, and a two-car garage, for $150,000 to $200,000. In cities that have had growth-management planning for ten to fifteen years, that same home costs $300,000 to $400,000. In cities that have had it for twenty-five years or more, the same house costs from $500,000 to as much as $1.5 million.

These estimates are consistent with estimates made by the nationwide real estate company Coldwell Banker, comparing the price of the same house in Houston and San Jose. Houston has been a city at the opposite pole from various California cities like San Jose, in terms of laws affecting the use of land. Houston has not even had zoning laws, much less the vast array of other government constraints common in San Jose or other places with severe land use restrictions.

Coldwell Banker has estimated that a house that costs $155,000 in Houston would cost more than a million dollars in San Jose.

Instead of comparing the price of the same house in different places, we can compare what a similar amount of money will buy in different places. For example, on March 1, 2009, a six-bedroom "executive style" house with a four-car garage, located on 5 acres of land, was advertised in the *St. Louis Post-Dispatch* for $668,999. That same day, a 1,300 square foot, two-bedroom condominium was advertised in the *San Francisco Chronicle* as "PRICE REDUCED" for $699,000.

We can also compare what happens to housing prices over time in different places. Even rising incomes and growing populations in places without severe land use restrictions have seldom produced housing price increases at all comparable to those in places with severe land use restrictions. While housing prices skyrocketed in California during the 1970s, even though incomes in California were *not* rising as fast as incomes nationwide, in Houston incomes were rising *faster* than the national average and yet Houston continued to have some of the most affordable housing in the nation. Dallas likewise has long had family incomes above the national average and housing prices below the national average.

Open space laws are not the only laws or policies that drive up home prices by restricting the building of houses. Among the arsenal of weapons available to those who want to prevent development are zoning laws, height restrictions, minimum lot size laws, historical preservation laws, building permit limits and farmland preservation laws. In some jurisdictions, planning commissions have arbitrary powers to grant or deny permission to build, which means that they can impose costs by requiring the builder to make whatever modifications they wish, at whatever costs these modifications might require, in addition to the accumulating costs of delay as more and more hearings are scheduled in a building approval process that can go on for years before permission is finally granted to actually begin building— if that permission ever comes.

In some communities, private citizens or groups can make objections to building plans, and the adjudications of such objections take more time, regardless of the merits or lack of merits of the objections. While these costs are initially imposed on the builder, those who buy or rent the housing can end up paying for all these things.

It is not only in the building of single-family homes that the presence or absence of these impediments affects the costs of housing, both directly and by preventing or discouraging housing from being built in the first place. Conversely, when and where there are few impediments to building, even a growing demand for housing can be met without forcing up prices the way they are forced up in more restrictive environments. In Manhattan during the 1950s, for example, tens of thousands of new housing units were built without apartment rents or condominium prices increasing in real terms— that is, money prices adjusted for inflation. But, in later years, after new building restrictions began to be imposed in the 1970s, a later study found "skyrocketing prices" (in real terms) in Manhattan, while the total housing stock there increased by less than 10 percent in a quarter of a century.

It was much the same story in Las Vegas, where the population almost tripled between 1980 and 2000, but the median price of housing did not change in real terms, that is, correcting for inflation. However, since 90 percent of the land in Nevada is owned by the federal government, the supply of land for building depends on the government's willingness to continue to sell land to be developed. After environmentalist groups raised objections to such sales in the twenty-first century, land use restrictions were followed by rapidly rising housing prices in Las Vegas, as has happened elsewhere under stringent land use constraints.

Much of the impetus for severe land use restrictions comes from individuals and groups who create an impression that they are trying to prevent the last few patches of greenery from being paved over. In reality, less than 10 percent of the land area of the United States has been developed. Trees alone cover more than six times the area of all the cities and towns in the country put together. But, for political decision-making, impressions can carry more weight than facts. As former Congressman Dick Armey put it: "Demagoguery beats data."

As housing prices rose from 2000 to 2005, this was widely conceived as a national problem, especially by Washington politicians seeking to create a national program to deal with it. However, the wide disparities in housing prices from community to community— even between coastal California and that state's inland valleys— show a very different picture. In 2005, the *New York Times* reported:

> Despite a widespread sense that real estate has never been more expensive, families in the vast majority of the country can still buy a house for a smaller share of their income than they could have a generation ago.
>
> A sharp fall in mortgage rates since the early 1980's, a decline in mortgage fees and a rise in incomes have more than made up for rising house prices in almost every place outside of New York, Washington, Miami and along the coast in California. *See p.* 189

There were places like San Diego and San Francisco, where more than 90 percent of the homes were selling for at least 140 percent of the cost of constructing them, and other places like Houston where only 27 percent of the homes were priced that far above construction costs. In other words, most of the country was *not* suffering from skyrocketing housing prices, which were largely confined to particular communities in which there were severe limitations on the building of housing. During the housing boom, home prices in the 10 most expensive metropolitan areas were more than twice as high as the national average.

In these high-price enclaves, people buying a home for the first time— and therefore not having the equity in an existing home to use as a down payment— "often must spend more than half of their income on mortgage payments" in places like New York and Los Angeles, the *New York Times* reported. But the percentage of median family income required to buy a house in Tampa was 21 percent and in Dallas 13 percent. Dallas, like Houston, has relatively few building restrictions.

A fundamental misconception of the housing market existed both during the housing boom and after the bust. That misconception was that the free market failed to produce affordable housing, and that government intervention was therefore necessary, in order to enable ordinary people to find a place to live that was within their means. Yet the hard evidence points in the opposite direction: It has been precisely where there was massive government intervention, in the form of severe building restrictions, that housing prices skyrocketed. Where the market was more or less left alone— places like Houston and Dallas, for example— housing prices took a smaller share of family income than in the past.

In short, the problem of a lack of "affordable housing," as conceived by many in the media and in politics, bore little resemblance to the situation in the real world. It was not a national problem but a severe problem in particular places. Washington politicians who set out to solve a problem that they misconceived contributed instead to the housing boom and bust, as will become clear in the following chapters.

"CREATIVE" FINANCING

At extremely high prices for even modest homes in places like coastal California, home buyers were especially prone to resort to risky ways of financing their purchases, in order to be able to buy a home at all. Regarded as "creative" or "innovative" ways of coping with high housing prices, these methods of financing the purchase of homes spread, especially to other areas with very high housing prices.

Among the new "creative" ways of financing a home purchase have been low-down-payment and no-down-payment mortgages, as well as mortgages on which only the interest is paid at first. Another variation widely used has been an adjustable rate mortgage. Unlike conventional 30-year mortgages with a fixed interest rate, adjustable rate mortgages have had interest rates that varied with the interest rate in the economy at large. While such mortgages existed before the mortgage boom of the early twenty-first century, they became especially prevalent among subprime mortgages during the housing boom. Ninety percent of subprime mortgage loans made by 2006 were adjustable rate mortgages. That same year, the average subprime borrower made only a 5 percent down payment on a home.

Some lenders made mortgage loans to borrowers with no down payment at all, and sometimes on the basis of income information that was not verified. By 2006, more than half of all subprime mortgage loans were what were called "stated income" loans in polite circles and "liar loans" in less polite circles. Moreover, subprime borrowers were making commitments to pay more than 40 percent of their incomes for the mortgages. Such risky loans were made less risky when the mortgage could be sold to Fannie Mae, Freddie Mac or some other financial institution.

Since Fannie Mae and Freddie Mac had quotas set for them by the Department of Housing and Urban Development to buy mortgages that lenders had made with borrowers in what was called "the underserved population"— people whose financial situation or credit history made them less likely to get conventional mortgages— these government-sponsored enterprises could accept these mortgages, earning the higher rates of return that such riskier investments paid, secure in the knowledge that the federal government was almost certain to rescue them in the event of serious trouble.

Among the variations on interest-only loans, a common one has been making monthly mortgage payments covering only the interest for the first two years of a 30-year mortgage, followed by larger monthly payments over the next 28 years to pay off the loan itself. Interest-only mortgages were typically mortgages with interest rates that would also vary over time, according to what interest rates were in the economy at large. In other words, the monthly mortgage payments could go up, even during the first two years when only the interest on the loan was being paid, if interest rates in the economy as a whole went up during those years.

Adjustable-rate mortgages— known as ARMs— had a number of variations. One of the more adventurous versions of the ARMs was one in which the home buyer had the option to pay less than the amount of the interest in some months during the interest-only period. While convenient for dealing with temporary financial problems, these option ARMs meant that paying less than the interest in some months meant that the unpaid interest was added to the principal, so that the home buyer who used that option could end up owing more than the original amount of the mortgage.

These various kinds of adjustable-rate mortgages, taken out when interest rates were unusually low, brought monthly mortgage payments down below what they would be in a conventional 30-year fixed-rate mortgage, thus enabling more people to stretch their incomes to cover the price of buying homes that they might otherwise be unable to afford. Put differently, these temporary arrangements concealed the fact that some people were buying homes that they would not be able to afford in the long run.

Long-run costs were also concealed by what were called "teaser" interest rates. These were interest rates charged during the early months of a new mortgage that were below even the unusually low interest rates being charged on mortgages in general during the housing boom. For example, if the prevailing interest rate on conventional mortgages was 6 percent, a so-called "teaser" rate of 4 percent might be charged for the first few months on a new mortgage, in order to attract people seeking to buy a home that was something of a stretch for someone with their income. The unusually low initial monthly mortgage payments, made possible by the temporary "teaser" rate, would then be followed by higher monthly mortgage payments when the prevailing interest rate replaced the teaser rate— followed still later by another increase in monthly mortgage payments when time came to begin repaying the principal on the mortgage loan.

During the height of the housing boom in 2005 and 2006, an estimated 15 percent of adjustable-rate mortgages that were issued had initial interest rates *below two percent*. In short, within a matter of months, the mortgage payments under such "creative" arrangements could rise well above their initial level under low introductory "teaser" interest rates, followed by another rise if market interest rates rose, and followed by yet another rise when time came to begin repaying the principal— all of this happening within the span of just two years. How many of those who signed up for such loans understood all this is a serious question.

ARMs were especially attractive methods of "creative financing" in places where housing was especially expensive. Thus, while housing prices were *rising* in the early years of the twenty-first century, initial monthly mortgage payments were *falling* during those same years, as a result of what the *Wall Street Journal* called "the onslaught of creative mortgage products— from interest-only loans to adjustable-rate mortgages carrying starter rates as low as 1%— that have allowed buyers to keep initial payments down even as home prices have soared."

The traditional fixed-rate 30-year mortgages, which were once a majority of all mortgages, were no longer a majority during the housing boom, as ARMs and other "creative" ways of financing the purchase of a home grew rapidly to cope with soaring housing prices. Such innovative mortgages quickly went from being rare to becoming common, especially in places with very high housing costs.

In 2002, less than 10 percent of new mortgages in the United States were interest-only mortgages, but that rose to 31 percent in 2005, as home prices rose. In a number of California cities, as well as in Denver, Washington, Phoenix and Seattle, interest-only loans were 40 percent of all mortgage loans made in 2005. In the San Francisco Bay Area, interest-only loans rose from being 11 percent of all new mortgages in 2002 to becoming 66 percent of all new mortgages in 2005, the height of the housing boom, in an area with some of the most expensive real estate in the country.

Such arrangements were especially attractive to people who expected their incomes to increase over time. By the time the higher monthly payments would become due, in order to begin paying off the principal; the borrowers' rising incomes would enable them to afford those higher payments— *if* all worked out according to plan. Another possibility was to refinance at the end of the two-year, interest-only period. In a rising housing market, the increased value of the house could make this an attractive option for both the borrower and the lender. Moreover, this process could be repeated again by taking out a new mortgage with interest-only payments for the first two years. But this repeated postponement of the day of reckoning depended on housing prices continuing to rise, so that lenders would continue to be willing to keep on refinancing the same house because of its rising value.

There was yet another reason for borrowers to take on risky "creative" financial arrangements during a housing boom. With housing prices rising substantially from year to year, home buyers could begin acquiring equity in their homes, even before time came for them to start paying off the principal on their mortgage loans.

For example, imagine someone buying a home in one of the places with booming housing prices, by taking out a no-down payment loan as a $600,000 mortgage, in which only the interest is paid during the first two years. Even if the home buyer turns out to be unable to make the larger monthly mortgage payments when these higher payments are scheduled to begin after the initial two years of interest-only payments are over, the increased value of the house in a rising housing market could enable the buyer to leave with considerable money, even if it was impossible for the buyer to continue living in the home after the monthly payments rose to an unaffordable level. If the house that initially cost $600,000 increased in value to $800,000 in the meantime, then the home buyer could sell the house for $800,000, paying off the $600,000 mortgage in order to do so, and walk away with $200,000 in cash.

Such scenarios became common during the housing boom, especially in the high-price enclaves, where home prices were skyrocketing. The only thing unrealistic about this example is that a $600,000 home would have to be a *very* modest home— if not a "fixer-upper"— in some coastal California communities during the housing boom. In other words, the gains to be made in such places were likely to be even greater than in this example.

· This was just one of the ways in which the rising value of houses could be turned into ready cash during the housing boom. Home equity loans also became common during the boom, whether the home was owned outright or the buyer was still making mortgage payments. For homes bought and paid for before the housing boom, the amount of money that could be borrowed, based on the house's rising value during the boom, could easily exceed the total amount paid for the house. For example, a Chicago man bought a 100-year-old house for $90,000 in 1992 and, during the housing boom, took out a $200,000 home equity loan on that house, which was now worth about $700,000.

In more expensive housing markets and over longer periods of time, the situation could get even more extreme. In Oakland, California, a couple bought a two-bedroom bungalow back in 1954 for $11,500. It was refinanced several times over the years by their children and, in the end, was lost to foreclosure with the family owing more than $450,000 for the money they had borrowed on that home.

Income tax rules also made borrowing against a home's equity attractive. Because mortgage interest payments can be deducted for income tax purposes, the interest paid on home equity loans could also be deducted, although interest on credit card debt or other debt was not deductible. Therefore it often paid anyone with any other kind of debt to pay off that debt with a home equity loan, whose interest would be deductible for income tax purposes. More and more people began to do this during the housing boom. In 2003, home equity loans totaled $593 billion. Such loans soared during the housing boom, nearly doubling to $1.13 trillion in 2007.

A special variation on the home equity loan was what was called "cash-out refinancing." Someone owing $300,000 on a mortgage with a fixed interest rate of 8 percent could take out a new loan to replace the old loan when the interest rate fell to 6 percent. But instead of taking out another $300,000 mortgage loan at 6 percent, the homeowner could take out a $400,000 loan at 6 percent, paying off the existing mortgage loan from the proceeds of the new loan and keeping $100,000 in cash. In an era of rising home prices, lenders were often quite willing to lend more money on a house that now had a higher market value. For the borrower, refinancing at a lower interest rate could mean that the monthly mortgage payment would not increase, even with a larger mortgage. These kinds of home-equity loans increased more than ten-fold during the housing boom, rising from $26 billion in 2000 to $318 billion in 2006.

As of 2006, 86 percent of all home mortgage refinances were "cash-out" refinances. In a period of five years, according to *The Economist* magazine, "American households extracted $2.3 trillion of equity from their homes."

Many home equity loans for the elderly did not require any repayment at all by the borrower, but simply transferred part of the equity to the lender, who could turn that equity into cash after the death of the borrower. These "reverse mortgages," as they were called, also increased greatly during the housing boom. There were fewer than 8,000 reverse mortgages in 2001 but the number soared to more than 40,000 in 2005.

Given all the ways of tapping the equity in a home to take out hard cash, it should not be surprising that the average equity in a home, which was 86 percent of its value back in 1945, was just 55 percent of its value in 2003.

There were many incentives to buy houses in a rising market, including buying for the purpose of re-selling at a higher price, even if the buyer never intended to live in the house, or bought several houses on credit at the same time, speculating on future appreciation. Such speculations in turn contributed to the rising demand for housing, with a resulting continuation of home price increases. Low initial "teaser" interest rates, and the resulting low initial monthly mortgage payments, made speculation profitable in a rising housing market. By buying a house, or multiple houses, with low initial monthly mortgage payments and then selling them later for a higher price before higher mortgage payments became due, many speculators could carry on very profitable speculations in very expensive houses with relatively little hard cash of their own.

Often speculators bought homes that needed fixing up or sprucing up and then quickly sold them— a process called "flipping." As *Money* magazine described the process:

> In hot spots like Las Vegas and Florida, real estate flippers have discovered that a modest down payment and a little patience can net them tens (even hundreds) of thousands of dollars in profits, sometimes tax-free. The most aggressive of them figure that some combo of paint, new flooring and kitchen upgrades can turn the dumpy house they bought for $300,000 in February into a $400,000 property they can unload in July. And in the most sizzling markets, they're absolutely right.

Fast turnarounds were not uncommon, as *Forbes* magazine reported:

> "It was disgusting," says Alan Washer. Grime coated the walls of the 1,600-square-foot, four-bedroom home; the musty air reeked of a cat colony that had played havoc with the wood floors. But one man's wreck is another guy's riches. Washer bought the house, in the leafy Chicago suburb of Oak Park, for $225,000 in July, spending an additional $5,000 to haul away heaps of rubbish left inside. Fixed up, he figured, it was worth $430,000. But two weeks after he closed on the place— and before he could refinish the floors or replace a rotting soffit or the old roof— Washer got a call from someone offering $315,000. He took it.

With housing speculation, however, comes risk. If home prices merely level off, that can create serious problems for speculative home buyers— especially those owing money on multiple homes bought with mortgages whose monthly payments are scheduled to increase. If rising home prices merely leveled off, that would tend to cut off the escape route of refinancing in order to avoid having to begin repaying the principal on the mortgage. A mere leveling off of home prices would mean that lenders were no longer willing to refinance as they did when prices were rising. If home prices actually fell, that would create even more serious problems for both home buyers in general and the financial institutions that had lent to them.

Many people who were not professional speculators were nevertheless, in effect, speculating not only on home prices but also on their own incomes rising fast enough to be able to begin making larger monthly mortgage payments after the initial interest-only payments period had passed. Adjustable-rate mortgages meant that buyers were also speculating on how long interest rates would stay at historic lows and how fast they would rise afterwards.

One of the inherent problems of speculation— whether in housing or elsewhere— is that the resulting prices during a boom may bear no relationship to anything other than what people believe or hope. And once those beliefs or hopes change, for whatever reason, the prices can plummet.

KNOWLEDGE AND DECISIONS

In any aspect of life, regardless of how much or how little knowledge we have, we must make decisions. The housing market is no exception. Sometimes we can draw upon our own experience or depend on the knowledge of other people but, in some cases, no one is really very knowledgeable when new and untried things are involved, such as the exotic new financial arrangements growing out of the "creative" financing of home purchases that became increasingly common during the housing boom.

Because both low interest rates and lowered mortgage eligibility standards enabled many low-income people, sometimes less educated people, to buy houses who could not have done so in earlier years, some of the least knowledgeable and least experienced home buyers were now financing their purchases with some of the newest and most complicated mortgages. There are indications that many of these less sophisticated home buyers may not have fully understood how much their monthly payments could rise under adjustable rate mortgages with initially very low interest rates and sometimes an initial period of perhaps two years when they were paying only interest on their mortgage loan.

For those buying houses for speculation, in order to sell them before the initial "teaser" rates rose, this could be a rational— and very profitable— arrangement. In California, for example, the median time that a home remained on the Multiple Listing Service before being sold was less than two weeks in 2004 and just over two weeks in 2005. During those two years, at least half of all homes on sale had multiple offers from prospective buyers. It was not uncommon in some California communities for the initial asking price to be bid up further, rather than compromised downward.

In this frenzied and booming market, "teaser" rate mortgages were a boon for speculators who could buy a house, perhaps fix it up or spruce it up, and sell it again very soon. Nationwide, a survey by the National Association of Realtors found that, during the housing boom, homes were bought as investments, rather than to live in, by 28 percent of home buyers in 2005 and by 22 percent of home buyers in 2006.

But for people buying a home to live in, low "teaser" rates could be a trap, if not understood. One study found that subprime borrowers "are disproportionately minority and lower income, older, less well educated, less financially sophisticated" people. However, getting in over their heads in complex adjustable-rate loans with initially low "teaser" rates may be more of a symptom, rather than a cause, of an unstable situation that could end in default and foreclosure. A study of adjustable-rate, subprime home mortgage foreclosures found the great majority were foreclosed even *before* the interest rate rose.

At the other end of the knowledge scale, sophisticated financial firms like Moody's and Standard & Poor's, whose ratings of the relative risks of different kinds of investments were depended upon by Wall Street firms and investors around the world, had only a very limited amount of hard data available to use when making ratings of stocks and bonds that were based on new and exotic mortgages. As one financial expert put it, "Wall Street produced a blizzard of increasingly complex new securities," based on mortgages that these Wall Street firms had purchased. But neither the creators nor the purchasers of securities based on bundles of mortgages knew the incomes, credit ratings or relevant facts about the home buyers whose mortgages they were handling. Neither did the securities-rating firms on whom investors were relying. As the *New York Times* reported:

> Moody's did not have access to the individual loan files, much less did it communicate with the borrowers or try to verify the information they provided in their loan applications. "We aren't loan officers," Claire Robinson, a 20-year veteran who is in charge of asset-backed finance for Moody's, told me. "Our expertise is as statisticians on an aggregate basis."

Such statistical approaches worked on other kinds of financial securities, including conventional mortgages. But many of these new mortgages were subprime mortgages, with "creative" financial arrangements, for which there was no long statistical track record. There were data on conventional mortgages, going back for generations, including periods of inflation or deflation, war and peace, and other changing conditions. But many of the new kinds of mortgages had become a major part of the housing market within very recent years. As one former official at Moody's put it, using the same statistical methods that had proved successful in evaluating conventional mortgages when evaluating these new "creative" mortgages was "like observing 100 years of weather in Antarctica to forecast the weather in Hawaii."

Nevertheless, the long-established, worldwide reputation of financial rating firms like Moody's and Standard & Poor's caused many investors to rely heavily on the good ratings they gave to many of the new financial securities. Investors around the world were later caught short when some of these securities turned out to be far less reliable than their ratings would have indicated.

Another element in the housing markets were lenders who knew how to take advantage of less knowledgeable homeowners, some of whom already owned their homes outright. Unscrupulous lenders would lend, not with the goal of being repaid but with the prospect of being able to foreclose on the property of homeowners who had signed agreements they did not understand. These were called "predatory lenders." Sometimes such racketeers did repairs or remodeling on credit, at inflated prices, and with contracts that only the uninformed or unwary were likely to sign.

Such shady operators are basically a problem for the criminal justice system. Yet the concept of "predatory lenders" has become widely applied loosely to all kinds of *other* situations and institutions whose only common denominator is that critics don't like them or don't understand them. The Federal Reserve System, which collects vast amounts of data on many aspects of lending, has no definition of "predatory lending." Many in politics have acted as if predatory lenders are what caused the housing crisis— a view especially common among those who themselves had a major role in bringing on the crisis.

All these things added to the growing riskiness of housing market finances.

When it comes to the home mortgage boom and bust, who was to blame? The borrowers? The lenders? The government? The financial markets?

The answer is yes. All were responsible and many were irresponsible.

Economics cannot explain such things. For that, we must turn to the politics of housing.

Chapter 2

The Politics of the Housing Boom

The fact that politicians know something to be madness does not stop them doing it.

The Economist

T he new and risky methods of financing home purchases that rose to dominance in the early years of the twenty-first century could not have replaced more traditional rules and standards for granting mortgage loans unless those who regulated banks and other lending institutions had agreed to such changes. In reality, government agencies not only approved the more lax standards for mortgage loan applicants, government officials were in fact the driving force behind the loosening of mortgage loan requirements.

Members of Congress from both political parties have urged federal regulatory agencies to press banks and other lenders to lower mortgage loan requirements, and have passed legislation to that end and to subsidize or guarantee loans made under lowered standards. Presidents of both parties, in different ways, pushed the idea that a higher rate of home ownership was "a good thing." In 1999, the *New York Times* reported:

> In a move that could help increase home ownership rates among minorities and low-income consumers, the Fannie Mae Corporation is easing the credit requirements on loans that it will purchase from banks and other lenders. . .
> Fannie Mae, the nation's biggest underwriter of home mortgages, has been under increasing pressure from the Clinton Administration to expand mortgage loans among low and moderate income people and felt

pressure from stock holders to maintain its phenomenal growth in profits.

Higher risk investments usually pay higher profits, so both the political incentives and the market incentives were for Fannie Mae and Freddie Mac to buy riskier mortgages, which pay higher interest rates, since the profits went to them and any runaway losses would be the taxpayers' problem.

The fact that Fannie Mae and Freddie Mac would now purchase mortgages made under less stringent credit requirements than in the past meant that banks and other lending institutions could now profit from making such riskier mortgages, selling these mortgages and passing their risks on to others. What began as pressure on Fannie Mae and Freddie Mac to lower the lending standards that banks and other lenders had to meet, in order for these government-sponsored enterprises to buy their mortgages, escalated over the years to actual percentage goals— quotas— being set by the Department of Housing and Urban Development for Fannie Mae and Freddie Mac to meet in purchasing mortgages made to people in what was called "the underserved population."

As the U.S. Commission on Civil Rights recounted this history:

> Prior to 1992, federal law only required that a "reasonable portion" of Fannie Mae and Freddie Mac's mortgage purchases advanced the goal of providing affordable housing to low- and moderate-income families. This amorphous goal was changed upon the adoption of the Federal Housing Enterprise Financial Safety and Soundness Act (FHEFSSA) of 1992. Prior to said statute, HUD promulgated rules requiring "30 percent of GSE conventional mortgage purchase be devoted to mortgages for (1) low- and moderate-income housing; or (2) housing located in central cities."

By 1996, the goal established by the Department of Housing and Urban Development (HUD) was raised to 40 percent and, a decade later, it was 53 percent. A HUD publication urged "creativity" to overcome "financial barriers to homeownership."

This was just one of the ways in which the federal government promoted lower mortgage lending standards. Others included requiring banks to report their loan approvals and denials to regulatory agencies that were charged with rating these banks on the extent to which they had met "community needs" under the Community Reinvestment Act of 1977. Like the pressures on Fannie *1977* Mae and Freddie Mac, these pressures on banks escalated over the years. Moreover, non-bank lending institutions that were not covered by the Community Reinvestment Act were pressured into signing "voluntary" agreements with the Department of Housing and Urban Development to essentially do what banks were mandated to do under the Community Reinvestment Act.

Before getting into the details of how all this came about politically, it is necessary to be clear that this was not a matter of the regulatory agencies *permitting* lower mortgage lending standards but of those federal agencies *requiring* lower standards, in order to meet politically defined goals. There were many who shared the responsibility— or, in this case, the irresponsibility— for the housing boom that was fueled by easier credit, lower mortgage approval standards and "creative" financing.

While such developments escalated during the Clinton administration, these developments began under the preceding George H.W. Bush administration and continued under the subsequent George W. Bush administration. Neither political party was blameless.

Like many disasters, this one began with good intentions, or at least intentions that sounded good politically. At the heart of those good intentions was the quest for "affordable housing," another way of expressing the crusade for more home ownership among a wider range of people.

"AFFORDABLE HOUSING"

While the term "affordable housing" has not been defined in any absolute sense, the usual way of measuring whether housing is more affordable or less affordable in one place compared to another, or in one time period compared to another, is by comparing what percentage of an average income has to be paid for the average rent or the average monthly mortgage payment. At one time, the rule of thumb was that housing costs should not take more than one-fourth of a family's income. Others have suggested 30 percent but, whatever the number, it is meaningful only for comparing one place with another or one time period with another.

Affordability can also be measured by comparing the *total* cost—not just the monthly mortgage payments— of the average house at a given place with the average annual income of the people who live there. For example, the median home price in Youngstown, Ohio, has been found to be roughly double the median income in Youngstown. The median home price in Las Vegas has been about six times the median income in that city and, in San Diego, the median home price has been ten times the median income.

As a rough rule of thumb for making comparisons, "affordable housing" can be a useful concept. In another sense, however, the concept of "affordable housing" conceals an assumption and an agenda that are very much in need of scrutiny. Each individual knows what can and cannot be afforded on that individual's income. In other words, those who can afford mansions can buy mansions and those who can afford bungalows can buy bungalows. Those who cannot afford to buy any house can rent a house or rent an apartment, and those who cannot yet afford even that can double up with relatives or roommates, or can rent a room. Many people have done some or all of these things at one period of their lives or another.

But that is *not* what is meant by those who set up a political goal of "affordable housing." The *political* meaning of affordable housing is that individuals choose their housing and government somehow makes it financially possible for them to have it. This is seldom spelled out explicitly, much less reasoned out in terms of its implications. Much of political rhetoric serves as a substitute for reasoning.

A National Problem?

At the heart of many arguments for federal intervention in housing markets has been the belief that a shortage of affordable housing is a nationwide problem, for which local solutions are inadequate. According to a *New York Times* editorial in 2002, "the housing crisis will never be solved unless the federal government gets back into the game." *Washington Post* columnist David Broder likewise saw the problem as national in scope, that "in almost every city I've visited this year, from Sacramento to Tallahassee to Boston, the shortage of affordable housing is close to the top of people's concerns."

There is, of course, no way to know how representative either the cities that Mr. Broder visited or the people that he talked to were, much less whether their perceptions or interests corresponded to empirical reality. As J.A. Schumpeter said: "You can travel far and wide and yet wear blinkers wherever you go."

p. 192

Indeed, a *New York Times* news report flatly contradicted what was said in the *New York Times* editorial just cited: "A sharp fall in mortgage rates since the early 1980's, a decline in mortgage fees and a rise in incomes have more than made up for rising house prices in almost every place outside of New York, Washington, Miami and along the coast in California." An earlier study by the Heritage Foundation likewise found that "the ratio of monthly cost-to-gross income decreased"— rather than increased— again, with the exception of "a few metropolitan markets on the East and West coasts."

Other scholarly research has likewise found that affordable housing, by common standards, has been the norm across most of the country, but with glaring exceptions in places where average housing prices are some multiple of what they are in the nation as a whole. Almost invariably, as noted in Chapter 1, these are places where severe local government restrictions on land use, and other impediments to building, have driven the cost of houses and of apartment rents to levels that take as much as half of the average family's income just to put a roof over their heads. For the country as a whole, however, home buyers have paid no more than the old-fashioned standard of 25 percent of their incomes for housing in any year since 1985. Renters have in recent years paid a somewhat higher percentage of their smaller incomes but not more than 30 percent in any year over the past several decades.

Neither by comparison with the recent past nor by comparison with other countries today is most housing in the United States unaffordable. The median-priced home in the United States as a whole is 3.6 times the median income of Americans. For Great Britain, the median-priced home is 5.5 times the median income and, in Australia and New Zealand, the ratio of home prices to income is 6.3.

Acknowledging this reality would cause a widely accepted vision, and the national crusades and policies built upon it, to collapse like a house of cards. Instead, facts that would undermine this vision and this political crusade have been largely ignored.

Despite the widespread assumption that government intervention is the key to making housing affordable to people of moderate or low incomes, history shows that it has been precisely in the times and places where government intervention has been greatest that housing costs have been both highest in absolute terms and have taken a larger share of the average income. This is true whether we compare different places at the same time or different time periods with one another. If we look back to the beginning of the twentieth century, when government played a much smaller role in the housing market and there were far fewer restrictions on building, the average American's housing costs were a *smaller* share of consumer expenditures than at the end of that century.

Back in 1901, housing costs were 23 percent of consumer expenditures. But, by 2003, housing costs were 33 percent of much higher consumer expenditures. There are local data that tell a very similar story:

Until 1970, median homes in nearly all U.S. metropolitan areas typically cost about twice as much as median family incomes in those areas. Depending on the prevailing interest rate, this meant that a family dedicating a quarter of its income to a mortgage could pay off a loan for a home in a little more than 10 years.

Even in coastal California, home prices were very affordable *before* the severe housing restrictions that began there during the 1970s. As late as 1969, the median-priced home in San Francisco cost no more than 2.3 times the median family income in San Francisco at that time. That same year, the median price of a home in San Jose was 2.2 times the median family income in San Jose. Spending one-fourth of the median family income on monthly mortgage payments would pay off a median mortgage in San Jose in 12 years. A decade later, the median family home in San Jose cost 4 times the median family income in San Jose— and now it would take 40 percent of the family's income to pay off the mortgage in 30 years. By 2005, at the height of the housing boom, the median price of a home in San Jose was 7.5 times the median family income there.

These variations in the affordability of housing prices over time tell essentially the same story as variations in the affordability of housing prices from place to place at a given time: Where there is the greatest government intervention, housing is least affordable. Nor is this pattern confined to the United States. As noted in Chapter 1, in 23 of the 26 urban areas around the world where housing is rated "severely unaffordable," there are severe land use restrictions under the heading of "smart-growth" policies.

Advocates of "affordable housing" seldom— if ever— seek to remove government restrictions that have led to higher housing prices. Instead, they seek various ways of either forcing the private sector to charge lower home prices and lower apartment rents, or else they seek to use the taxpayers' money to subsidize housing in one way or another. In other words, they do not seek to reduce the government's role in the housing market but to increase it. They do not seek to *lower* housing costs but to *conceal* housing costs with taxpayer-provided subsidies or with laws that prevent those costs from being expressed in the prices charged.

Lowering Lending Standards

One of the first federal government efforts to change the process of mortgage lending by private financial institutions was the Community Reinvestment Act of 1977. Like many government policies or programs, it began small and grew in scope and severity over the years.

The Community Reinvestment Act directed "each appropriate Federal financial supervisory agency to use its authority when examining financial institutions, to encourage such institutions to help meet the credit needs of the local communities in which they are chartered consistent with the safe and sound operation of such institutions."

Given the proviso of "safe and sound operation," these words seem almost innocuous. Apparently it was considered to be innocuous when it was passed, after just one day of debate on the Senate floor and no debate at all in the House of Representatives. Nevertheless, the implicit assumption that government officials are qualified to tell lenders to whom they should lend money entrusted to them by depositors or investors was fraught with consequences that became ever more clear with the passing years. Yet this remarkable assumption has received little scrutiny, either when the Community Reinvestment Act was passed or since.

Although the Community Reinvestment Act had no major immediate impact, over the years its underlying assumptions and provisions provided the basis for ever more insistent pressure on lenders from a variety of government officials and agencies to lend to those whom politicians and bureaucrats wanted them to lend to, rather than to those that lenders would have chosen to lend to on the basis of the lenders' own experience and expertise.

redlining

These pressures began to build especially strongly in the 1990s and increased exponentially thereafter. Studies in the early 1990s, showing different mortgage loan approval rates for blacks and whites, set off media sensations and denunciations, leading to both Congressional and White House pressures on agencies regulating banks to impose new lending rules, and to monitor statistics on the loan approval rates by race, by community and by income, with penalties on banks and other lenders for failing to meet politically-imposed norms or quotas.

However, these stepped-up pressures began even earlier, in 1989, during the George H.W. Bush administration. In April 1989, the *New York Times* reported:

> The Department of Justice has sent letters to major banks and savings and loans throughout Atlanta asking for access to loan records over the past five years. At issue is whether the lending institutions have a history of denying loans to neighborhoods because of racial composition or other factors.
> The Justice Department describes the inquiry into possible redlining as a preliminary investigation. But a spokeswoman for the department says it is perhaps the largest Federal inquiry ever into alleged discrimination in lending.

Pressures were also brought to bear on Fannie Mae and Freddie Mac to buy the riskier mortgages that lenders were being pressured to make. In 1992, Congress passed, and President George H.W. Bush signed into law, a bill establishing "an annual goal for the purchase by each enterprise of mortgages on housing located in central cities, rural areas, and other underserved areas." In the subsequent Clinton administration, Attorney General Janet Reno threatened legal action against lenders whose racial statistics raised her suspicions.

It would be too much of a detour at this point to go into the details of these claims of racial discrimination by mortgage lenders, but that will be done in Chapter 4. However, even at this point, the idea that lenders would be offended by receiving monthly mortgage payment checks in the mail from blacks should at least give us pause to assess whether or not that seems plausible— especially since a majority of both blacks and whites had their mortgage loan applications approved. The issue has been about the statistical difference between these approval rates, not any claim that most blacks could not get mortgage loans.

Although many in the media and in politics treat statistical differences in outcomes as evidence of differences in the way people are treated— rather than being a result of those people's own track records— this is still another remarkable, unsubstantiated and yet largely unchallenged assumption. Moreover, it is an assumption that is inconsistent with the plain fact that statistical differences among groups are both large and common, as well as long-enduring, in countries around the world, even in situations where these differences cannot be explained by discrimination.*

Applying the assumption that statistical differences mean discrimination to mortgage lending ignores the plain fact that mortgage lenders are in business to make money. Yet even people who are quick to denounce corporate "greed" often also argue inconsistently as if lenders are arbitrarily withholding their favors from people they don't like. Lenders are not doing favors by making loans, any more than Campbell's is doing favors by selling soup. Lenders would be cutting their own throats financially if they arbitrarily denied loans to people with good prospects of paying them back with interest. Moreover, the fact that black-owned banks have been found to turn down black mortgage loan applicants more often than white-owned banks undermines racial discrimination as an explanation. It also undermines the implicit assumption that different loan denial rates reflect the decision-makers, rather than the applicants. It cannot be assumed that black applicants who apply to black-owned banks are the same as black applicants who apply to white-owned banks.

---

* For dozens of examples from countries around the world, just in books of mine, see *The Vision of the Anointed*, pp. 35–37; *Conquests and Cultures*, p. 125; *Migrations and Cultures*, pp. 4, 17, 30, 31, 56–57, 118, 121, 122–123, 126, 130, 135, 152, 154, 158, 167, 176, 179, 196, 211, 212, 224, 251, 258, 264, 265, 275, 277, 278, 289, 290, 298, 300, 305, 306, 318, 320, 324, 345–346, 353–356, 358, 366, 373.

Whatever the merits, or lack of merits, of the logic or evidence on which charges of biased lending were based, the political impact of such beliefs has been powerful. Moreover, even though racial bias charges provided much of the initial impetus for greater federal government involvement in private mortgage lending decisions, once federal regulatory agencies became involved that involvement spread far beyond issues of race, and the policies imposed required a lowering of mortgage loan approval standards to people of all races.

It is by no means clear that minority mortgage loan applicants were the main beneficiaries— or that they necessarily benefitted at all, on net balance, when their loan default rates and home foreclosure rates were especially high during the later housing bust. In any event, the *application* of the principles of the Community Reinvestment Act evolved in practice over time. In 1993, the Department of Housing and Urban Development started taking legal action against mortgage bankers who turned down a higher percentage of minority applicants than white applicants for mortgage loans. Lenders then began lowering their down payment requirements and income requirements. HUD also brought pressures to bear on Fannie Mae and Freddie Mac to increase their purchases of mortgages made to low-income and moderate-income home buyers. In 1996 HUD set a target that 42 percent of the mortgages bought by Fannie Mae and Freddie Mac were to be financed for people with incomes below the median income in their areas.

In plain English, the regulators imposed quotas— and, if lenders had to resort to "innovative or flexible" standards and methods to meet those quotas, so be it. The Federal Reserve Bank of Boston issued a manual advising banks on non-discriminatory lending, which advised against using "arbitrary or unreasonable measures of creditworthiness."

Because banks are federally regulated enterprises, they need government permission to do many things that other businesses do as they see fit. That permission can be delayed or denied when objections are made that banks or other lenders are not living up to their obligations under the Community Reinvestment Act. For example, when legislation was pending in 1999 to permit banks to diversify into selling investment securities, the White House urged "that banks given unsatisfactory ratings under the 1977 Community Reinvestment Act be prohibited from enjoying the new diversification privileges" of this legislation.

Accordingly, when Congress passed legislation removing existing prohibitions against banks affiliating with securities or insurance firms, this new scope of banking operations was in fact reserved for those banks with a "rating of 'satisfactory record of meeting community credit needs', or better, at the most recent examination of each such institution"— that is, banks that met government-imposed quotas.

Various community activists across the country have been able to pressure banks into making concessions in money or in kind. These pressures could take various forms. For example, community activists could raise objections when banks sought permission from regulators to merge with other banks or to open new branches in another state, and banks would often find it expedient to make some concessions to these activists, in order to get the objections retracted, rather than go through the long delays that adjudication of objections and claims could entail. Sometimes the pressures were more direct, as when "left-wing groups like ACORN blocked drive-up lanes and made business impossible for banks until they surrendered to demands that they make billions in loans they wouldn't otherwise have made." The *Wall Street Journal* reported:

> Increasingly, community activists are taking banks to task— and winning large financial concessions— under the federal Community Reinvestment Act. . . This year alone, banks are expected to pony up $1 billion in low-cost loans and other aid for such causes as housing for the poor and the development of inner-city businesses. Wells Fargo Bank is providing low-cost financing for a shelter for battered women. First National Bank of Chicago is helping finance work on the headquarters of the National Training and Information Center, a major community-action group.

As regulatory agencies began to require reports on banks' "community service" activities under the Community Reinvestment Act before granting permission for mergers or opening branch offices, banks began to expand such things as donations to local non-profit agencies, establishing quotas for hiring of bank employees and set aside a certain amount of business for firms owned by ethnic minorities. Sumitomo Bank of California, for example, declared that it would give 20 to 25 percent of its contracts to minority-owned businesses.

Despite the title of the Community Reinvestment Act, it was not just in particular communities that lenders were pressured to make loans that they would not have made otherwise. Banks' qualification standards for lending to individuals in general were also attacked as too stringent as regards down payments, income, credit histories and other standards. In the housing markets, lenders were increasingly pressured by federal officials to relax lending standards, so as to make mortgage loans to people whose incomes and credit histories would not make them eligible under the traditional standards. With Fannie Mae and Freddie Mac ready to buy these mortgages from the original lenders, these lenders had every incentive to make such loans, whose risks could be passed on to these government-sponsored enterprises.

While these pressures became strong under the Clinton administration, they continued under the George W. Bush administration which, in 2002, urged Congress to pass the American Dream Downpayment Act. That Act subsidized the down payments of prospective home buyers whose incomes were below a certain level. After its passage, President Bush also urged Congress to pass legislation permitting the Federal Housing Administration to begin making zero-down-payment loans at low interest rates to low-income Americans. In 2004, Federal Housing Commissioner John Weicher said, "the White House doesn't think those who can afford the monthly payment but have been unable to save for a down payment should be deprived from owning a home." He added, "We do not anticipate any costs to taxpayers." Who, if not the taxpayers, would pay for these government subsidies— much less the defaults from making riskier loans— was not revealed.

Under these political pressures, traditional mortgage loans with traditional safeguards began to decline and mortgage loans made under the "innovative" and "flexible" standards urged by government increased. Traditional 30-year mortgages with a fixed interest rate, which were still 57 percent of all mortgages in 2001, fell to 33 percent of all mortgages by the end of 2006. Meanwhile, subprime loans rose from 7 percent of all mortgage loans to become 19 percent of such loans over the same span of years. Other non-traditional loans rose from less than 3 percent of all mortgage loans to nearly 14 percent.

Between 2005 and 2007, Fannie Mae and Freddie Mac acquired an estimated trillion dollars' worth of subprime and other non-traditional mortgages. This was approximately 40 percent of the value of all the mortgages they purchased from banks and other lenders during those years. In other words, these two major institutions of the mortgage markets were acquiring increasingly risky assets. Although pressures and quotas from government regulatory agencies were applied directly to banks, much mortgage lending is also done by other institutions, such as mortgage and finance companies and credit unions. However, the ability to resell mortgages to Fannie Mae and Freddie Mac provided incentives for lending to people who might not get mortgage loans in a free market.

What was crucial was that the Department of Housing and Urban Development, which was among the federal agencies pushing Fannie Mae and Freddie Mac to make more loans to people who would not normally be approved for loans— the "underserved" population, in the phrase often used— "allowed Freddie Mac and Fannie Mae to count billions of dollars they invested in subprime loans as a public good that would foster affordable housing," according to the *Washington Post*.

In short, riskier loans were accepted as good loans by one of the key regulators of the housing markets. Moreover, HUD was not just accepting subprime lending but pushing for more. After HUD became a regulator of Fannie Mae and Freddie Mac in 1992, these government-sponsored enterprises were set numerical goals— quotas— for what share of their lending was to be for "affordable housing" mortgages. In practice, they were pushed to acquire more subprime mortgages.

This was important not only because of the risk to the assets of these two enterprises themselves but, because they are dominant forces in the housing market and major gigantic financial institutions, there were dangers to the whole financial market if things went wrong with Fannie Mae and Freddie Mac, whose securities were widely held by other financial institutions in Wall Street and beyond. The importance of Fannie Mae and Freddie Mac in the housing markets is demonstrated by the magnitude of their mortgage guarantees, which total more than two *trillion* dollars. That is larger than the Gross Domestic Product of all but six nations.

Ordinarily, financial markets would become less willing to invest in an enterprise with ever growing risks. But, although Fannie Mae and Freddie Mac are officially private, profit-making enterprises, their size and the federal government's involvement in both their creation and their on-going operations led many investors to assume that the federal government would never allow them to fail— which is to say, the increasing riskiness of the assets of these two mortgage market giants was an increasing riskiness for the taxpayers, whether the taxpayers knew it or not.

Since more and riskier mortgages meant more profits to Fannie Mae and Freddie Mac, who could rely on the federal government to cover major losses, it was perfectly rational for them to expand their purchases of riskier mortgages from the banks and other mortgage lenders. Moreover, "creative" accounting *within* Fannie Mae and Freddie Mac themselves concealed the full extent of the risk until independent audits turned up discrepancies at both places, which led to the resignation of the heads of both institutions.

In short, the policies and practices of many institutions, local and national, public and private, set the stage for the housing boom and the housing bust that followed. Placing the roots of the housing boom and bust in the free market and the solution in government is very convenient for politicians and for those who favor government interventions. But such explanations are inconsistent with facts, however impressive they might be as exercises in rhetoric.

Both the genesis of unaffordable housing in particular local areas and the responses with national policies to make buying a home easier were political in origin, and government regulation is what forced lenders to meet arbitrary quotas by eroding traditional mortgage lending safeguards. The facts could not be plainer. Market criteria had long required such things as substantial down payments, as well as income and credit histories that made continuing payments likely. But all that was brushed aside in the political crusade for "affordable housing" and bigger home ownership statistics.

Both the unrealistic nature of policies pursued in the name of "affordable housing" and the serious dangers that such policies posed to the entire economy provoked many warnings from economists and others. But these warnings were repeatedly brushed aside by political leaders, often by shifting the focus to the supposed benefits of creating more home ownership through "affordable housing."

WARNINGS

Many people (including the author of this book)* pointed out some of the problems and risks during the housing boom. As far away as London, the distinguished British magazine *The Economist* in 2003 reiterated a warning it had made before, that "house prices would fall by 10% in America over the next four years," though it acknowledged that many of its readers "reject our gloomy warnings." In reality, American house prices fell sooner and more steeply. By 2005, *The Economist* repeated their warning yet again, but more urgently:

---

* A column of mine in the *Wall Street Journal* of May 26, 2005 warned that "this whole financial arrangement can collapse like a house of cards" and "the whole economy is affected if and when a speculative bubble bursts."

"America's house prices have reached dangerous levels" and added: "The whole world economy is at risk."

In 2003, U.S. Secretary of the Treasury John W. Snow asked Congress to "enact legislation to create a new Federal agency to regulate and supervise" Fannie Mae and Freddie Mac, because of his concerns about the risks they were taking. Two years later, testifying before the same Congressional committee, he returned to the same theme, citing the "systemic risk" arising from the fact that securities issued by Fannie Mae and Freddie Mac were "out there in the marketplace, held by all sorts of financial institutions— insurance companies, pension plans, community banks, thrifts, commercial banks." He added: "The concern is, if something unravels, it could cause systemic risk to the whole financial system."

In 2004, Josh Rosner, an analyst at Medley Global Advisors in New York, said, "The move to push homeownership on people that historically would not have had the finances or credit to qualify could conceivably and ultimately turn Fannie Mae's American dream of homeownership into the American nightmare of homeownership where people are trapped in their homes." He added: "If incomes don't rise or home values don't keep rising, or if interest rates rose considerably, you could quickly end up with significantly more people underwater with their mortgages and unable to pay."*

That same year, Professor Gregory Mankiw of Harvard, Chairman of the Council of Economic Advisors to the President, warned of the "systemic risk" posed by the "implicit public guarantee" of Fannie Mae and Freddie Mac, which encouraged these government-sponsored enterprises to take bigger risks. "The savings and loan crisis of the 1980s illustrates the adverse incentive effects that can rise as a result of government guarantees," Professor Mankiw warned.

A 2004 article in *Fortune* magazine warned of housing speculation that "is rapidly losing touch with reality" and of the risks

---

* The phrase "underwater" was widely used to refer to a situation where the value of the house has fallen below the amount owed on the mortgage.

created by the growing practice of borrowing against the equity in one's home. It added that "there's a real danger that a downturn in prices, or even a stall, could slam the economy, especially all-important consumer spending. Americans have used their homes like ATMs, taking out $662 billion in home-equity loans and refinancings since 2001."

In 2005, resident scholar Peter J. Wallison of the American Enterprise Institute, a Washington think tank, warned that, if Congress did not rein in Fannie Mae and Freddie Mac, "there will be a massive default with huge losses to the taxpayers and systemic effects on the economy."

Although most of the strongest supporters of lowering mortgage approval standards were Democrats, President George W. Bush joined in the political push for more home ownership. In 2002, he said, "I've set this goal for the country. We want 5.5 million more homeowners by 2010"— including a million more minority homeowners. The following year he signed the American Dream Downpayment Act, which provided money to help low-income home buyers by providing down payments and closing costs. *Barron's* magazine saw the dangers in all this:

> One of the proudest elements of President Bush's "compassionate conservative" agenda has been government financial support to home buyers for down payments. . . . But he is exposing taxpayers to tens of billions of dollars of possible losses, luring thousands of moderate-income families into bankruptcy, and risking the destruction of entire neighborhoods. . . . Free down payments carry catastrophic risks. . . Transferring the risk of homeownership from buyers to taxpayers does not endow virtue in America. Giving people a handout that leads them to financial ruin is wrecking-ball benevolence.

The head of the Federal Deposit Insurance Corporation warned Congress about "increasing numbers of problem loans, and concentrations of higher risk loans as a percentage of capital."

Federal Reserve Chairman Alan Greenspan was the best-known public figure to issue warnings on the housing boom. His warnings, like those of the Secretary of the Treasury and the head of the Federal

Deposit Insurance Corporation, were delivered directly to Congress, while testifying there. Alan Greenspan over the years moved from expressions of mild concern to a more dire view of the situation.

In 2005, Chairman Greenspan testified: "Although a bubbling in home prices for the Nation as a whole does not appear likely, there do appear to be at a minimum signs of froth in some local markets where home prices seem to have risen to unsustainable levels." Greenspan did note "the prevalence of interest-only loans, as well as the introduction of other relatively exotic forms of adjustable rate mortgages" as "developments of particular concern." But he added: "Although we certainly cannot rule out home price declines, especially in some local markets, these declines, were they to occur, likely would not have substantial macro-economic implications."

Although Chairman Greenspan at this point seemed not to expect major problems from the housing booms in various localities around the country, he was already apprehensive about the longer-run consequences of the expansion of Fannie Mae and Freddie Mac. He said, "if they continue to grow, continue to have the low capital that they have," then "they potentially create ever growing potential systemic risks down the road." There was, in his judgment, "no risk now at the moment," so there was time "to do something to fend off problems, which in my judgment seem almost inevitable as we look forward into the remainder of this decade." He opposed "enabling these institutions to increase in size," and added:

> We are placing the total financial system of the future at a substantial risk. Fortunately, at this stage, the risk is, the best I can judge, virtually negligible. I don't believe that will be the case if we continue to expand in this system.

By 2007, however, after Alan Greenspan was no longer chairman of the Federal Reserve System, and after housing prices had begun to fall, his concerns were heightened. He told the *Financial Times* of London that turmoil in the financial markets was "an accident waiting to happen." In a television interview on *60 Minutes*, Greenspan admitted that he had not fully assessed the extent of the dangers from the new ways of financing home mortgages. "While I was aware a lot of these practices were going on, I had no notion of how significant they had become until very late," he said. "I really didn't get it until very late in 2005 and 2006."

Many in Congress and elsewhere never really got it.

In response to warnings about the growing riskiness in housing markets, Congressman Barney Frank said in 2003, "Fannie Mae and Freddie Mac have played a very useful role in helping make housing more affordable." Critics "exaggerate a threat of safety" and "conjure up the possibility of serious financial losses to the Treasury, which I do not see."

As for government pressures on Fannie Mae and Freddie Mac to loosen their mortgage lending standards, he said: "I believe that we, as the Federal Government, have probably done too little rather than too much to push them to meet the goals of affordable housing and to set reasonable goals." He said, "I would like to get Fannie and Freddie more deeply into helping low-income housing and possibly moving into something that is more explicitly a subsidy." He added: "I want to roll the dice a little bit more in this situation towards subsidized housing."

Congressman Frank expressed a fear that criticisms of lower lending standards could create pressures to tighten those standards, because "the more pressure there is there, then the less I think we see in terms of affordable housing."

Congressman Frank dismissed fears expressed by those who saw an implicit commitment by the federal government to bail out Fannie Mae and Freddie Mac that could lead these giants to engage in more risky financial operations, because they felt they were backed up by the government, and this could lead investors to go along with accepting their risky securities, based on the same implicit reliance on the federal treasury. "But there is no guarantee," Congressman Frank asserted, "there is no explicit guarantee, there is no implicit guarantee, there is no wink-and-nod guarantee."

Such statements were not just some popping off by an isolated politician. Barney Frank was in 2003 the ranking member of the House Committee on Financial Services and would later become chairman of that powerful committee in 2006. He was a very influential force in the housing market.

Later events, however, were not kind to Congressman Frank's assertions. Those investors who had relied on taxpayer bailouts of Fannie Mae and Freddie Mac turned out to be right and Barney Frank wrong. As of January 2009, Fannie Mae and Freddie Mac were in line to receive $238 billion in federal bailout money and were asking for $70 billion more.

Congressman Frank was by no means the only member of Congress to dismiss warnings and assert that Fannie Mae and Freddie Mac were safe and sound institutions. His counterpart in the Senate, Chairman Christopher Dodd of the Senate Banking Committee, was equally adamant on the subject and continued to be so equally long— well into 2008, long after the financial system had already gone into a historic collapse. Back in 2004, when Fannie Mae and Freddie Mac were under criticism, Senator Dodd called them "one of the great success stories of all time" and urged "caution" in restricting their activities, out of fear of "doing great damage to what has been one of the great engines of economic success in the last 30 or 40 years."

After accounting errors totaling $11 billion were discovered in the books of Fannie Mae and Freddie Mac, President Bush in 2007 said that these government-sponsored enterprises should complete a "robust reform package" before being allowed to expand their mortgage portfolios. Senator Dodd said that President Bush should "immediately reconsider his ill-advised" position. As late as July 2008, after the housing market had collapsed, Senator Dodd continued to defend Fannie Mae and Freddie Mac as being "on a sound footing." Later events did not deal kindly with this assertion either, as both these hybrid enterprises were bailed out to prevent their collapse and were taken over by the federal government.

Over the years, both houses of Congress had many defenders of Fannie Mae and Freddie Mac as promoters of the political crusade for "affordable housing" through lower mortgage lending standards. Congresswoman Maxine Waters said in 2003, "we do not have a crisis at Freddie Mac, and in particular at Fannie Mae, under the outstanding leadership of Mr. Frank Raines." (This was the same Franklin Raines who would later take early retirement after the accounting scandals at Fannie Mae came to light.) Maxine Waters added that any regulatory reforms "must be done in a manner so as not to impede their affordable housing mission, a mission that has seen innovation flourish from desktop underwriting to 100 percent loans."

It was precisely these "desktop loans" based on unsubstantiated income claims by applicants— "liar loans" critics called them— and loans with no down payment at all ("100 percent loans") that many saw as especially dangerous.

Congressman Joe Baca likewise made "affordable housing" his over-riding concern. "According to Fannie Mae's own research," he said, with each rise of a quarter of a percent in the interest rate "some 78,166 Hispanic and 107,158 African American families become unable to afford to purchase a home." Moreover, "a long protracted debate on regulation" could cause "instability of the markets." In other words, just talking about the risks and the need for regulation could reduce the over-riding goal of more home ownership through "affordable housing." Such statements are reminiscent of Admiral Farragut's famous battle cry, "Damn the torpedoes, full speed ahead!" In this case, however, the financial markets got torpedoed and the whole economy sank.

In June 2004, in response to President Bush's expressed concerns about the riskiness of Fannie Mae and Freddie Mac, seventy-six Democrats in the House of Representatives sent him a letter defending these government-sponsored enterprises, and again making the case that "an exclusive focus on safety and soundness is likely to come, in practice, at the expense of affordable housing."

These 76 House members included such prominent individuals as Nancy Pelosi, Barney Frank, Maxine Waters and Charles Rangel.

Not only members of Congress, but others with a vested interest in lower mortgage lending standards, staunchly defended those standards in general and Fannie Mae and Freddie Mac in particular, during the housing boom that others were warning about. People in the business of building homes obviously have a vested interest in government policies and programs that cause more homes to be built. Therefore it should not be surprising that a representative of the National Association of Homebuilders testified before the House Committee on Financial Services in favor of existing low standards for mortgage loan approval:

> In focusing on the safety and soundness regulation, we urge the committee not to lose sight of the core missions, which is. . .to provide liquidity, capital and stability to the housing market. . .
>
> The objective and focus of program oversight is not safety and soundness, as HUD Secretary Martinez testified, it is mission compliance. An example would be furthering the Administration's goal of increasing minority home ownership.

In other words, so long as more homes got built, the National Association of Homebuilders was not going to sweat the details, which would ultimately be the taxpayers' problem. The National Urban League likewise saw the whole issue in terms of its own constituency. An official of the Urban League testified before the same committee that any oversight of Fannie Mae and Freddie Mac should "fit into a coherent set of programs at HUD to create the largest affordable housing stock available for America, and that huge disparities in home ownership faced by African-Americans and Hispanics can be closed."

The heads of Fannie Mae and Freddie Mac also went on record in favor of mortgage lending standards that focused on "affordable housing" more so than on financial standards. The Director of Freddie Mac, after gingerly referring in passing to "the resolution of Freddie Mac's accounting issues," went on to say that "we have consistently met the permanent affordable housing goals" and that "Freddie Mac is safe, sound and strong."

The CEO of Fannie Mae, the already mentioned Franklin Raines, likewise said that every year "we have met or exceeded our affordable housing goals, even as they have increased" and that Fannie Mae has "also set a voluntary goal: to lead the market in serving minority families." Moreover, CEO Raines pointed out in passing that Fannie Mae had "amassed over $30 billion of private equity capital to finance $2 trillion of mortgages today." He did not address the critics' charge that it was precisely this very high ratio of business done to the amount of capital available, to cover any problems that might arise, which posed a major risk to Fannie Mae and to the financial system in general, which held such vast amounts of Fannie Mae's securities.

Congressional support for Fannie Mae and Freddie Mac went far beyond words. When the Office of Federal Housing Enterprise Oversight— the agency overseeing these government-sponsored enterprises— turned up irregularities in Fannie Mae's accounting and in 2004 issued what *Barron's* magazine called "a blistering 211-page report," Republican Senator Kit Bond called for an investigation *of the Office of Federal Housing Enterprise Oversight*, tried to have their budget slashed, and sought to have the leadership of the regulatory agency removed. Democratic Congressman Barney Frank likewise declared: "It is clear that a leadership change at OFHEO is overdue."

In short, Fannie Mae's political support in Congress has been bipartisan. "Fannie Mae and Freddie Mac's employees and political action committees donated nearly $5 million to current members of Congress since 1989," according to the *St. Louis Post-Dispatch*. Republican Senator Kit Bond received $95,000 and Democratic Senator Christopher Dodd received $165,000. According to the *Wall Street Journal*:

> The two companies employ armies of lobbyists and consultants and are major campaign donors. "There has been no more powerful organization in Washington than Fannie Mae," said Rep. Chris Shays (R., Conn.).

"They have been able to manipulate the regulatory and legislative process for years."

Such criticisms of the political protection of Fannie Mae and Freddie Mac were not confined to conservative publications like the *Wall Street Journal*. Essentially the same criticisms were made in the liberal *Washington Post*:

> Blessed with the advantages of a government agency and a private company at the same time, Fannie Mae and Freddie Mac used their windfall profits to co-opt the politicians who were supposed to control them. The companies fought successfully against increased regulation by cultivating their friends and hounding their enemies.
>
> The agencies that regulated the companies were outmatched: They lacked the money, the staff, the sophistication and the political support to serve as an effective check.

This pattern went back for years. The *Washington Post* recalled a 1992 attempt by Congressman Jim Leach to get stronger regulation of Fannie Mae and Freddie Mac— and the opposition by Congressman Barney Frank to prevent it. The *Washington Post* also pointed out how the budget of the Office of Federal Housing Enterprise Oversight, which regulated Fannie Mae and Freddie Mac, was more tightly controlled by Congress than were the budgets of agencies regulating banks, giving the two hybrid companies' "congressional allies an easy way to exert pressure" on OFHEO and limit its ability to regulate. Moreover, the rules on capital requirements for Fannie Mae and Freddie Mac were less strict than the rules for banks, allowing these government-sponsored enterprises greater opportunities for profit, by expanding their transactions without as much capital as banks would be required to have in order to do the same things.

A few members of Congress warned about the dangers in the way Fannie Mae and Freddie Mac were operating. In addition to Congressman Jim Leach, there was Congressman Richard Baker and Congressman Christopher Shays. They got nowhere. Congressman Shays said that these government-sponsored enterprises "are going to crash if this Congress doesn't wake up and do something about it."

But Congress was not about to wake up, much less do something about it. Too many members of both houses of Congress, and of both political parties, as well as people in the Executive branch, were benefitting from Fannie Mae, Freddie Mac, and other financial institutions involved in creating the housing boom.

Corruption of the political process can take many forms. Senator Christopher Dodd, for example, received mortgages from Countrywide Financial Corporation on unusually favorable terms, saving him an estimated $75,000.* Among politically well-connected people put on the payroll of Countrywide were former Secretary of Housing and Urban Development Henry Cisneros and the son of Nancy Pelosi. Senator Bob Bennett of Utah not only received more campaign contributions from Fannie Mae and Freddie Mac than any other Republican in Congress over the years, his son was employed by Fannie Mae. In addition, *The Economist* magazine reported: "Ex-politicians were given jobs" by Fannie Mae and Freddie Mac.

Among those who have been appointed to various lucrative positions on the payroll of these government-sponsored enterprises have been former White House aide Harold Ickes, former Democratic Congressman Thomas Downey, former Republican Senator Alfonse D'Amato, former Deputy Attorney General Jamie Gorelick, former Secretary of Commerce William M. Daley, former Congressman Harold E. Ford, the wife of former Republican Governor John Engler, as well as former Clinton White House adviser, former Democratic Congressman and current Obama White House chief of staff, Rahm Emanuel.

One of the other perquisites of power, in addition to being able to place political allies and aides in lucrative positions, has long been simply the ability to throw one's weight around, in order to extort

---

* In June 2009 the *Wall Street Journal* said: "Mr. Dodd denies receiving any special treatment, and nearly a year ago he promised to release the Countrywide mortgage documents and clear up the matter. We are still waiting, though he did attempt to placate the Connecticut press with a peek-a-boo release of a few select documents and a review by his own lawyers in February." "Dodd's Irish Luck," *Wall Street Journal*, June 20, 2009, p. A12.

favors for one's constituents. Although the Massachusetts-based bank called OneUnited was ineligible to receive money from the Troubled Asset Relief Program (TARP) under its general guidelines, Massachusetts Congressman Barney Frank intervened and suddenly it became eligible to receive $12 million of the taxpayers' money. According to the *Wall Street Journal*, "Mr. Frank, by his own account, wrote into the TARP bill a provision specifically aimed at helping this particular home-state bank. And later, he acknowledges, he spoke to regulators urging that OneUnited be considered for a cash injection."

At a meeting with U.S. Treasury Department officials were not only representatives of Congressman Barney Frank but also representatives of Senator John Kerry of Massachusetts and of Congresswoman Maxine Waters of Los Angeles, whose husband had served on the board of directors of the OneUnited Bank and has had at least a quarter of a million dollars worth of stock in the bank. Similarly, after General Motors was bailed out by the government and began shutting down dealerships and other facilities around the country, their plan to shut down a facility in Massachusetts was cancelled after a phone call from Congressman Frank.

Fear, as well as favors, help explain how some programs and institutions become sacred cows. According to economist Gerald P. O'Driscoll, a former official of the Federal Reserve System and a former executive in private banking, before becoming a Senior Fellow at the Cato Institute:

> At heart, Fannie and Freddie had become classic examples of "crony capitalism." The "cronies" were businessmen and politicians working together to line each other's pockets while claiming to serve the public good. The politicians created the mortgage giants, which then returned some of the profits to the pols— sometimes directly, as campaign funds; sometimes as "contributions" to favored constituents. . . And, because government backing let Fannie and Freddie dominate the mortgage-underwriting market, private-sector criticism was silenced. Local banks that wanted to offer mortgages dared not speak out against them. Large banks dared not complain about the giants' government-given advantage because they needed to be able to buy securities from Fannie/Freddie.

The very existence of Fannie Mae and Freddie Mac is hard to explain by any public benefit derived from having these hybrid enterprises buying home mortgages that can be— and are— bought by ordinary private financial institutions. The benefits to politicians are far more obvious. As the housing boom turned to bust, the dangers of Fannie Mae and Freddie Mac to the taxpayers, and to the economy as a whole, also became painfully clear.

Chapter 3

The Housing Bust

The great irony is that those who unleashed this economic calamity appear to be the main beneficiaries of the crisis they helped to create.

Peter Schweizer

Back in 2002, *Newsweek* economic columnist Robert J. Samuelson wrote:

> To anyone with a sense of history, the home boom must be a source of wonder. Housing usually leads the economy into recession. Mortgage rates rise, then housing construction and home sales fall.

This historical pattern repeated yet again, just four years later. The "blame game" of finger-pointing began immediately, many in politics and the media saying that the problem was that the market was left unregulated and now the government had to step in.

The development of lax lending standards, both by banks and by Fannie Mae and Freddie Mac standing behind the banks, came *not* from a lack of government regulation and oversight, but precisely as a *result* of government regulation and oversight, directed toward the politically popular goal of more "home ownership" through "affordable housing," especially for low-income home buyers. These lax lending standards were the foundation for a house of cards that was ready to collapse with a relatively small nudge.

That nudge came as the Federal Reserve System, having lowered its own interest rates to an extremely low one percent, began slowly raising the interest rate back toward more normal levels in 2004. Unusually low interest rates had been used earlier by the Federal

Reserve, in order to maintain credit spending in the economy at large, at a time when the economy seemed about to decline otherwise. But such extremely low interest rates could not be maintained indefinitely, without an unending supply of easy credit leading to inflation. Federal Reserve authorities therefore began gradually but steadily raising their interest rate over time, from its low of one percent in 2004 until the Federal Reserve's interest rate reached 5.25 percent in 2006.

As financial institutions had to pay more to get money, they of course began raising their own interest rates charged to borrowers— including those borrowing to buy homes. This affected not only new borrowers but also existing home buyers with adjustable rate mortgages. Just as mortgage interest rates had followed Federal Reserve interest rates down, now mortgage interest rates rose as Federal Reserve interest rates rose. Then, just as unusually low interest rates had made monthly mortgage payments more affordable for more people, increasing the demand for houses and therefore their prices, conversely the rise of interest rates to more normal levels made monthly mortgage payments more expensive, and thereby reduced the demand for houses.

DECLINING HOME PRICES

Housing prices began falling in 2006, for the first time in more than a decade— and they fell by record amounts. They fell especially sharply in places where they had risen especially sharply before, which was where more people had gone farthest out on a limb with risky "creative" financing, in order to be able to buy a house, and so were most likely to default when rising interest rates meant rising monthly mortgage payments. Speculators caught owing money on mortgages on multiple houses that could no longer be sold for rising prices— or even for the prices at which the speculators bought them— were also especially likely to default, even if that meant going bankrupt. As lenders repossessed more houses and put them up for sale, this increase in the number of houses for sale further lowered the prices of houses in general through supply and demand.

As housing prices declined in September 2006, California led the nation in mortgage foreclosures. The numbers of foreclosures in San Francisco and in adjoining San Mateo County were double what they had been a year earlier, and foreclosures in Alameda County across the Bay from San Francisco more than tripled in just one year.

These were not one-time events, but a continuing trend in the following years. In June 2007, foreclosure notices nationwide rose 87 percent over the previous year. In the San Francisco Bay Area, foreclosures continued to increase, nearly tripling in one year. For California as a whole, there was an 800 percent increase in the number of homes whose deeds reverted to bank ownership. This was a major problem for the banks, as well as for those who lost their homes, since banks lose an estimated $40,000 per home foreclosed. Not being in the business of managing real estate, banks have every incentive to quickly dump repossessed houses on the market at whatever price they can get for them.

Large-scale foreclosures meant falling home prices, as the foreclosed homes added to the supply without any corresponding increase in demand. "Fully half of all existing homes sold in the Bay Area in December [2008] were foreclosures unloaded by banks at fire-sale prices," the *San Francisco Chronicle* reported. Those sales sent housing prices "tumbling to new lows and attracted droves of buyers." For the nine-county Bay Area, prices were "down 46.8 percent from a year ago," the *San Francisco Chronicle* reported. Those places outside California that had had similar sky-high prices went through a similar experience when the housing bubble burst.

Phoenix, Arizona, was described in the *New York Times* as "an epicenter of the nation's recent building boom" but that changed drastically when the housing bubble burst in 2006:

> Until recently, this fast-growing area was a paradise on earth for home builders. Fulton Homes' developments, for example, were so popular last

year that it was able to raise prices on its new homes by $1,000 to $10,000 almost every week.

"People were standing in line for lotteries," recalled Douglas S. Fulton, president of the company, one of the largest private builders in the Phoenix area. And they were "camping overnight begging to be the next number in the next lot in the next house."

No more.

Today, it is the company's sales agents that do most of the waiting. Not only are there few new customers to talk to, but many buyers who put down a deposit are not even bothering to come back for the walk-through.

"All of a sudden, they just don't show up," Mr. Fulton said, noting that such cancellations often mean the buyers forfeit as much as 5 percent of the price. The reason? The prospective buyers got cold feet or simply could not sell their old home.

Sharp declines in housing prices still continued in 2008. At the end of that year, Standard & Poor's reported that its home-price index for October, compared to October of the previous year, declined more sharply than at any time in the two decades' history of that index. In October 2008, six metropolitan areas showed housing price declines of more than 25 percent, compared to the previous October, and three— Phoenix, Las Vegas and San Francisco— had housing price declines of more than 30 percent compared to October of the previous year.

Coastal California was especially hard hit. In just one year, home prices fell by 27 percent in San Diego, 28 percent in Los Angeles and 31 percent in San Francisco. A few other places had similar declines in just one year— 29 percent in Miami, 32 percent in Las Vegas and 33 percent in Phoenix. But, of the 25 metropolitan areas with the steepest home price declines, 16 were in California. For California as a whole, home prices dropped by an average of $100,000 between 2007 and 2008. San Diego, where housing prices had more than doubled between 2000 and 2005, saw its average home price decline by more than $200,000 from 2006 to 2008.

Differential Impacts

The very different conditions in different local housing markets was demonstrated by the fact that, despite drastic declines in home prices in some areas, the nationwide housing price decline was somewhere between 2 percent and 9 percent in 2007, depending on what index was used. The home price decline was 5 percent or less in more than 50 of the metropolitan areas in the country. In fewer than 10 of these metropolitan areas had home prices declined by more than 20 percent. Meanwhile, in more than 20 metropolitan areas, home prices were still rising. Neither the sharp rise in home prices to unaffordable levels nor the subsequent fall was a nationwide phenomenon. Both were severe problems in particular localities.

In Dallas the home price decline was only 3 percent. This was in a city with few building restrictions, where housing prices took just 13 percent of the average income, even during the boom. Where housing can be had for 13 percent of the average income, there is far less incentive to go out on a limb with risky financing to buy a home— and therefore far less risk of a boom and bust in the housing market. There is also far less incentive for speculation in such a housing market. As Alan Greenspan had said back in 2005, "We don't perceive that there is a national bubble, but it's hard not to see that there are a lot of local bubbles."

There was also a differential impact of rising interest rates on people with different kinds of mortgages. While interest rate changes did not affect existing home buyers who already had fixed-rate mortgages, these rising rates very much affected both new prospective home buyers and existing home buyers with adjustable rate mortgages, as the rise of interest rates meant increases in their monthly mortgage payments. One group particularly hard hit by the housing downturn were borrowers who used what were called "option ARMS"— adjustable rate mortgages (ARMs) with an option to vary the monthly payments at the borrower's discretion. In January 2009, the *Wall Street Journal* reported, "with home prices falling, more than

55% of borrowers with option ARMs owe more than their homes are valued at, according to J.P. Morgan Securities Inc." Twenty-eight percent of such borrowers were either delinquent or in foreclosure.

Although monthly mortgage payments by existing home buyers with the old-fashioned, fixed-rate mortgages were of course not directly affected by the rising interest rates, the value of their houses declined with that of all the rest. However, traditional fixed-rate 30-year mortgages were no longer standard but were now only about one-third of all mortgages.

Many people who had stretched to buy homes with interest-only, adjustable-rate mortgages now often found themselves pushed over the edge financially when their monthly mortgage payment rose because of rising interest rates, even before the interest-only period expired. Such borrowers were doubly affected if interest rates rose at the same time as the already scheduled monthly payment increase needed to begin paying off the principal on their mortgage loan. By 2007, about one-fourth of all adjustable-rate mortgage loans, interest-only loans and payment-option loans were at least 60 days late on their mortgage payments. This was more than double the rate of payment delinquencies on conventional 30-year fixed-rate mortgages.

The special vulnerability of borrowers with adjustable rate loans, as compared to 30-year fixed-interest-rate mortgages, was reflected in the default rates and foreclosure rates during the housing downturn. In 2007, Federal Reserve Board Chairman Ben Bernanke announced: "About 320,000 foreclosures were initiated in each of the first two quarters of this year, just more than half of them on subprime mortgages, up from an average of about 220,000 during the past 6 years." According to the *New York Times*: "Minority homeowners take out a disproportionate share of subprime loans. The most recent Home Mortgage Disclosure Act data from lending institutions show that over half of African-Americans and 40 percent of Hispanics received subprime loans." Both groups were especially hard hit by the foreclosures that followed the housing bust. So much for the favor being done to minorities.

Speculators, who could make remarkable sums of money in a remarkably short amount of time during the housing boom, by borrowing at low "teaser" rates of interest and then selling quickly before these below-market rates of interest moved up to market rates, now found themselves stuck with having to pay for multiple mortgages on expensive houses that took longer to sell and could no longer be sold for more than they cost— or even for as much as they had cost. Not all of those trapped by the housing bust were innocent homeowners. Substantial numbers were people who had profited handsomely from the boom and who now wanted to be rescued from the bust with the taxpayers' money.

Research by the *San Francisco Chronicle* in 2007 turned up nearly a thousand homes in foreclosure in the San Francisco Bay Area that were "owned by 439 people who had multiple properties foreclosed upon from January to September." In addition, "349 foreclosures were owned by people who listed mailing ZIP codes different from their property's address at the time of purchase— suggesting the properties were an investment, not a primary residence." The *Las Vegas Sun* "found that 74 percent of single-family homes in foreclosure during a six-month period this year were owned by investors who did not live there." Like other aspects of the housing markets, foreclosures on property owned by absentee owners were "much more common among defaults in California, Nevada, Arizona and Florida— all states with particularly rapid price appreciation that attracted speculators."

It was actually even more localized than that. Holman Jenkins of the *Wall Street Journal* called attention to "the striking fact" that much of the subprime crisis originated in particular counties in just four states. It was much the same story with foreclosures. In April 2009, *USA Today* reported: "Five states— California, Florida, Arizona, Nevada and Illinois— accounted for almost 60% of the first-quarter foreclosure activity." Neither the shortage of "affordable housing" that led to government intervention in housing markets, nor the boom and bust brought on by that intervention, spread evenly across the nation.

Nor were the foreclosures. What did spread across the nation, and even overseas, were the financial repercussions.

Financial Market Repercussions

While, in a sense, the worst of the housing market collapse was geographically concentrated in places with the highest and previously fastest growing housing prices, the repercussions were nationwide and even international.

These *locally* high housing prices, and then locally sharp declines in housing prices, in such places as coastal California, Miami or Phoenix, which had led to especially high rates of mortgage defaults, had national repercussions, because the inflated values of houses in these places were accepted by *national* organizations like Fannie Mae and Freddie Mac, which bought these mortgages, and by Wall Street firms that also bought such mortgages and then created and sold securities based on the inflated values of these mortgages across the country and overseas. Securities issued by Fannie Mae and Freddie Mac were likewise bought by both American and foreign investors. That is why a bank in Germany had to be bailed out when American housing prices fell.

As a scholarly study noted, "many of those who either sold or bought these securities were highly-sophisticated investors such as Bear Stearns, Merrill Lynch, or Citibank." But their sophistication did not save them:

> Nonetheless, numerous Wall Street titans have taken multi-billion dollar write-downs as a result of investing in securities backed by subprime loans. . . In fact, significant losses have been suffered at virtually every level of the subprime chain. . .

How suddenly subprime mortgages had become a major part of the financial scene was shown by the dollar volume of their growth. The value of subprime mortgages created in 1995 was $65 billion but this swelled more than five-fold to $332 billion in 2003. Because the era of widespread use of subprime mortgages was new, neither the

Wall Street firms that bought them nor the securities-rating firms, like Moody's or Standard & Poor's, on whose ratings the Wall Street investors relied when buying mortgage-backed securities, had much history to draw on in assessing the risks of these kinds of securities. Moreover, that history of esoteric new financial instruments was not only brief but concentrated in a period of prosperity, rather than being a history going back through decades of varied economic conditions, as the history of more conventional mortgages and other financial instruments did. As one study pointed out:

> Mortgage credit conditions couldn't have seemed better in those years. By 2005, with unemployment declining and house prices surging, delinquencies and defaults had dropped to record lows. Hardly a borrower in San Diego or Miami was even late with a payment.

Even subprime mortgages had only a low rate of foreclosure at the height of the housing boom in 2005. Moreover, the foreclosure rate for subprime mortgages was not dramatically higher than that for prime mortgages at that time— though subprime mortgages' foreclosure rate would shoot up both absolutely and relative to that of prime mortgages after the housing bust began in 2006. Although many critics have blamed the securities-rating companies for giving high ratings to new kinds of securities whose values later collapsed, it is not clear what hard evidence existed, before the housing market collapse, that would have led to lower ratings.

There was ignorance, which might have led to caution, but no hard evidence on which to base a specific lower rating. Many investors were remote from the direct participants who made the original mortgages. These mortgages were sold to other financial institutions and were then bundled together to create bonds, each backed by many mortgages. Nor did the process always stop there. These bonds could in turn be bundled together to create what were called "collateralized debt obligations"— which were even further removed from original mortgages and from any knowledge of the homeowners involved, the reliability of the appraisals that had been made of the properties,* and other factors that affect risk. *The Economist* magazine called the purchase of some of these securities "a leap in the dark."

The collapse of the housing market in 2006 forced changes in the ratings of mortgage-based securities. According to the *New York Times*:

> In April 2007, Moody's announced it was revising the model it used to evaluate subprime mortgages. It noted that the model "was first introduced in 2002. Since then, the mortgage market has evolved considerably." This was a rather stunning admission; its model had been based on a world that no longer existed.

The sudden surge in subprime mortgages and the securities based on them was not the only reason for over-optimistic credit ratings being given to the securities. Those who issued mortgage-backed securities "would 'shop' the securities at each of the three major rating entities and have the securities rated by the one that was willing to give the best rating." These credit-rating agencies were among the many contributors to the financial crisis by their insufficient caution in giving the new and untested securities favorable ratings.

The fundamental problem, however, was in the housing market. Even existing home buyers who did *not* have either subprime mortgages or adjustable-rate mortgages were nevertheless affected indirectly by the rising interest rates, when higher interest rates caused rising home prices to suddenly turn into falling home prices. Therefore many home buyers, regardless of what kind of mortgage they had, could find the value of their home falling below the amount that they owed on the mortgage. That could confront them with a

---

* According to the *Wall Street Journal* in 2002: "Few of the people involved in making mortgage loans these days have a long-term interest in them. Traditionally, bankers had made loans directly and held them, giving the lenders a strong incentive to find fair appraisals to protect their interests. Today, many appraisers are picked by independent mortgage brokers, who are paid per transaction and have little stake in the long-term health of the loans. Many lenders also have lost a long-term interest in their loans, because they sell them off to investors." John Hechinger, "Shaky Foundation: Rising Home Prices Cast Appraisers in a Harsh Light," *Wall Street Journal*, December 13, 2002, pp. A1, A10.

painful question: "Why continue to pay off a $500,000 mortgage on a home that is now worth only $350,000?"

In short, even some people who could afford to pay off their mortgages were now faced with incentives to stop doing so. People who had borrowed against the equity in their homes were of course at increased risk of finding that what they owed now exceeded the value of the remaining equity in their home, when they had both a mortgage to pay and a home-equity loan to repay. Here too were people who were *not* trapped by circumstances beyond their control but who had simply chosen risky ways of getting money and lost.

Home buyers in a variety of circumstances now had reasons to default on their mortgages— and they proceeded to do so, whether they had to or whether they simply chose to. This set in motion a sequence of events— beginning with rising rates of defaults and foreclosures, followed by declining values of financial institutions' assets based on the declining values of the mortgages they held. Those who owned stock in those financial institutions saw the value of their stock decline and some financial institutions on the other side of the Atlantic suffered heavy losses because of their investments in securities based on the value of American home mortgages.

The spread of financial disaster from local housing markets to national and international financial markets was much like a heavy rainfall high in the mountains, filling a thousand little creeks and streams that empty into a big river, ultimately flooding people living far downstream from the source of the water. Perhaps better levees might have saved the people downstream. But that does not change the fact that the flood originated in heavy rainfalls in the mountains. In the case of the housing market collapse, much has been made of the claim that there was inadequate regulatory agency oversight of the financial markets that turned home mortgages into esoteric Wall Street securities, which added to the risk. But these securities would have remained secure if people had continued to make their monthly mortgage payments.

It was ultimately the skyrocketing rates of mortgage delinquencies and defaults that were like the heavy rain in the mountains that caused the flooding downstream. As Professor Stanley Liebowitz of the University of Texas at Dallas put it: "From the current handwringing, you'd think that the banks came up with the idea of looser underwriting standards on their own, with regulators just asleep on the job." Government was not passively inefficient. It was actively zealous in promoting risky mortgage lending practices.

ECONOMIC AND POLITICAL ADJUSTMENTS

Since people make mistakes, whether they are in the market, in the government or elsewhere, the salient question is how they adjust to their mistakes in a market economy, compared to how they adjust in political institutions. More specifically, the question is how people have adjusted to the housing boom and bust in these two settings, with their very different incentives and constraints.

Responses in the Market

The market's adjustments to the bursting of the housing bubble took place quickly and in predictable ways. In California, for example, the mixtures of homes purchased shifted toward what were, for California, less expensive homes. Homes costing less than half a million dollars were just 43 percent of all homes sold in California in 2007 but became 78 percent of all homes sold there the following year. In short, people were learning to stay within what their incomes could afford.

Although the median down payment during the housing boom was a record low 12 percent of the sales price in California in 2006, after the riskiness of low down payments became painfully clear to both borrowers and lenders in the wake of the housing bust, the median down payment rose to the traditional 20 percent level in 2008.

The proportion of California home buyers who made no down payment at all dropped from 18 percent in 2007 to 3 percent in 2008, the lowest proportion in years.

The proportion of interest-only, adjustable-rate mortgages in the state also fell, from 16 percent of all mortgages in 2007 to 2 percent in 2008. Even first-time home buyers, who had financed 24 percent of their housing purchases with interest-only, adjustable rate mortgages at the height of the housing boom in 2005, financed only 2 percent of their home purchases that way in 2008. The old-fashioned fixed-rate, 30-year mortgage made a dramatic comeback, rising from just 55 percent of all mortgages in the state in 2005 to more than 90 percent of all California mortgages in 2008.

There were correspondingly large changes in the use of second mortgages. More than 60 percent of first-time home buyers in California had used second mortgages to purchase their homes in 2006 but that fell to 12 percent just two years later.

National trends were similar. Adjustable-rate mortgages, which were 35 percent of all mortgages in 2004, were down to 10 percent of all mortgages by 2007. While the total amount lent in subprime mortgages nationwide was nearly $140 billion in the fourth quarter of 2006, that fell to less that $20 billion in the fourth quarter of 2007. Every major racial or ethnic group in the country— blacks, whites, Hispanics, Asian Americans, American Indians and Native Hawaiians— reduced the share of their loans that were subprime. Lenders also adjusted. According to the *New York Times*, "lenders have become more cautious about whom they will lend to," and both refinancing and mortgage insurance now had more stringent requirements that borrowers must meet. In May 2009, the *New York Times* reported that "half of all banks recently tightened their lending standards on prime mortgages" and that many would-be home buyers "simply cannot get financing."

Consumers, as well as businesses, adjusted substantially within a very few years, according to a 2009 account in the *New York Times*:

> The personal saving rate, which dipped below zero during the housing boom as Americans tapped home equity loans and other easy lines of credit, rose to 6.9 percent in May, the Commerce Department reported. That was its highest point since December 1993.

Holders of mortgage-backed securities began dumping on the market the houses behind those securities. According to the *Wall Street Journal* in July 2009:

> While nationwide figures are scarce, a review of thousands of foreclosures in the Atlanta area shows that trusts managing pools of securitized mortgages sold six times as many properties as banks during the six months ended March 31. And homes dumped by subprime bondholders sold for thousands of dollars less on average than bank-owned properties, the data show.

Among the foreclosed homes in the Atlanta area that were sold by holders of mortgage-backed securities, one that had been bought for $151,000 in June 2006 was sold for $90,000 in April 2009. Another purchased for $292,000 in March 2006 was sold for $164,000 in January 2009. Yet another home that had been bought for $236,000 at the height of the housing boom in August 2005 was sold in January 2009 for just $30,000. Among nearly 3,000 homes in the Atlanta area sold by holders of mortgage-backed securities in a six-month period, the average selling price was just 62 percent of the original mortgage loan amount.

In short, the market learns— even if only the hard way— and adjusts with remarkable speed, when staring financial ruin in the face is the alternative. The question is whether politicians and government bureaucrats learn, especially when they pay no price for being wrong, and are able to deflect blame toward the market with denunciations of "greed," "Wall Street" or whatever other convenient scapegoats are available.

Political Responses

While those in the market— both businesses and consumers— have made major changes in the wake of the economic crisis, politicians on the other hand have opted for more of the same, even in the wake of the housing market boom and bust. While banks and securities firms dumped foreclosed houses on the market at whatever discounted price they could get, the government set up multi-billion-dollar programs to try to prop up housing prices with the taxpayers' money. As banks and other private lenders pulled back and tightened up as regards mortgage lending, the Federal Housing Administration (FHA) surged ahead. As the *Wall Street Journal* reported in May 2009:

> Last year banks issued $180 billion of new mortgages insured by the FHA, which means they carry a 100% taxpayer guarantee. Many of these have the same characteristics as subprime loans: low downpayment requirements, high-risk borrowers, and in many cases shady mortgage originators. FHA now insures nearly one of every three new mortgages, up from 2% in 2006. . . According to Mortgage Bankers Association data, more than one in eight FHA loans is now delinquent— nearly triple the rate on conventional, nonsubprime loan portfolios. Another 7.5% of recent FHA loans are in "serious delinquency," which means at least three months overdue.

Meanwhile, in the face of innumerable problems and costly bailouts in the housing financing sector, Congress in 2008 authorized an *increase* in the size of the loans that the Federal Housing Administration could insure— nearly doubling the mortgage loan limit from $362,500 to $719,000. Since most Americans cannot afford a mortgage loan of more than $700,000, the case for forcing taxpayers to subsidize those who take out such large mortgage loans is far from clear, even aside from the risky ways that so many of the FHA loans are financed. One of these risks is that the minimum down payment for FHA mortgage loans is less than 4 percent. But that is only one of the risks, as the *Wall Street Journal* reported:

> In a rational world, Congress and the White House would tighten FHA underwriting standards, in particular by eliminating the 100% guarantee. That guarantee means banks and mortgage lenders have no skin in the game; lenders collect the 2% to 3% origination fees on as many FHA loans as they can push out the door regardless of whether the borrower has a likelihood of repaying the mortgage. The Washington Post

reported in March a near-tripling in the past year in the number of loans in which a borrower failed to make more than a single payment. One Florida bank, Great Country Mortgage of Coral Gables, had a 64% default rate on its FHA properties.

While it may not be "a rational world" as far as the federal government's policies affect the taxpayers, it is quite rational from the standpoint of elected officials who benefit by catering to special interest groups such as mortgage lenders, home builders and others who profit from loose mortgage lending standards, while politicians pay no price politically from doing so, despite whatever economic disasters have already been created by such policies or what new disasters may be on the horizon from a continuation of such policies. The ability of politicians to shift blame to others is the key to their not having to pay a price for promoting policies that increase the risks for taxpayers and for the economy as a whole.

The government has even leaned on those banks that have scaled back on risky loans that had been made to fulfill goals under the Community Reinvestment Act. In March 2009, an official of the Federal Reserve System declared: "We don't view the current credit environment as a free pass in terms of a bank meeting its CRA requirements." The Federal Deposit Insurance Corporation gave the small East Bridgewater Savings Bank in Boston a "needs to improve" rating, even though this bank had had no foreclosures and no delinquent loans. "Improvement" would presumably mean making the kinds of risky loans under government pressures that had gotten other banks into trouble.

The Politics of Blame

In addition to the more or less ad hoc scapegoating of others, many of the architects of the lower mortgage lending standards at the heart of the housing boom and bust have more systematically created scapegoats by summoning before Congressional committees various business leaders or federal employees to be denounced on nationwide television or before other members of the mass media. As the *New York Times* reported in September 2008: "Almost every member of the Senate Banking Committee wagged a finger at what they described as Wall Street's greed and lax regulatory oversight." This is the committee chaired by Senator Christopher Dodd. It was much the same story in hearings before the House Financial Services Committee— chaired by Congressman Barney Frank— in February 2009, where "the leaders of some of the country's largest banks endured hours of hectoring Wednesday by indignant lawmakers," as the *Los Angeles Times* reported.

Often those summoned before these committees to be publicly browbeaten or humiliated on television were in no position to answer in kind, whether because their jobs and their agencies' appropriations were at risk or because they were leaders of private businesses currently under federal regulation or which could be singled out for adverse new legislation.

This was just one of the ways in which Washington politicians demonstrated their understanding that the best defense is a good offense. Senator Christopher Dodd said: "I have a lot of questions about where was the administration over the last eight years." Repeatedly the Bush administration had sought increased power to rein in Fannie Mae and Freddie Mac during those years, while Senator Dodd fought adamantly against granting such powers.

Senator Dodd also blamed Federal Reserve Board chairman Alan Greenspan for the mortgage crisis, even though Greenspan had warned against the riskiness of policies that Dodd had defended in the name of "affordable housing." According to Senator Dodd in 2007, after the housing bubble had burst, Alan Greenspan "seemed to encourage the development and use of adjustable-rate mortgages that today are defaulting and going into foreclosure at record rates." But adjustable-rate mortgages have been the norm in Europe for decades, without causing a mortgage crisis.

Lax lending standards used to meet "affordable housing" quotas were the key to the American mortgage crisis. That many of those who could not meet the regular American standards for a conventional 30-year fixed-rate mortgage resorted to adjustable-rate, often subprime, mortgages was an effect, rather than a cause.* If mortgage loans had been made to the same people with risky prospects, but in the form of 30-year fixed-rate mortgages, there is no reason to believe that the same people would have made the payments due on these more conventional mortgages and thereby avoided defaults and foreclosures.

Whatever Alan Greenspan's contribution to the housing boom and bust, whether through Federal Reserve monetary policy or through warnings that were not as strong as they could have been, the bottom line is that he did warn and Christopher Dodd dismissed his warnings, along with all the other warnings. The radically different history of housing prices skyrocketing and then plummeting in places like coastal California, as compared to places like Dallas where housing prices changed very little during both the boom and the bust, suggests that Alan Greenspan could hardly have been the main factor, since Federal Reserve policies applied nationwide while housing booms and busts were highly localized, however much the financial repercussions spread beyond these localities.

While attacking Alan Greenspan, Senator Dodd continued to defend Fannie Mae and Freddie Mac. In February 2008, long after the housing bubble bust and its spreading damage was well underway, Senator Dodd said "we have sat through hours of hearings over the years with witnesses repeatedly raising alarm bells about the risks Fannie and Freddie pose to the financial system." But now these government-sponsored enterprises were "the only part of the housing finance system where credit is still flowing." Thus, while the financial

---

* These new (to many Americans) mortgages grew to prominence at a time of unusually low interest rates that made the purchase of a home look more affordable than it was to less experienced people, who may not have been aware of how substantially their monthly mortgage payment would increase. Variations like below market "teaser" rates that might last for a matter of months added to the difference between initial monthly mortgage payments and the payments that would have to be made later.

system was now "under siege," Dodd said, it was Fannie Mae and Freddie Mac "that are riding to the rescue."

That private financial institutions, which were risking their own money, were reluctant to continue extending credit as freely as before under dire new conditions, while government-sponsored enterprises that could pass their risks on to the taxpayers were still going full steam ahead was not surprising, much less a reason for congratulating them for getting in deeper, ultimately requiring hundreds of billions of dollars in bailouts. Yet Senator Dodd acted as if those who had issued the warnings he had consistently rejected were now discredited by the continued risky lending of Fannie Mae and Freddie Mac.

In reality, the government ended up taking over both of these enterprises and, in January 2009, the Congressional Budget Office estimated that covering Fannie Mae's and Freddie Mac's losses would cost the government $238 billion for the year. That was *before* the two enterprises requested an additional $70 billion. Altogether, the bailouts of Fannie Mae and Freddie Mac would cost the taxpayers more than the bailouts of the Bank of America, Citigroup, J.P. Morgan Chase, and Wells Fargo *combined*.

In July 2008, the *Wall Street Journal* reported: "On Friday, Senate Banking Chairman Christopher Dodd (D., Conn.) declared that Fannie and Freddie are 'fundamentally strong,' that fears about their capital are overwrought, and that 'this is not a time to be panicking about this. These are viable, strong institutions.'" A week later, an editorial in the *Wall Street Journal* said "In any other business, Mr. Dodd would be begging forgiveness." But, in politics, the ability to brazen out your mistakes can be a crucial skill for the survival of a career.

Congressman Barney Frank likewise went on the offensive after the mortgage bust. In 2007, Congressman Frank said in the *Financial Times* of London that "the subprime crisis demonstrates the serious negative economic and social consequences that result from too little regulation." The financial crisis was caused by "bad decisions that were made by people in the private sector," Congressman Frank said in 2008, "thanks to a conservative philosophy that says the market knows best." "We are in a worldwide crisis now because of excessive deregulation," he said. According to Barney Frank, "mortgages made and sold in the unregulated sector led to the crisis."

The theme that the unregulated market was the source of the financial crisis was echoed by others, including Senator Charles Schumer:

> These unprecedented events have made it clear to the country what many of us have been saying for some time. We are in the midst of the greatest financial crisis since the Great Depression. After 8 years of deregulatory zeal by the Bush administration, an attitude of "the market can do no wrong" has led it down a short path to economic recession.

In the wake of the housing bust, Congressman Barney Frank and Senator Christopher Dodd, as chairmen of the House and Senate committees most involved in the housing market— and long-time promoters of the very policies that led to the housing boom and bust— were all over the media, where they were treated as experts, able to explain the problems and provide solutions.

Television financial program hostess Maria Bartiromo was one of the few to challenge either Senator Dodd or Congressman Frank on their own roles in the housing mortgage crisis. After Congressman Frank gave his views on the causes and cure of the crisis, there was this exchange:

> *With all due respect, congressman, I saw videotapes of you saying in the past: "Oh, let's open up the lending. The housing market is fine."*
> No, you didn't see any such tapes.
>
> *I did. I saw them on TV.*
> Yeah, well, I never said open up the housing market, the market is fine. . . .
>
> *So whose fault is this?*
> The right-wing Republicans who took the position that regulation was always bad, the market was self-correcting, and you should not have any restrictions on the free flow of capital.

This revisionist history ignored both the ill-advised and the well-advised interventions of the Bush administration, including their attempts to get stronger regulatory constraints put on Fannie Mae and Freddie Mac— attempts rejected by both Barney Frank in the House of Representatives and Christopher Dodd in the Senate, among others in Congress who obstructed those attempts.

Perhaps the crowning gem of Congressman Frank's revisionist history was his statement in 2009: "I publicly opposed giving mortgages to unqualified borrowers because I believed that some families are better off renting." His years of responding to warnings about the riskiness of Fannie Mae and Freddie Mac by saying that such emphasis on risk— exaggerated, as he had characterized it in 2003— imperiled the goal of "affordable housing" were blithely forgotten. Indeed, by the middle of 2009, Congressman Barney Frank was writing letters to the heads of Fannie Mae and Freddie Mac, saying that their lending standards for condominium buyers "may be too onerous." It was as if the previous political imposition of lower mortgage underwriting standards on Fannie Mae and Freddie Mac had never happened— and as if the dire consequences for the national and international financial markets had never happened. What had not happened were any dire political consequences for Congressman Frank.

On the Republican side, Senator Kit Bond, who had also tried to obstruct the regulators overseeing Fannie Mae and Freddie Mac, now came out in favor of "a new regulator with more expansive powers to oversee the two mortgage government-sponsored enterprises, Fannie Mae and Freddie Mac, if they continue to exist," adding that this was "a long overdue and necessary step." Moreover, he said that OFHEO "did not examine, did not look at the practices" that Fannie Mae and Freddie Mac had engaged in and that OFHEO had said "that these were sound operations." But it was precisely OFHEO's cracking down on Fannie Mae that had aroused Senator Bond's wrath in the past. Revisionist history has been bipartisan. A front-page article in the *St. Louis Post-Dispatch* recalled the facts, in contrast to Senator

Bond's version, under the title "Bond's Tough Talk on Fannie, Freddie Rings Hollow to Some."

POLITICAL "SOLUTIONS"

Whatever the problem, there always seems to be a political "solution." These proposed solutions range from ad hoc interventions to major institutional changes such as more regulation of housing and financial markets. Advocates of a more active role for government have also sought to defend previous government interventions such as those under the Community Reinvestment Act.

Ad Hoc Interventions

Short-sighted suggestions of solutions to the housing crisis have also been bipartisan. Democratic Senator Barbara Boxer wanted more government intervention in the housing market. "Allow bankruptcy judges to modify loans on principal residences," Senator Boxer said—and Congressman John Conyers and Senator Richard Durbin introduced legislation to do just that. Senator Harry Reid endorsed the same idea. How empowering judges to void contracts would affect the future willingness of lenders to lend to millions of other people was a subject not addressed. It was a classic example of politicians "solving" one problem without regard to how many new problems that solution created.

The same short-sighted perspective was apparent when Republican Senator Mitch McConnell suggested "providing government-backed, 4% fixed mortgages to any credit-worthy borrower." Professor Edward Glaeser of Harvard, a specialist in the economics of housing markets, said the Republicans' plan would be both "wildly expensive and ineffective."

Senator Dodd's solution to the housing boom and bust was very much like his advocacy of what brought on the boom and bust—

specify an end result, with no consideration of its ramifications. The mantra of "home ownership" was now joined by the mantra of "foreclosure mitigation." How people got into a situation where they faced foreclosure, or what would happen to housing markets after government intervention in foreclosures, were not matters addressed. However, the additional arbitrary goal did not replace the previous arbitrary goal. In sponsoring legislation to replace the existing regulator of Fannie Mae and Freddie Mac with a new regulatory agency, Senator Dodd said this would allow these government-sponsored enterprises to "better meet their mission of providing a source of affordable financing for homeownership."

Congressman Barney Frank likewise introduced legislation in the House of Representatives to save people facing foreclosure, with their financial responsibility to be mitigated by either the taxpayers or the lenders. Putting the cost of people's mistakes on other people hardly seems reasonable after the fact, and even less so as a prospective policy to discourage future mistakes.

Considering how quickly people in California drastically reduced their use of "creative" financing schemes when they had to pay the consequences, the case for sheltering people from consequences with federal legislation is by no means obvious. Unlike the bailouts of financial institutions, where the argument could be made that the shrinkage of credit if these institutions collapsed would hurt the whole economy, no such claim could be made for preventing mortgage foreclosures. While the decline of housing prices may be painful for their current owners, these declining prices make home purchases more affordable to prospective buyers— the very goal that politicians have been claiming to be pursuing for years. Yet affordable housing through the operations of the marketplace provides no political benefit to elected officials and elicits no support from them.

In the prevailing vision, foreclosure is a "problem" with a political "solution" and the people facing foreclosure are "victims"— and, needless to say, it is politically incorrect to "blame the victim." Unfortunately, facts from the world of reality tell a different story.

Changing the terms of mortgage loans to help borrowers who are behind in their payments has not proven to be the end of the story. As *The Economist* magazine reported in February 2009: "Of 73,000 loans modified in the first quarter of last year, 43% were again delinquent eight months later."

Foreclosure is not something that just happens to people, like being struck by lightning. Foreclosure is the end result of a process that borrowers and lenders entered into in the past and that more borrowers and lenders will enter into in the future. An arbitrary intervention at some point in time in this ongoing process has to be assessed not only in terms of its justification as of that moment, given the choices that people made in the past, but also in terms of what incentives and constraints are created for those who consider entering that process in the future.

Almost certainly such political interventions will make lenders more reluctant to lend when their chances of getting their money back are reduced by the prospect of more political interventions in the years ahead. As a result, borrowers are likely to find it harder to get mortgage loans and the loans are likely to carry higher interest rates, in order to cover the increased risk of more political interventions. In short, the costs of bad decisions made in the past will result in more onerous terms for future borrowers, who had nothing to do with the decisions of others in the past.

Why those who made those decisions should be spared the consequences, and those who had nothing to do with their mistakes should be forced to suffer the consequences, is a question seldom raised, much less answered. The political answer is of course that elected officials have every incentive to hand out favors with the taxpayers' money. But politicians have no incentives to learn from the policy fiascoes they create when they can shift blame to others. Whole successive generations of politicians have in fact repeated the same mistakes in the housing markets and survived the repeated crises and collapses in those markets resulting from political intervention.

As far back as 1922, Secretary of Commerce Herbert Hoover launched a crusade to turn tenants into homeowners and, by 1927, Congressional legislation encouraged banks to make more mortgage loans. The net result was increased home ownership, followed by increased rates of foreclosures. The very same pattern reappeared during the Roosevelt administration of the 1930s, which created new government agencies to facilitate home ownership, and one of these agencies ended up with more than 200,000 foreclosures. After the Second World War, yet another round of federal interventions in the housing market led to yet another round of risky lending and resulting foreclosures. What has happened in recent years is just a bigger and more disastrous repetition of what has happened before.

If it seems that politicians never learn, the question must be faced: Why should they? What they do learn is that there is much political mileage to be gained by promoting more home ownership and no political price to be paid for the foreclosures that eventually follow. Politicians' behavior is perfectly rational under these circumstances. Whether it is rational for others to expect political interventions to improve housing markets is another question entirely.

Regulation

Widespread calls for more or better regulation do not come to grips with the fact that there is no such thing as generic "regulation." The regulation of Fannie Mae and Freddie Mac by the Office of Federal Housing Enterprise Oversight (OFHEO) was radically different from the regulation of banks by various agencies that forced these banks into quota lending and lower loan approval standards. These latter regulators micro-managed mortgage standards while the former simply held Fannie Mae and Freddie Mac to the existing accounting rules, which they were violating. More important, those regulators who pushed for lower mortgage approval standards were doing what politicians wanted done, while OFHEO, by holding Fannie Mae and Freddie Mac to the accounting rules, was limiting the scope of these hybrid enterprises' operations, bringing down on OFHEO the wrath of Senator Kit Bond and Congressman Barney Frank, among others.

Regulation which simply enforces clear and concrete rules, as highway patrolmen do when they give out tickets to motorists who exceed the posted speed limits, or as OFHEO did when it caught Fannie Mae violating accounting rules, is very different from regulation based on the arbitrary power to withhold permission to make ordinary business decisions from banks if the demographic makeup of those whose mortgage loan applications were approved do not fit the preconceptions of government officials or if banks have in other ways not lived up to their responsibilities under the Community Reinvestment Act.

As we have already seen, government regulation and intervention have been at the heart of the conditions that set the stage for the current housing market disaster. That does not mean that all regulation must be futile or counterproductive. What it does mean is that the specifics of any proposed regulation are crucial. Among these specifics must be answers to such questions as: Regulate with what powers? How clearly defined? With what insulation from political interference? With what accountability for what results? Such specifics would tell us much more than political rhetoric about a need for more generic "regulation."

There is already overlapping regulation of banks and other lending institutions by various federal agencies with varying jurisdictions and agendas, and a substantial portion of the lending institutions are regulated by state agencies. Moreover, mortgages as they pass from banks to Wall Street firms that bundle them into stocks and bonds pass from the jurisdiction of bank regulators into the jurisdiction of the Securities and Exchange Commission. Any hope of consistent coordination among all these overlapping regulatory organizations seems almost Utopian.

Those who speak of regulation in the abstract not only overlook how radically different one kind of regulation can be from another, they seldom bother to consider how many individual regulators there are to oversee how many varied lenders with ever growing kinds of complex and exotic lending arrangements. "At the peak of California's housing boom," according to one study, "no more than 30 state examiners watched over nearly 5,000 consumer finance companies," with the net result that mortgage companies "could expect an examination from state regulators about once every four years." That is longer than it took the housing market to go from boom to bust. Moreover, many of these regulators "felt pressure from local politicians to keep mortgage credit flowing freely to their constituents."

A question can also be raised as to whether members of the general public who enter the housing market or the financial markets are better off being told to rely on the government's protecting their interests— which, if done thoroughly, might require regulators as numerous as the hordes of Genghis Khan, each with a degree in accounting and some with degrees in law and economics as well— or to be told frankly that they had better watch their backs themselves. In other words, is the illusion of government protection better than *caveat emptor*? It all depends on the specifics, not on the generalities of political rhetoric.

In the years before the Civil War, when there was no Federal Reserve System, no Federal Deposit Insurance Corporation and none of the federal agencies regulating banks today, "bank capital/asset ratios were substantially higher than today," according to Alan Greenspan. In other words, the pressures of market competition kept banks from the risky practice of operating with as little capital, in proportion to their volume of business, as they do today, because depositors would have taken their money elsewhere if a bank in that era had taken such risks as the banks of today take.

BAILOUTS AND "STIMULUS"

As the housing market continued to decline in 2008, taking down with it the stock market and major financial institutions, some of which went bankrupt, while unemployment increased, Congress voted $700 billion to be spent under the Troubled Asset Relief Program (TARP) in the last months of the Bush administration, ostensibly to rescue financial institutions— and later, during the Obama administration, Congress passed legislation appropriating another $787 billion "stimulus" package to try to revive the economy.

The rationale of the first bailout, TARP, was to prevent more financial institutions from collapsing, which could reduce the availability of credit, on which demand, output and employment depended. As of February 2009, the largest recipients of TARP money included J.P. Morgan Chase ($25 billion), Wells Fargo ($25 billion), AIG ($40 billion), Bank of America ($45 billion) and Citigroup ($50 billion). However, the government financial institution bailout money soon began to be spent for other things, such as bailing out General Motors and other non-financial enterprises.

Although many in Congress professed to be shocked at the way the money had been used for things different from what it had been said to be for, such a change was not unprecedented— nor even surprising, given the political incentives and given the history of government spending in many places and times. As far back as 1776, Adam Smith warned that a fund set aside by the British government for paying off the national debt was "an obvious and easy expedient" to be "misapplied" to other purposes. The next great classical economist, David Ricardo, objected to a similar fund in his time, on grounds that "we have, I fear, neither wisdom enough, nor virtue enough" for such a plan. Later, he said that this fund "has encouraged expenditure" and called it a "delusion" and "deceitful."

There may have been a more realistic understanding of the incentives and constraints of politics back in what are sometimes called "earlier and simpler times." Perhaps it is our time that is more naive in its expectations of politicians and government.

In today's emphasis on rescuing people arbitrarily singled out to be given the taxpayers' money, seldom has there been much discussion of homeowners who got themselves in over their heads with risky financial arrangements, not to mention speculators who had profited greatly from the housing boom and were now stuck with some of the inevitable losses that go with speculation. Both the bailout and the stimulus programs have serious problems, not always addressed seriously, including the timing of their effects and the dangers of inflation from so much unprecedented deficit spending, and— a key question— whether a "stimulus" program would in fact stimulate the economy.

Timing Problems

Even with the best intentions and the best expertise, it is not easy to know what the net effect of a given expenditure will be, much less when that effect will take place. Even in the normal course of actions taken by the Federal Reserve System to increase or reduce the money supply, the full effects may be delayed more than a year— and no one can be sure what the situation in the economy will be after a year or more has passed. An increase in the money supply begun when the economy has insufficient demand can take its full effect at a time when there are inflationary pressures, which the new infusion of money can aggravate.

Where the current large increases in government spending are said to be for infrastructure, the delayed impact may take an especially long time to be felt, since building almost anything can require complying with all sorts of federal, state and local rules involving environmental studies that must first be performed and hearings that must be held by various agencies, where all sorts of objections must be considered and adjudicated. Predicting when all the money currently being appropriated will actually be spent is especially challenging under these conditions.

If the money appropriated for infrastructure were spent for repairs of existing roads, bridges and the like, instead of for building new structures, the money might well enter the economy sooner and more predictably. However, the very reason for the widespread neglect of the maintenance and repair of infrastructure is that political incentives favor building new things, rather than repairing or maintaining existing things. Building a plaza, a community center or a marina creates occasions for ribbon-cutting ceremonies that provide valuable favorable publicity for elected officials. But there are no ribbon-cutting ceremonies for filling in potholes or repairing bridges and sewers.

Inflation

Regardless of when the "stimulus" money takes effect in the economy, the sheer size of the stimulus package ensures that its effect will be huge. The federal deficit in 2008, under the Bush administration, which was by no means frugal, was $459 billion. But that would more than *triple* to $1.4 trillion in just one year under the new administration, according to the Congressional Budget Office, which also estimates that the deficit would still be running at more than a trillion dollars a year, as late as 2019. Within living memory, there was a time when the entire national output of the United States was less than a trillion dollars. Today, there are many countries— in fact, *most* of the countries in the world— whose entire national output still does not reach a trillion dollars a year.

Since many people have trouble grasping what a trillion means, one way to visualize it is that a trillion seconds ago, no one on this planet could read or write. The ancient Chinese dynasties and the Roman Empire had not yet come into being. None of the founders of Christianity, Judaism or Islam had yet been born. That was a trillion *seconds* ago— and we are talking about trillions of dollars.

The potential for inflation is huge. More than that, even Wall Street does not have an unlimited amount of money, so that borrowing money through the sale of government bonds absorbs funds that would otherwise be available to go into private investments that create private jobs.

After twenty years of very low rates of inflation, it may be too easy for the public to forget what dangers inflation can pose. At least half of the American population today had either not been born, or not yet reached adulthood, at the time of the "stagflation" of the 1970s, when the economy suffered both high inflation and stagnant growth at the same time, with high unemployment and interest rates in double digits. Many of today's Americans may even be unaware of the wrenching economic problems of the early 1980s— widespread business failures and unemployment— as the Federal Reserve followed restrictive monetary policies to break the back of inflation.

In the process, Federal Reserve Chairman Paul Volcker became one of the most hated men in America, and President Ronald Reagan saw his popularity in the polls plummet for supporting what Volcker was doing. Eventually it worked and the country enjoyed two decades of economic growth with low inflation afterwards. But no one at the time knew when "eventually" would be, and many suffered in the meantime. They would undoubtedly have suffered even more had inflation continued to rise out of control. But the existing pain was what people felt.

Inflation is not the only legacy of runaway government spending. A growing national debt can be regarded as the ghost of Christmas past. At one time, Keynesian economists downplayed the problem of running up a huge national debt, saying, "We owe it to ourselves," since most of the government securities that constitute the national debt were sold to Americans. It was not quite that simple, even back in the heyday of Keynesian economics.* But, as of 2007, approximately 45 percent of the publicly held American national debt

---

* See my *Basic Economics*, third edition, pp. 404–405.

was held by individuals and organizations in other countries. This means that future generations of Americans will have to ship trillions of dollars' worth of their output to China and other countries to whom that debt is owed.

"Stimulation" of the Private Sector

A "stimulus" is supposed to stimulate somebody or something. In other words, stimulus spending— even on the unprecedented scale in the current stimulus package— is not by itself supposed to restore the economy to prosperity and rising employment. As the President of the United States and other spokesmen for the Obama administration have repeated, this spending is supposed to stimulate *other* spending, as the money works its way through the economy, so that others are thereby encouraged to invest or spend their own money. In other words, government sector spending is supposed to stimulate business and consumer spending in the private sector.

The idea sounds fine, as most political ideas do. But the real question is: Is that what has actually happened? Is that what usually happens?

At the end of 2008, after hundreds of billions of dollars of the Bush administration's stimulus package and TARP bailout money had been spent in the preceding months, what was actually happening in the private sector? According to the *Wall Street Journal*, business spending on equipment and software in the last quarter of 2008 "fell 27.8%, the worst in a half-century. Spending on durable goods fell 22.4%. The only spending that increased was by government." Several months into the new Obama administration, the *Wall Street Journal* reported in August 2009 that creditors were taking control of companies that could not pay their debts at "close to double the pace of 2008."

Banks were also holding on to their money, as the *New York Times* reported in January 2009:

With new capital, Congress and the Bush administration hoped, banks would resume normal lending to businesses and consumers. But worried banks are holding onto the money, so there has been scant benefit to the economy from the government help to the banks.

It was much the same story in the new administration. Under the headline "Bank Lending Keeps Dropping," the *Wall Street Journal* in April 2009 reported, "the biggest recipients of taxpayer aid made or refinanced 23% less in new loans in February, the latest available data, than in October, the month the Treasury kicked off the Troubled Asset Relief Program." In October 2009, *The Economist* reported that credit extended by American banks *declined* from $7.14 trillion in May to $6.78 trillion in September. Having money is only one factor in banks' lending decisions. The prospect of having loans repaid is obviously another.

In short, a costly government program that was supposed to increase bank lending has in fact been followed by *reduced* bank lending. Moreover, the velocity of circulation of money in the economy as a whole fell faster than it had in 50 years. When money moves more *slowly* through the economy than before, that does not sound like a stimulus but more like a sedative. Calling something a stimulus does not make it a stimulus.

Although the new President of the United States spoke often of the new jobs created by various government stimulus initiatives, unemployment in the economy as a whole continued to grow, so whatever jobs were created by federal government spending or hiring did not amount to a *net* increase in jobs. In August 2009, the *New York Times* reported a continuing decline in jobs in the private sector and less than a one percent increase in jobs in state and local governments— a worse record than in previous recessions over the preceding forty years. As job losses continued to grow month by month in 2009, much was made of the fact that the *rate* of growth of job losses was declining.* As the *New York Times* reported:

---

* In mathematical terms, the second derivative was negative, even though the first derivative was positive.

Employers eliminated 247,000 jobs in July, a huge number by the standards of an ordinary recession, but the smallest monthly loss since last August, the Bureau of Labor Statistics reported. And the unemployment rate, rising for months, actually ticked down, to 9.4 percent from 9.5 percent in June, mainly because so many people dropped out of the hunt for work, ceasing to list themselves as unemployed. . .

Obama administration officials credited the stimulus package, enacted in February, for the continuing improvement, from a peak of 741,000 jobs lost in January. Some said the July loss would have been closer to 500,000 without the American Recovery and Reinvestment Act. The president, appearing briefly in the White House Rose Garden, said his administration had "rescued our economy from catastrophe."

There is, of course, no way to know whether there would in fact have been half a million jobs lost in July without the stimulus package, just as there is no way to know how many jobs were lost in the private sector by the money withdrawn from the private economy to create government jobs with the stimulus money. What is clear is that there was no net increase in jobs in the economy as a whole, after many months of stimulus programs under both the Bush and Obama administrations. In August 2009, unemployment rose to 9.7 percent, the highest level since 1983— and among teenagers, the unemployment rate was 25.5 percent, the highest since 1948, when the government began keeping such records. However, as a front page story in the *New York Times* chose to be put it, "the losses continued to moderate from their worst numbers of the year." In other words, things were getting worse more slowly. In October 2009, unemployment hit double digits— 10.2 percent— for the first time in more than a quarter of a century.

The effect of stimulus spending is not entirely clear in the stock market as well. In February 2009, the Dow Jones Industrial Average fell to *one-half* of where it had been just 16 months earlier. In April 2009, the *Wall Street Journal* reported that business investment "fell another 38%" in the first quarter of 2009. While the stock market eventually began to rise in 2009, in the wake of the Obama administration's stimulus package, that is hardly decisive evidence, since the stock market rose considerably *more* during the same period in China, Indonesia, Singapore and South Korea, without that stimulus.

Similarly, industrial production in the second quarter of 2009 was growing in these other countries, while industrial production in the United States continued falling. In Europe, the Gross Domestic Products of France and Germany were growing, while that of the United States was still declining. Under the headline "Europe Recovers as U.S. Lags," the *Wall Street Journal* reported in August 2009:

> The news that Europe's economic engine is rebounding suggests the region is joining the recovery under way in China and increasingly elsewhere in Asia, exemplified by India's announcement Wednesday that industrial production in June rose nearly 8% from a year earlier.
>
> That contrasts with uneven consumer spending in the U.S., where retail sales unexpectedly fell 0.1% in July, as American households are hurting from job losses, a weak housing market and tight credit.
>
> This week, Federal Reserve officials said U.S. "economic activity is leveling out," but cautioned that it is likely to remain "weak for a time."

When American industrial production turned around and rose by one-half of one percent in July 2009, it was the first increase since the previous year, but that was far lower than the increase in industrial production in various Asian countries, which could hardly be credited to the "stimulus" in America.

Among the attempts to escape the conclusion that the stimulus has simply failed has been the claim that most of the Obama administration's stimulus money has yet to be spent. However plausible that might seem at first, money is money— and whether the Obama administration is spending the money appropriated in its own stimulus bill or the hundreds of billions appropriated in the Bush administration's bill, vast sums of money are still being spent, and are still showing little or no sign of actually stimulating the economy.

Amid a chorus of demands that government "do something" about the economic downturn, there has been remarkably little interest in comparing what happens when government does something with what happens when it does not. Nor has there been much attention paid to the fact that generic "something" is as meaningless as generic "regulation" or generic "change." Government can only do something *specific*— and just what that specific something is determines whether it is likely to make things better or worse. In the long history of the United States, it has been only since the Great Depression of the 1930s that the federal government has intervened in the economy in response to an economic downturn. Since markets recovered on their own faster from previous depressions, it is by no means unambiguously clear that an imperative to "do something" speeds recovery.

One of the things that government can do more effectively than any other institution is generate uncertainty, simply because government decisions constrain everyone else's decisions— and changing government policies make it difficult or impossible to know what to expect when making either business or personal economic plans. For example, with Senator Barbara Boxer blithely talking about empowering judges to rewrite mortgage contracts to suit the judges' notions, would that encourage or discourage lenders to write more mortgages, when they would have no idea what their chances were of getting their money back, in accordance with the terms of the contract made with the borrower? Many political quick fixes pay little or no attention to how those quick fixes change incentives and constraints on future behavior.

Far more momentous than Senator Boxer's suggestion have been the ad hoc— and therefore unpredictable— policies at the end of the Bush administration and the beginning of the Obama administration. First there was the Troubled Asset Relief Program, submitted to Congress in 2008 by Chairman Ben Bernanke of the Federal Reserve Board and Secretary of the Treasury Henry Paulson, as "a two-and-a-half-page legislation, with no mention of oversight and few restrictions on the use" of the $700 billion involved, as monetary economist John B. Taylor of Stanford University characterized it. A survey of securities firms and banks showed that 94 percent of them "found the TARP lacking in clarity about its operations." Moreover, bailout decisions in general— rescuing Bear Stearns but letting Lehman Brothers collapse— provided no basis for financial markets to figure out what the rules or principles of this program were, leading to a "lack of predictability about Treasury-Fed intervention policy."

The point here is not that these particular decisions were bad in themselves. Everyone has to make ad hoc judgment calls at some point or other. But a *government's* ad hoc decisions provide no reliable framework for the decisions to be made by millions of other people subject to the government's rules, when those rules are difficult to discern, both in their specifics and in their duration. One of the hardest things for a market to adjust to is uncertainty, whether it is uncertainty about how judges will change mortgage contracts when given a free hand to do so or— even more important— what new government interventions in the financial markets will strike like a bolt from the blue. When money appropriated to rescue financial institutions began to be spent to bail out General Motors, that signalled ad hoc decision-making, whatever the merits or demerits of bailing out General Motors might be.

Still more uncertainty was generated by the new Obama administration, when the President announced on February 9, 2009 that the next day Secretary of the Treasury Timothy Geithner "will be announcing some very clear and specific plans for how we are going to start loosening up credit once again." But when Secretary Geithner appeared on nationwide television the next day with no concrete policy but only vague generalities, the stock market took a nosedive. Even newspapers generally sympathetic to the administration— the *New York Times*, the *Washington Post*, and the *St. Louis Post-Dispatch*, for example— complained of the lack of specifics. A *New York Times* editorial referred to the "lead-balloon reception of Mr. Geithner's plan"; *Washington Post* writers said such things as "after watching his debut this week, I don't see how he could get much worse" and "it contributed to the very public anxiety and investor uncertainty that Geithner criticized."

With the Bush administration, the uncertainty was over what they were going to do. With the Obama administration, the uncertainty seemed to be over whether those in the administration themselves knew what they were going to do.

Perhaps the housing market collapse and its repercussions so threatened the whole financial system that government intervention was imperative, in order to prevent a domino effect of collapsing financial institutions and a drying up of the credit on which the whole economy depends. But, if so, that would not justify spending vast sums of money on automobile companies and innumerable pet projects from coast to coast. Moreover, an urgent need to prop up tottering financial institutions is completely incompatible with arranging the spending from the Obama administration's stimulus bill in such a way that most of it will not be done within a year of the hastily passed stimulus bill of 2009.

Despite the rhetoric of urgency and the great haste with which this legislation was rushed through Congress to spend hundreds of billions of dollars, the actual programs and policies created are very *slow*-acting. In February 2009, the Congressional Budget Office estimated that it would be September 2010 before even three-quarters of the money would be spent. *The Economist* magazine commented: "Too much of the boost to demand is backloaded to 2010 and beyond." This is a very strange combination of unprecedented haste to pass legislation appropriating money that would be spent at a very slow pace.

In mid-2009, the *Los Angeles Times* reported: "As of May 29, just over 100 days since Obama signed the bill into law, only about 6% of the funds had been spent." Later, in August 2009, the *Wall Street Journal* reported "only a little more than 10%" of the money had been spent.

Shortly before taking office, President-elect Barack Obama said:

> We've got shovel-ready projects all across the country that governors and mayors are pleading to fund. And the minute we can get those investments to the state level, jobs are going to be created.

Despite repeated claims about "shovel-ready projects" waiting for stimulus money to get started immediately to repair infrastructure, actual spending on infrastructure after the bill was passed turned out to be very slow. As of August 2009, the Federal Transit Administration had spent about $500 million— or 6 percent of the $8.4 billion it received. The government's General Services Administration (GSA) decided to spend one billion dollars upgrading federal buildings, but only about one percent of the money for that project had been spent by August 2009. The GSA estimated that it would be 2011 before choices would be made about all the projects on which all the money would be spent.

Why there was such *haste* to pass a *slow*-acting bill is a question to return to in the last chapter.

Chapter 4

Housing Mystiques and Housing Mistakes

It is not for the State to enforce philanthropy by law.

John Stuart Mill

The current housing crisis and its economic repercussions, within the United States and beyond, have evolved within a set of assumptions and beliefs that are part of an older and wider vision. That older and wider vision has remained as little examined by many of those who have believed it as has the set of ideas behind the policies that created the current housing crisis.

VISIONS AND REALITIES

Housing is too important in most people's lives to expect it to always be discussed dispassionately. "Home" is, after all, a word with emotional overtones, quite aside from its physical or economic significance. It would be hard to understand the evolution of housing policies in the United States over the years without understanding the framework of values, beliefs and assumptions— in short, the vision— on which they are founded. We have already seen one aspect of the prevailing vision, namely the notion that unaffordable housing prices are produced by the free market and that making housing affordable requires government intervention. However, there are other aspects of the prevailing vision which would also require government intervention, and those also require an examination that they seldom receive.

This is not to say that sheer idealism drives housing policies. Regardless of how sincerely a particular vision may be conceived and believed by some, both politicians and special interests can use the prevailing vision to advance their own interests. It was, for example, the *National Real Estate Investor* magazine which said in 2002:

> A new report by the Millennial Housing Commission confirms what advocates of affordable housing have claimed: More Americans are finding it impossible to find affordable housing.

Heartening as it might be to imagine that real estate investors were worried about people unable to afford housing, it is hard to overlook the possibility that they might also be interested in how "affordable housing" programs can create opportunities for real estate investors. Similarly, when the bipartisan Millennial Housing Commission, appointed by Congress in 2000, presented a picture of a *national* lack of affordable housing, requiring a variety of national programs, it is hard to overlook what political opportunities such national— that is, federal government— programs would present to Congressional Democrats and Republicans alike, to visibly dramatize a concern for the less fortunate with new laws and new appropriations of the taxpayers' money.

Other aspects of the prevailing vision have promoted many other government policies, from the local level to the national level. As with the affordability argument, we must compare the vision with the empirical reality.

Visions may be generated by all sorts of people for all sorts of reasons, including genuine concerns for the well-being of other people and of the country as a whole. But once a particular vision has become widely accepted, so many people may have such a vested interest— whether financial, political or ideological— that the vision can become remarkably resistant to the facts of the real world. Visions of housing have long been classic examples.

The Millennial Housing Commission set forth a vision of housing that has been prevalent for at least a century:

> Decent and affordable housing has a demonstrable impact on family stability and the life outcomes of children. Decent housing is an indispensable building block of healthy neighborhoods, and thus shapes the quality of community life. . . . Better housing can lead to better outcomes for individuals, communities, and American society as a whole.

It is certainly true that neighborhoods with better housing also usually have more stable families, better educated children and lower crime rates. But statisticians have long pointed out that correlation is not causation, though that may be the most often ignored lesson in statistics. American families that travel to Monaco are probably better off in many ways than families that never leave the United States. But that does not mean that the federal government should subsidize trips to Monaco or expect social benefits if they do.

The presumed causal role of housing in behavior patterns has a long pedigree. Nineteenth century reporter-reformer Jacob Riis called the "places and domiciles" of New York's rundown Lower East Side "nurseries of crime." He strongly favored slum-clearance programs, though noting in passing that in many cases "the police had to drag the tenants out by force" before the demolition could begin— which might suggest that these tenants had a different view of their best interests than that of Riis and the reformers he inspired. Yet this vision of the causal role of housing in social behavior, and of the superior wisdom of third party observers, has persisted to this day, despite an accumulation of far more evidence to the contrary than was available in Jacob Riis' time.

Perhaps the most dramatic evidence to the contrary was provided in the twentieth century by massive transfers of people from crime-ridden slums into brand new public housing projects— which quickly became new centers of crime and quickly deteriorated into new slums. Even in Jacob Riis' time, he noted that some people "carry their slums with them wherever they go." But somehow this did not dim his crusading zeal for slum clearance, much less change his over-all vision of the role of housing in social outcomes. Nor have the repeated, massive and multiple failures of public housing projects in later times caused others to abandon that vision.

Even after many public housing projects had become such social disaster areas that they have been demolished with explosives, what was not demolished were the assumptions that had led to such hugely costly failures in the first place. When that particular way of trying to change people's behavior by moving them into better housing failed, it simply led to other ways of attempting to do the same thing, such as issuing Section 8 housing vouchers to enable some people to go rent in middle class neighborhoods, where they could not otherwise afford to live.

Bitter complaints about the behavior of such people in their new surroundings by neighbors, landlords and law enforcement officials have largely fallen on deaf ears, and the vision has remained unchanged. Apparently those with direct personal experience must be wrong and a vision shared among distant elites must be right. Some complaints have been dismissed as "racism" when the voucher tenants have been black, but some of the bitterest complaints have come from black neighbors, who in many cases moved away from ghettos in order to get away from the very kinds of dysfunctional people that the government sends to live among them in their new neighborhoods. Not all voucher tenants are dysfunctional but it takes very few who are to make life miserable for their neighbors.

Nor has the vision of housing's effect on behavior been re-examined in light of the opposite phenomenon— namely, the existence of neighborhoods with older and unprepossessing housing, but with low crime rates and low rates of disease and other social pathology. In Jane Jacobs' classic, *The Death and Life of Great American Cities*, she recalled an Italian neighborhood in Boston that an urban planning expert described as "the worst slum in the city," but which his own data showed to have "among the lowest delinquency, disease and infant mortality rates in the city." Social dogmas and the visions behind them die hard, and sometimes they refuse to die at all, when those who have those visions pay no price for being wrong.

The vision that Jacob Riis had in the nineteenth century was still going strong in the Millennial Housing Commission's report in the twenty-first century. The only difference was that now it had more political muscle behind it, despite more empirical evidence against it. That vision now served to promote widespread government interventions in the housing market to create "affordable housing" and to protect people considered to be vulnerable, such as racial or ethnic minorities. The actual, counterproductive track record of government intervention as regards the affordability of housing has made no dent on the social vision behind such interventions. Nor has the evidence on the actual effects of government interventions on minorities been examined with any such scrutiny as might dim the enthusiasm for that activity.

This long-standing social crusading mentality has played a major role in pushing policies of lowered mortgage lending standards that led to the housing market collapse and its repercussions throughout the economy today.

While Democrats have been prominent in these crusades at both the local and national levels, some Republicans have been part of the picture as well. It was none other than President George W. Bush who said, in 2002: "We can put light where there's darkness, and hope where there's despondency in this country. And part of it is working together as a nation to encourage folks to own their own home." Six years later, when his own Secretary of the Treasury explained to him the magnitude of the economic disaster, he asked "How did we get here?" Apparently, neither he nor many others in politics and the media saw any connection between their housing crusades and the economic crisis now facing the nation.

MINORITIES AND HOUSING

One of the driving forces behind the strong pressures brought to bear against financial institutions, to lend to people they were not lending to as often as to others, has been a widespread belief that lenders' existing standards and practices discriminated against non-white applicants for mortgage loans, whether intentionally or systemically. Federal Reserve studies which seemed to support this view have been highly publicized in the media, accompanied by expressions of indignation and outrage, along with demands that government officials "do something" to put a stop to such discrimination. The many criticisms of these studies— including criticisms by academic economists and government economists in such agencies as the Federal Deposit Insurance Corporation and even the Federal Reserve System itself— receive little, if any, attention in the media.

Minorities and Mortgages

The methods used in statistical studies that have been widely cited to claim that there is mortgage lending discrimination are based on comparing approval and denial rates of mortgage loan applications between blacks and whites, or between blacks and Hispanics, on the one hand, compared to non-Hispanic whites on the other. However, the data in a 1991 study by the Federal Reserve System that set off a nationwide outcry against differences in mortgage loan approval rates between whites and non-whites nevertheless showed that most applicants of any race were approved.

Among those applying for government-backed loans, the approval rates were 61 percent for blacks and 77 percent for whites. For conventional loans, the approval rates were 56 percent for blacks and 76 percent for whites. For refinancing loans, the approval rates were 61 percent for blacks and 74 percent for whites. So the issue is the cause of statistical differences in approval rates, not whether any group is shut out of the market. Significantly, seldom do widely publicized racial comparisons include Asian Americans, even when data on Asian Americans are readily available in the same set of data from which black-white comparisons are made. This is a crucial omission, as we shall see, for including Asian Americans would undermine both the conclusions and the methods used to reach those conclusions.

In a mortgage loan approval process where innumerable factors affect outcomes, only those factors which these studies choose to take into account, and for which there are also statistics available, are studied. Moreover, large intergroup differences are found in virtually all the loan approval factors that are compared, such as income, credit ratings, the kind of housing for which financing is being sought, whether it is initial financing or refinancing being sought, home purchase loans or home improvement loans, and other differences. Loan approval rates vary with all these factors and with other factors, so that racial differences in these factors make racial differences in loan approval rates virtually inevitable, whether there is racial discrimination or not— even in situations where the person who makes the actual approval or denial decision never sees the applicant, but only the applicant's paperwork, and has no way of knowing what the applicant's race is.

The 1991 empirical study by the Federal Reserve System that evoked widespread outcries against mortgage lending discrimination was very upfront about the shortcomings of the data that were used:

> Differences in approval and denial rates among groups and neighborhoods revealed by the new data can be expected to raise questions about the adequacy and fairness of the home lending process. The data have important limitations, however, and care must be taken in drawing conclusions from observed lending patterns. Foremost among these limitations is a lack of information about factors that are important in determining the creditworthiness of applicants and the adequacy of the collateral offered as security for their loans. Without taking into account such information, one cannot determine whether individual applicants or applicants grouped by a common characteristic (such as race or gender) have been treated fairly.

Many in politics and the media, however, proceeded to do exactly what this study said could not be done. They took the data as virtual proof of racial discrimination in mortgage lending. An editorial in *USA Today* began "Getting turned down for a mortgage may have more to do with how you look than how much you make" and ended "How you look must not be allowed to determine where you live." An editorial in the *St. Louis Post-Dispatch* said:

> A report by the Federal Reserve Board gives weight to the charge that blacks, Hispanics and some other minorities are rejected for mortgage loans far more frequently than whites with comparable income. The study makes a strong case for fairer mortgage-lending standards. . . Federal bank regulators must now step in and insist that these institutions adopt strong measures to end discriminatory lending patterns.

The *St. Louis Post-Dispatch* also opined that "lending institutions are being far more conservative than they have to be in determining the creditworthiness of minorities." Subsequent default rates suggest otherwise.

It was not only in editorial comment, but in the way that news stories were presented, that made it appear that the Federal Reserve data proved racial discrimination. Many news accounts led off with statements pointing clearly to that conclusion. A front page news story in the *Wall Street Journal* began: "When it comes to buying a home, not all Americans are created equal. If you're black, it's twice as likely your mortgage application will be rejected as it is if you're white." A *New York Times* news story began: "The most comprehensive report on mortgage lending nationwide ever issued by the Government shows that even within the same income group whites are nearly twice as likely as blacks to get loans."

What many seemed to consider damning evidence was that blacks and whites in the same income bracket still had different mortgage loan acceptance rates. Yet the very study they cited pointed out that "Income is the only financial characteristic of the applicant" in the data that were used, and that "several consumer financial characteristics" enter into a decision to approve or disapprove a mortgage loan application, including "the proportion of the consumer's income that will need to be dedicated to the repayment of the proposed loan plus other outstanding debts, the level of equity (through the downpayment) that the consumer is able and willing to put into the property, the consumer's employment experience and prospects, and the consumer's history of repaying debts."

The wealth or net worth of mortgage loan applicants is also a factor. Blacks and whites in the same *income* bracket have very different amounts of *wealth*. Census data show that even blacks in the highest income quintile have less than one-third the net worth of whites in the highest income quintile. Indeed, blacks in the highest income quintile have less net worth than whites in the second-highest income quintile. Therefore comparing black and white mortgage loan applicants in the same *income* bracket, in order to see if there is discrimination, is still comparing apples and oranges in terms of one of the determinants of mortgage loan eligibility— namely, wealth or net worth. Not surprisingly, in view of history, there are greater differences between blacks and whites in inherited wealth than in current incomes. A study of mortgage loan applicants in the Boston area found the net worth of white applicants to be three times that of black and Hispanic applicants.

Significantly, data in later studies by the Federal Reserve System and by the U.S. Commission on Civil Rights showed that whites were denied conventional home mortgage loans more often than Asian Americans. In 2000, for example, while 44.6 percent of blacks were turned down for conventional mortgage loans compared to 22.3 percent of whites, only 12.4 percent of "Asian Americans and Native Hawaiians" were turned down. Studies also showed that whites resorted to higher-priced subprime loans more often than Asian Americans— but these facts were almost never reported in the media.

What such omitted facts might imply was that financial and behavioral differences among groups can lead to differences in mortgage loan approval rates, among other things, whether or not race as such was the basis for approval or non-approval. But this inconvenient possibility was eliminated by leaving Asian Americans out of the picture.

Credit history is another of the factors influencing mortgage loan approval, and credit ratings differ among groups. Just as whites average higher credit scores than blacks or Hispanics, so Asian Americans average higher credit scores than whites. One of the few places in the press where any of these kinds of data were even mentioned was in an op-ed column in the *Atlanta Journal-Constitution*:

> Among blacks, 52 percent have credit scores that would classify them as subprime borrowers.
>
> In metro Atlanta, 49 percent of blacks wind up with a subprime mortgage.
>
> Among whites, 16 percent have managed their personal credit so poorly that they'd be classified as subprime borrowers.
>
> In metro Atlanta, 13 percent of whites end up with subprime mortgages. . . Without question, more blacks (49 percent) than Hispanics (34 percent), more Hispanics than whites (13 percent) and more whites than Asians (10 percent) used subprime loans to buy a house.

Data like these are usually buried in ponderous research papers that the general public does not read. A research paper from Freddie Mac, for example, found that whites earning less than $25,000 a year had better credit records as a group than blacks earning between $65,000 and $75,000. In short, comparing blacks and whites on the basis of income did not mean comparing people with equal credit risks, so it is hardly surprising that they did not end up with equal mortgage loan approval rates. Although the race of the mortgage loan applicants may not have been known to the lending officials in charge of approving or denying loan applications, the credit histories that were known were enough to produce racial differences in the outcomes. The fact that the same (or larger) racial differences have been found in decisions by black-owned banks reinforces the point.

It is no wonder that these plain facts are so seldom reported in most of the media. Such hard data would undermine the moral melodrama that is more in keeping with the prevailing vision and with the interests of politicians, activists and the media. All too typical of media coverage was a *Washington Post* story that began: "About 29 percent of African Americans who bought or refinanced homes last year ended up with high-cost loans, compared with only about 10 percent of white Americans," according to what was described as "a consumer advocacy group's analysis of new data from 15 large national lenders."

A 2002 statistical study, done by a research organization for the Department of Housing and Urban Development, included credit histories among its variables and concluded: "More substantive conclusions, particularly with regard to implications for the existence of racial discrimination in mortgage lending, are hazardous." But many in the media and in politics seemed undaunted by such hazards. Differences in credit scores between groups are just one of the salient factors usually missing in statistical comparisons of mortgage loan approval rates or rates of using subprime mortgages.

Another Federal Reserve study of subprime borrowing, in 2006, also using Home Mortgage Disclosure Act data, noted: "The HMDA data do not include many of the factors considered in credit underwriting and pricing." But such crucial caveats are seldom mentioned in most political and media alarms about statistical disparities in mortgage loan approval rates. This later Federal Reserve study showed a pattern similar to what earlier studies had shown, namely that "black and Hispanic borrowers are more likely, and Asians [sic] borrowers less likely, to obtain loans with prices above the pricing thresholds than are non-Hispanic white borrowers."

Including the differential mortgage loan denial rates between Asian Americans and whites shows that the same methods used to conclude that blacks are discriminated against in mortgage lending would also lead to the conclusion that whites are discriminated against in favor of Asian Americans, reducing this whole procedure to absurdity, since no one believes that white-owned banks are discriminating against whites. Nor does it seem likely that black-owned banks are discriminating against blacks. To continue believing in such statistical methods of determining discrimination would mean accepting empirical evidence when it fits the prevailing vision and rejecting it when it does not.

Not only the omission of data on white-Asian American differences in news accounts of racial differences in mortgage lending approval rates, but the way other data are presented, clearly indicate how supposedly straight news accounts lead readers toward a preconceived conclusion. For example, when loan *approval* rates are not cited, but loan *denial* rates are, that creates a larger statistical disparity, since most loans are approved, for all the racial groups concerned. But even if 98 percent of blacks had their mortgage loan applications approved, if 99 percent of whites were approved then by quoting denial rates alone it could be said that blacks were rejected twice as often as whites.

Although this hypothetical example is only an illustration of the difference between citing loan approval rates and citing loan denial rates, the same principle has been very much in evidence in the real world. For example, a 1992 study of mortgage loan application outcome differences in the Boston area by the Federal Reserve Bank of Boston did not mention loan *approval* rates even once in its 71 pages. Instead, it gave loan *denial* rates among those blacks, Hispanics and whites who were comparable on a wider range of variables than in the 1991 Federal Reserve study. These loan denial rates were 11 percent for whites and 17 percent for non-whites. The way this was reported was "even after controlling for financial, employment, and neighborhood characteristics, black and Hispanic mortgage applicants in the Boston metropolitan area are roughly 60 percent more likely to be turned down than whites."

It is certainly true that a 17 percent rejection rate is higher than an 11 percent rejection rate— 55 percent higher, which can be considered "roughly 60 percent" only by being very rough. But it is also true that the very same information could be conveyed by saying that there was simply a 6 percentage point difference in loan denial rates and that the great majority of both white and non-white applicants were approved among people who were comparable in some of the factors that go into mortgage lending decisions. But such careful distinctions were seldom, if ever, made in the media.

Again, news stories opened with statements that turned them into de facto editorials. The *Boston Globe*, for example, reported this study by beginning: "A landmark study released yesterday shows that banks in Greater Boston discriminate against black and Hispanic mortgage applicants, offering the most damning evidence to date of racial hurdles facing minority homebuyers." Under the headline "Boston Fed Finds Racial Discrimination in Mortgage Lending Is Still Widespread," a *Wall Street Journal* news story reported the Boston Federal Reserve study, with a comment from an unnamed "spokeswoman for the Office of the Comptroller of the Currency" who declared the study "definitive." A headline in *BusinessWeek* magazine said, "There's No 'Whites Only' Sign, But..." and this story likewise declared the study "definitive."

The head of the Federal Reserve Bank of Boston also declared, "no more studies needed." But apparently the Federal Reserve Board in Washington did not consider this study the last word, for a later research paper from the Federal Reserve in Washington found the conclusions of the Boston Federal Reserve Bank "difficult to justify" in view of a re-examination of the same data.

Among others who did not find this study "definitive" was financial specialist Mark Zandi, who pointed out that blacks and Hispanics tended to buy lower-priced houses— and that these were precisely the kinds of houses whose prices were falling the fastest during the period of the survey, making such houses a more risky investment, regardless of who was buying them. Nobel-Prizewinning economist Gary Becker, who had pioneered in the economics of discrimination, found the Boston Federal Reserve study, among others, had "serious methodological flaws" that "make them of dubious value in formulating social policy."

Professor Stan J. Liebowitz of the University of Texas at Dallas was even more critical after examining what he called the "horribly mangled data" from the Boston Federal Reserve Bank. Among the various inconsistencies he found in the data were that "44 loans were supposedly rejected by the lender but then sold in the secondary market— which, of course, is impossible."* He added:

> When we attempted to conduct the statistical analysis removing the impact of these obvious data errors, we found that the evidence of discrimination vanished. Without discrimination, of course, there would be no reason to try to "fix" the mortgage market by changing lending standards. But the fix was in— there was no standing in the way of this train, to paraphrase a Fed economist who warned me not to waste my time.

Certainly the federal government was not slow to follow up these studies with increased pressures on lenders. The Federal Reserve Bank of Boston, for example, said that it wanted to be "helpful to lenders as they work to close the mortgage gap." It warned that it would be hard to serve "minority customers" if the "underwriting standards contain arbitrary or unreasonable measures of creditworthiness," that lending standards should be used that "are appropriate to the economic culture of urban, lower-income, and nontraditional consumers," that in reviewing "past credit problems, lenders should be willing to consider extenuating circumstances." In short, mortgage lending standards should be brought down to the level at which more mortgages would be granted to those whom government officials wanted mortgages granted. Nor were these mere pious wishes, as subsequent government sanctions showed.

---

* For a fuller account of the statistical problems of the Boston Federal Reserve data in a scholarly journal, see Theodore E. Day and Stan J. Liebowitz, "Mortgage Lending to Minorities: Where's the Bias?" *Economic Inquiry*, January 1998. This article mentions (p. 7) other studies by other researchers who found inconsistencies and errors in the Boston Federal Reserve study.

Discrimination and the Law

Whatever the empirical weaknesses of the evidence for attributing intergroup differentials in mortgage loan approval rates to racial discrimination, the *legal* case for lending discrimination has been much easier to make, given the standards used in civil rights law, where the existence of statistical disparities is enough to establish a *prima facie* case against the accused— after which the burden of proof shifts to the accused to prove his innocence.

When neither side can convincingly prove anything— as is often the case— the accused stands to lose, since the burden of proof has been shifted to the accused in such cases, contrary to the usual practice in civil cases, not to mention criminal cases. Moreover, the process costs of fighting a discrimination charge can be enormous, whether the charge is racial discrimination or sex discrimination— and regardless of whether the accused is guilty or innocent. The Sears department store chain, for example, spent $20 million fighting a sex discrimination case for 15 years, even though the Equal Employment Opportunity Commission that brought charges against Sears did not produce even one woman, either currently or previously employed in any of Sears' hundreds of stores across the country, to claim that she personally had been discriminated against.

Statistics alone were enough to establish a *prima facie* case that kept the litigation going. Even though Sears eventually won in the Circuit Court of Appeals, few businesses could afford to spend the kind of money that Sears spent and endure years of bad publicity that go with accusations of discrimination. Most businesses— even large corporations like General Motors— have found it prudent to settle such cases out of court on whatever terms they can get. These settlements are then cited by activists and others as proof of widespread discrimination by race or sex.

Banks and other lending institutions are especially vulnerable, because they have to get the approval of government regulatory agencies in order to make business decisions that Sears and other businesses are free to make without government permission. Banks cannot open new branches or close existing branches without the approval of federal regulators. Even if a bank might be willing to pay out vast sums of money to fight discrimination charges for years, federal regulatory agencies can hold up approval for that bank's mergers, acquisitions and other business decisions, pending the outcome of those cases. Against that background, it is easier to understand the responses of banks to political pressures that developed and escalated.

In the wake of the highly publicized statistical studies of racial disparities in mortgage loan approval rates in the early 1990s that have already been noted, the Clinton administration went into action on a number of fronts. The first prosecution of a bank for racial discrimination in mortgage lending was made in 1992, when the Justice Department charged the Decatur Federal Savings & Loan Association with racial discrimination, based on statistical differences between mortgage loan approval rates between blacks and whites. According to the *Wall Street Journal*, "Decatur denied the charges and said it chose settlement over protracted litigation." Given the standards used by courts in such cases and the arbitrary powers of federal regulatory agencies to withhold their approval of various business decisions by banks, it is hard to imagine a bank doing otherwise.

A year later, the Federal Reserve Board refused to approve an application by the Shawmut National Corporation to acquire the New Dartmouth Bank, "because of the bank's record on racial fairness," as the *New York Times* put it. The bank had not been convicted of anything in a court of law but the Federal Reserve Board was not required to use such legal standards. After the Federal Reserve referred the case to the Justice Department, the mortgage subsidiary of Shawmut National Corporation settled out of court by agreeing to "pay at least $960,000 to compensate minority applicants who may have been unfairly denied loans," according to the *Washington Times*.

Attorney General Janet Reno warned other banks that those who "closely examine their lending practices and make necessary changes to eliminate discrimination" would "fare better in this department's stepped-up enforcement effort than those who do not." She said: "Do not wait for the Justice Department to come knocking."

After Shawmut's settlement, the Federal Reserve Board then withdrew its opposition to Shawmut's acquisition of the New Dartmouth Bank. In a column titled "How to Rob a Bank Legally," economist Paul Craig Roberts said: "Believe it or not, there were no individual complaints from minorities." Here, as in the Sears case, statistical disparities were enough for a lawsuit, even if there was not one flesh-and-blood human being who even claimed to have been discriminated against personally. In the case of a bank, just the existence of such a lawsuit can freeze the bank's ability to make and carry out business decisions that require the approval of government regulatory agencies, regardless of how the litigation eventually turns out.

With both regulatory agencies and law-enforcement agencies equating statistical disparities with discrimination, banks across the country began to settle cases out of court. Attorney General Janet Reno expanded the definition of discrimination, bringing a case against the Chevy Chase Federal Savings Bank because it did not have branches in minority neighborhoods. The bank settled, like many other banks. The *New York Times* reported: "Under the settlement, the Chevy Chase Federal Savings Bank will open new branches and mortgage offices in poor neighborhoods to help redress what the Justice Department called racial bias."

How much any of this actually helped blacks is another question entirely. Being granted loans because the bank needs to meet statistical targets— quotas— in order to keep federal agencies off their backs, rather than because you are likely to be able to repay the loans, is not unequivocally a benefit to the borrower. As already noted in earlier chapters, members of minority groups have been disproportionately represented among those who took out subprime mortgages with initially low "teaser" rates that were for many a financial trap.

"Redlining" and "Community" Investment

The process that brought Washington politicians increasingly into mortgage lending decisions began with a wave of alarming rhetoric about "redlining" in the 1970s. Senator William Proxmire, sponsor of legislation against redlining, put the case this way:

> By redlining let me make it clear what I am talking about. I am talking about the fact that banks and savings and loans will take their deposits from a community and instead of reinvesting them in that community, they will invest them elsewhere, and they will actually or figuratively draw a red line on a map around the areas of their city, sometimes in the inner city, sometimes in the older neighborhoods, sometimes ethnic and sometimes black, but often encompassing a great area of their neighborhood.

Senator Proxmire not only saw a problem, he offered a solution:

> We have found many cases where these institutions have invested virtually nothing in the local community. We think this ought to be taken into consideration as one element in deciding whether or not the institution would be allowed to grow.

Here we see the fundamental thinking that led to the Community Reinvestment Act and to other political interventions to direct bank depositors' money where politicians— with no expertise, experience or stake— want it to go, rather than where the people entrusted with that money by depositors and investors choose as the most promising investments. To implement this vision, the regulators of banks, whose powers were created to guard against risk for the sake of the depositors and the viability of the financial system in general, have been urged and directed by politicians to use those powers instead to carry out a social policy that was never contemplated by those who passed the laws setting up these regulatory agencies.

This is one of many things that makes talking about "regulation" in the abstract meaningless. There are not only many very different kinds of regulation, directed toward varied and even mutually contradictory goals, any regulatory powers, created for whatever purpose, can be directed toward completely different purposes— and often are. Just as the power to tax is the power to destroy, as Chief Justice John Marshall said in 1819, so the power to impose arbitrary decisions is the power to extort, whether those with that power are local planning commissions or federal regulators of financial institutions.

In the wake of the political uproar over redlining, banks were forced by the Home Mortgage Disclosure Act of 1975 to collect and disclose statistics on mortgage applications. The Act was expanded in 1989 to include data on the economic and demographic characteristics of the people they were lending to, and whose applications for loans they declined. In the meantime, the Community Reinvestment Act was passed in 1977.

Neither law produced any immediate and dramatic changes but, like many other laws and policies, they provided an entering wedge whose potential was revealed in later years, as the principles involved were applied more forcefully. These principles included the idea that (1) political decisions should determine where the money that people entrusted to banks should be invested, that (2) people who wanted that money to buy a house should be our focus, not those who earned that money and put it in the bank, and finally that (3) any difference in the extent to which different communities and different racial or ethnic groups were lent that money could only be due to unfair treatment of those groups, not to anything different in the circumstances or behavior of those groups. A Department of Housing and Urban Development document during the Clinton administration exemplified this third assumption when it expressed the problem as one of breaking down "racial and ethnic barriers" so as to create more "access" to home ownership.

The old nineteenth-century notion of Jacob Riis that bad housing causes bad behavior resurfaced in the fight against redlining. The *Wall Street Journal* quoted one of the leading advocates of laws against redlining:

"Redlining is one of your major causes of urban decline," says Mrs. Cincotta of National People's Action on Housing. "There's a whole set of problems that start— like flight to the suburbs and crime in the streets— and they definitely start somewhere. I think they start with the institutions pulling out the money from the neighborhoods."

In other words, according to Gale Cincotta, for some inexplicable reason banks stopped lending in certain neighborhoods and then— afterwards— those neighborhoods became scenes of crime in the streets and flight to the suburbs began. The painful history of urban neighborhood decline was turned upside down in this picture. Moreover, Cincotta was not some isolated voice. Friend and foe alike credited her with being one of the main forces behind passage of the Community Reinvestment Act of 1977.

The Home Mortgage Disclosure Act and the Community Reinvestment Act not only opened banks to public scrutiny of their lending patterns, they built on the presumption that differences in loan approval rates among people of different racial backgrounds, income levels or in different neighborhoods were due to biases in the banks, rather than differences in the behavior or circumstances among people in the different racial groups, income levels or neighborhoods. More was involved than a presumption, however. The Community Reinvestment Act mandated that regulatory agencies give ratings to individual banks on the extent to which they met the goals of the Act— and mandated that permission for banks to make various business decisions subject to regulatory approval be granted or withheld according to whether the particular bank had earned at least a "satisfactory" rating on serving "the community."

According to the U.S. Commission on Civil Rights, "the FDIC considers a bank's CRA performance when assessing that institution's application for the establishment of a domestic branch, the relocation of the bank's main office or a branch, the merger, consolidation, or acquisition of assets, and deposit insurance for a newly-chartered institution." The Federal Deposit Insurance Corporation (FDIC) is just one of four federal regulatory agencies with the authority to evaluate a bank or savings & loan association's record of making loans under the guidelines of the Community Reinvestment Act. These lenders must also satisfy the Federal Reserve System, the Office of the Comptroller of the Currency and the Office of Thrift Supervision that their performance under these guidelines merits a "satisfactory" or better rating.

The first denial of a merger application by a bank because its record of lending did not satisfy regulators that it had met the standards of the Community Reinvestment Act occurred in 1989. The fact that the Community Reinvestment Act was passed in 1977 says nothing about when it became a major factor in the mortgage lending market.

In addition, outside individuals and groups were now empowered to appear before regulatory bodies to charge banks with either specific misdeeds or just a failure to live up to whatever were said to be their responsibilities to "the community." Regulators could then take such charges into account when deciding whether to approve a bank's desire to open additional branches, close existing branches, or make other business decisions. Community activist groups such as ACORN* thus acquired legal leverage to extract large sums of money from banks as the price of withdrawing their objections to banks' getting approval from regulatory agencies to make ordinary business transactions.

This provision of the law proved to be very financially rewarding to a whole class of community activists who extracted literally millions of dollars each from financial institutions by raising claims of racial discrimination when these institutions were seeking government permission for such things as mergers, acquisitions, or the opening or closing of bank branches. As the *New York Times* reported in 1986:

> In Chicago, for example, Gale Cincotta, head of National People's Action, and representatives of other neighborhood groups, persuaded three large Chicago banks to commit themselves to making $173 million in low-interest loans for both housing and industrial development in poor neighborhoods. In return, the groups agreed not to challenge the banks' merger plans.

Jesse Jackson has also been prominent among those using similar tactics and, as a result, acquiring millions of dollars in donations for

---

* Association of Community Organizations for Reform Now

various organizations he controls. So has the community activist organization ACORN. As noted in Chapter 2, such activists also used more direct disruptions to increase their ability to gain concessions from banks.

Congressman Barney Frank has been among those who have defended activists whose interventions had extracted money and other concessions from lending institutions. He characterized these activists as "people who are trying very hard to preserve some equity and some social justice," and as "people whose only crime was to offend powerful political interests because they cared about equity." A similarly sanitized version of community activist organizations appeared in a report prepared for the Ford Foundation by the Joint Center for Housing Studies at Harvard:

> Community groups are responding, as they must, to this changing environment. Some have developed special skills to work cooperatively with mortgage lenders to provide homebuyer education and counseling services. Other advocates are forging new, and broader coalitions that have the capacity to confront large-scale banking organizations, or the sophistication to assess the characteristics of new mortgage products. Others seek to expand their advocacy beyond mortgage lending, and shift the focus of the debate to larger issues relating to access to financial services. In any event, community organizations are adapting as they continue their efforts to advocate for and serve the needs of the lower-income people and communities they represent.

However lofty the rhetoric used by others to describe community activists, prominent community activist and Saul Alinsky disciple Gale Cincotta was much more blunt when addressing her followers: "We want it. They've got it. Let's go get it."* Community activist groups' actions seem much more consistent with Cincotta's exhortation than with the more high-minded gloss put on their activities by others. According to the *Los Angeles Times*:

> ACORN, for example, has used the CRA [Community Reinvestment Act] as leverage to compel banks to create pools of loans for low- and

---

* Gale Cincotta's death was reported in the *New York Times* of August 17, 2001 under the headline, "Gale Cincotta, 72, Opponent of Biased Banking Policies."

moderate-income families. Its efforts have generated about $6 billion in loans to these borrowers, while also generating funds for ACORN's nonprofit housing corporation. Supporters call that a win-win scenario; critics say it's legalized extortion.

Congressman Paul Broun is one of those critics. The banks in his district "couldn't expand their services and they couldn't put in ATM machines unless they would make these bad loans." As noted in Chapter 2, ACORN's tactics have included disrupting business at banks. Other tactics include having shouting crowds of activists going to the homes of business people or government officials to harass or intimidate them and their families. In Baltimore, ACORN activists "piled garbage in front of City Hall," disrupted a bankers' dinner and "staged a profanity-laced protest in front of Mayor Martin O'Malley's home." According to the mayor: "They unloaded a busload of people shouting pretty ugly things and scared the daylights out of my wife and kids." Members of National People's Action showed up at the home of Senator Phil Gramm in 1999:

> Phil Gramm was preparing for an evening at the theater one recent Sunday when a convoy of 15 yellow school buses pulled up across the street from his two-story brick house. Hundreds of protesters streamed onto the Texas senator's front porch and lawn, demanding that he explain his crusade against the Community Reinvestment Act.

Senator Gramm had been singled out because of what Paul Gigot of the *Wall Street Journal* called "Sen. Phil Gramm's attempt to open a window on one of America's great political extortion rackets, the Community Reinvestment Act." He added:

> The CRA was sold in 1977 as a way to induce banks to lend more to inner cities. But its political uses weren't fully exploited until the Clinton presidency coincided with a wave of bank mergers in the 1990s. Liberal interest groups hit paydirt: They found they could use CRA to obstruct bank mergers, forcing costly regulatory delays.
> Banks concluded that if they wanted their mergers to be approved in any financially reasonable period of time, they had no choice but to pay up. So they wrote big checks to various "citizen action" groups, and in return the groups withdrew their objections to the mergers.

As a wealth redistribution scheme, CRA has proved even better than lawsuits. Sen. Gramm says it's leveraged some $9.5 billion in current and future cash payments. . .

The hypocrisy here is off the charts: Banks must jump through hoops to show they're obeying CRA rules, but the beneficiaries of those rules needn't report what they're doing with their cash windfall. In other words, the liberals who profit from claiming to speak for the poor don't have to reveal if their winnings are actually being spent on the poor.

Over the years, the sums of money extracted from financial and other business organizations by community activist organizations, using a variety of tactics, have amounted to more than a trillion dollars, according to the National Community Reinvestment Coalition— nearly all of this money being received since 1992. In short, although the Community Reinvestment Act was passed in 1977, its impact began to be felt much later, as new implementing regulations put teeth into its gentle words about "encouraging" lenders to lend where the government wanted them to lend.

How much redlining was there in fact? An empirical study by economics professor George J. Benston of Emory University found remarkably little evidence of it. But such empirical studies receive far less attention in the media than the alarming rhetoric of those with a vested interest in promoting the image of redlining and the reality of their own enhanced opportunities to benefit financially from laws and policies based on those alarms. But, whether redlining is common or uncommon, the premises of the laws and policies against it deserve more scrutiny than they have received.

The notion that financial institutions should invest according to where they are located geographically is a staggering assumption, for which no argument is given, unless incessant repetition is considered to be an argument. From the standpoint of risk, diversification is usually safer than concentration, whether with mortgage lending, commodity speculation, insurance, or innumerable other investments.

Sometimes the semblance of an argument is presented by saying that a given community's money is being exported to other communities. But this verbal collectivization of the *community* does not change the plain fact that the money involved is the money earned and deposited in banks by *individuals*. If those particular individuals want that money invested locally, they need only choose to deposit their money in banks or other institutions that invest locally. But if what most depositors in low-income neighborhoods want is what other depositors elsewhere want— to have their money safeguarded and to earn as good a return as it can safely— then it is not clear why their interests should be sacrificed to the interests of third-party activists who say, "you have to go into all neighborhoods across the city whether you make money or not," as a community activist spokesman said in Chicago. Nor is there any basis for the media to call it "discrimination" if lenders don't.

Neither depositors nor the risks to their money received much attention by either politicians or the media. When a spokesman for the banking industry said, in 1975, "You're asking us to put ourselves into a position where we will be social-pressured into making unsound loans," *Washington Post* columnist Nicholas von Hoffman found that statement simply fodder for dismissive humor. Moral condemnation of "redlining" was both widespread and vehement. People who would never go into certain neighborhoods after dark, or perhaps even in broad daylight, have nevertheless expressed moral outrage when they learned that banks were unwilling to put as much of their depositors' money into such neighborhoods as third parties wanted them to.

When Senator Jake Garn said that pending legislation would jeopardize the rights of depositors, it was one of the very few times when depositors have even been mentioned in discussions of mortgage lending, then or in later years. It is as if the only people who matter are those who want to borrow the depositors' money— as if, as community activist Gale Cincotta put it, owning a home is a "right."

Denying or down-playing the risks in political allocation of bank depositors' money has been common, both in the media and in politics. Senator Paul Sarbanes, for example, said that nothing in the Community Reinvestment Act would require lenders to "depart from safe and sound practices." A *Washington Post* editorial likewise conceded that lending institutions have both the right and the obligation "to be sure their investments are sound." But, it added: "Careful and even conservative business judgments, however, should not be confused with prejudice, no matter how entrenched in traditional habits that prejudice might be." In short, the *Washington Post* presumed to know better than those who spent their careers in banking that the pattern of their lending could only be due to prejudice. Whether in politics or in the media, those who make such statements pay no price when other people's money is put at risk, nor even when the economy as a whole is put at risk as a result of the financial repercussions of the policies they advocate.

THE MARKET VERSUS GOVERNMENT DEBATE

In the wake of the housing market collapse in 2006, and its repercussions in financial markets and in the economy as a whole since then, there have been heated controversies over the role of the Community Reinvestment Act. This has been part of a much wider debate over whether it was an unregulated free market or the government that was primarily responsible for the housing boom and bust, with its disastrous consequences for the economy. Those who say that it was defects in free market capitalism that brought on the economic problems, such as Professor Richard A. Posner in his book *A Failure of Capitalism*, say that neither the Community Reinvestment Act nor the loans made under it had a major role in the economic downturn. Even the role of Fannie Mae and Freddie Mac in the economic disaster was attributed by Professor Posner to their being private enterprises:

> Both companies got entangled with the lower-grade mortgage-backed securities and were collapsing in September 2008 and were taken over by the government. But although federally chartered, they were until then

private corporations. Had they not had shareholders and highly compensated managers, they would not have taken as many risks as they did because they would not have had the same profit opportunities.   .

The role of the Department of Housing and Urban Development in imposing escalating numerical "goals" on Fannie Mae and Freddie Mac to buy mortgages made to "the underserved population" seems to fade into the background in this picture, which features "government's inaction" as a "product of a free-market ideology" as what allowed market capitalism to bring the economy to dire straits. Others have likewise said that it was "a philosophical distaste for regulation" that was responsible for the country's economic problems.

While Professor Posner acknowledged that the Community Reinvestment Act "requires the federal bank regulatory authorities to encourage banks to lend money to people who are poor credit risks because they have modest incomes," and that other legislation passed in the 1990s "encouraged Fannie Mae and Freddie Mac to increase the number of mortgage loans to low- and middle-income families that it guarantees," he said "the laws did not actually *require* the banks to make risky loans." But this is making a distinction without a real difference. When costly sanctions can be imposed on banks at regulators' discretion for not coming up with the numbers they want to see, and when the Department of Justice threatens prosecutions if they don't see the kinds of numbers they expect, then for all practical purposes the laws *do* require making loans that would be too risky to make in the absence of such threats.*

Officials of the four federal agencies regulating banks under the Community Reinvestment Act— the Federal Reserve System, the

---

* Neither the Department of Housing and Urban Development, which had regulatory authority over Fannie Mae and Freddie Mac, nor ACORN which extracted vast sums of money from banks using the Community Reinvestment Act as well as its own disrupting tactics, is listed in the index to Professor Posner's book.

Federal Deposit Insurance Corporation, the Office of Thrift Supervision and the Office of the Comptroller of the Currency— have also denied that the Community Reinvestment Act was the cause of the housing boom and bust. They and their supporters advance four main arguments:

1. The Community Reinvestment Act became law in 1977, while the housing boom and bust occurred in the twenty-first century.
2. Most mortgage loans were not Community Reinvestment Act loans.
3. Most of the lending institutions which made the majority of subprime mortgage loans were not institutions covered by the Community Reinvestment Act, but were non-bank financial institutions such as mortgage companies, finance companies and credit unions.
4. Delinquency rates, default rates and mortgage foreclosure rates were not very different for CRA mortgage loans and other kinds of mortgage loans.

Whatever the plausibility of these arguments, they do not stand up well under scrutiny.

What matters are not the innocuous generalities of the Community Reinvestment Act as passed in 1977 but the implementing rules and practices that later developed under the general aegis of that Act, especially in the 1990s and beyond. New regulatory amendments in 1989, 1995 and 2005 put pressure on banks not merely to change their institutional "outreach" to the "underserved" population but to actually make more loans to them, even if this required "innovative or flexible" lending practices. As already noted, federal regulators rated each bank's record on lending to the "underserved" population, and these ratings were taken into account when banks' business decisions required the regulators' approval.

Although non-bank lenders— such as mortgage companies, finance companies and credit unions— were not covered by the Community Reinvestment Act, the same principles underlying the Community Reinvestment Act were enshrined in so-called "voluntary" agreements made in the 1990s by non-bank lenders with the Department of Housing and Urban Development, under threat of adverse regulatory or prosecutorial actions under laws against lending discrimination such as the Fair Housing Act and the Equal Credit Opportunity Act. Prosecution under these laws could be based on statistical disparities alone. Even a lender with a policy of not lending on houses worth less than $60,000 could be construed to be guilty of "institutional racism," since such houses might be disproportionately owned by low-income minorities, on whom such a policy would have a "disparate impact."

To say, as some supporters of "community investment" did, that Community Reinvestment Act loans were not more risky than other kinds of loans ignores the question of what other kinds of loans they were being compared with and during what time period. To the extent that CRA loans were compared with other loans made under similar government duress, the fact that a different mechanism was used to achieve the same results changes nothing in substance, however much it might provide a talking point.

When the housing boom was in full force, all sorts of high-risk loans were doing well. As one scholarly article in the *University of Pennsylvania Law Review* put it, "CRA loans (at least until now) have proven to be as creditworthy and profitable as non-CRA loans." But this was said in a rising market in 1995. At the height of the boom in 2005, as noted in Chapter 3, "Hardly a borrower in San Diego or Miami was even late with a payment." Even people who were unable to make the mortgage payments did not have to default because, as noted in Chapter 1, they often had the option, in a rapidly rising market, to sell the house for more than the mortgage and pocket the difference. As one investor put it, "In a rising market, even a bad loan is a good loan."

Many risky loans were doing well until the boom turned to bust. That is when a large chasm opened up between the foreclosure rate on subprime loans and those on conventional loans. Things may be going fine, right across the economy, right up to the moment of collapse. But that does not prove that there were no dangerous risks all the while.

Ultimately, however, the debate on market versus government is not about the Community Reinvestment Act, as such. That Act was part of a more general thrust of government pressures on private lenders to lend where politicians wanted them to lend, rather than where the incentives and constraints of a free market would lead them to lend. Whatever the symbolic value of the Community Reinvestment Act as a sign of the kind of thinking that pervaded both political parties and most of the media, there were many other concrete expressions of that thinking in the Justice Department prosecutions for statistical disparities equated with discrimination, the "voluntary" agreements imposed on lending institutions by the Department of Housing and Urban Development and HUD's numerical "goals" imposed on Fannie Mae and Freddie Mac to buy the increasingly risky mortgages that lenders were making.

However ready some observers have been to blame the housing boom and bust on the free market, both the boom and bust were products of government actions. The geographically concentrated enclaves in which most of the boom originated were areas where state and local government restrictions on building were the key factors in skyrocketing housing prices. The insistence of Washington politicians on regarding these heavily burdensome local housing prices as a national problem requiring a federal solution fueled the drive to pressure lenders to come up with "creative"— and risky— "solutions." Where housing markets were freer, home prices were a fraction of what they were where there were government restrictions on building, and housing took less than half as big a share of a family's income to put a roof over their heads.

Those local housing markets that led the housing boom were the farthest removed from a free market. Fannie Mae and Freddie Mac were likewise far removed from a free market. Among many differences from firms in a free market, not only were these hybrid organizations created by the federal government, the President of the United States was empowered to appoint 5 of its 18 board members, these enterprises are exempt from state and local taxes that their competitors have to pay, they are exempt from Securities and Exchange Commission fees and securities registration requirements to which their competitors are subject and, because of both explicit and implicit federal support, they are able to borrow at lower interest rates than their competitors. They meet virtually nobody's definition of firms in a free market.

Lenders— whether banks under the Community Reinvestment Act or other lenders subject to "voluntary" compliance with Department of Housing and Urban Development goals— likewise fit virtually no one's definition of a free market. Nor need we agonize over the precise definition of free markets. As with local housing markets, where there were clearly places with more free and less free markets— and the latter were where housing prices boomed and then plummeted— so with lending markets there have clearly been *times* that were less government-controlled and times where government control escalated. Here too, real estate was for generations one of the safest investments *before* massive federal intervention in innumerable forms, of which the Community Reinvestment Act was just one. It should go without saying that community activist goon squads extorting billions of dollars from lending institutions were not the free market.

Wall Street in general, and the firms there buying mortgages and issuing mortgage-backed securities in particular, might seem to be a venue where those who blame unregulated free markets have their strongest case. However, even here, a key role was played by the securities-rating agencies, whose high ratings for mortgage-backed securities led investors across the country and around the world to buy securities whose riskiness far exceeded what the ratings would suggest.

While Moody's, Standard & Poor's and Fitch are private enterprises, that did not make the market for securities ratings a free market. On the contrary, for most of the period of the housing boom, these three firms were a government-designated cartel when it came to rating mortgage-backed securities for approval by the Securities and Exchange Commission, a federal agency. There were many other securities-rating firms but only these three had the official SEC recognition required by law for various financial institutions (including insurance companies and money market funds) to comply with SEC rules. The failures of a government-created cartel are not the failures of a free market.

Here again, the question can be raised whether the investors would have been better off to have been told *"caveat emptor"* or to be told that the government was protecting them by authorizing three firms to rate the riskiness of the securities that the investors were buying. It is hard to believe that the new kinds of mortgage-backed securities, with little or no track record, would have been equally saleable without what turned out to be the false assurances of a government-created cartel.

The argument that it was the unregulated free market that brought on the housing boom and bust, with all its further dire consequences, can be made impregnable by reducing it to a tautology, by simply defining all the key institutions involved as part of the unregulated free market— in complete defiance of the evidence. While it is true that more of a very *different* kind of regulation might have reduced the risks in the housing and financial markets, it is also true that so would *less* of the kind of regulation that was actually imposed. Moreover, the political incentives are to create precisely the kinds of regulation that were in fact created, so that those who are urging more unspecified "regulation" may be setting the stage for more of what has created or exacerbated the problems in the first place.

THE RHETORIC OF HOUSING

Mortgage lending is not the only area in which lofty rhetoric—"community" investment, "access" to loans, the "democratization of capital"— has been crucial to the political success of policies that might not have survived scrutiny otherwise. The verbal packaging of many other housing policies has likewise been crucial to mobilizing wide political support from people who have no material vested interest in the issues at hand.

Land use restrictions, for example, would have far less appeal if called simply "land use restrictions," as they are by scholars specializing in the study of housing. But when verbally packaged as "open space" laws "protecting the environment," or policies "preserving farmland" for future generations, preventing "urban sprawl" or "preserving" places that are "historic," these impediments to building homes take on an idealistic glow that can attract much wider support from people with no such personal stake as might cause them to scrutinize the specifics behind these glowing generalities.

Despite much loudly expressed concern in the media and in politics about the possibility that minorities were being harmed by mortgage lenders, there has been remarkably little concern expressed about the effects on minorities of rhetorically well-packaged housing restrictions. For example, skyrocketing housing prices in particular communities around the country with severe building restrictions hit blacks especially hard, even though many of these communities have been overwhelmingly liberal in their politics, with emphasis on their concern for minorities, the poor and children. In fact, however, each of these groups, for whom much concern has been expressed, have been precisely the groups disproportionately forced *out* of these high housing cost communities.

In San Francisco, for example, the black population has been cut in half since 1970. In an even shorter span of time, between the 1990 and 2000 censuses, four California counties— Los Angeles County, San Mateo County, and Alameda County, as well as San Francisco

County— have had their black populations decline by more than ten thousand each, despite increases in the general populations of these counties. Nor are blacks the only group unable to continue living in San Francisco. Families with low or moderate incomes are another. Just between 2002 and 2006, the number of San Francisco households with incomes below $150,000 declined by more than 16,000, while the number of households with incomes of $150,000 and up increased by more than 17,000.

As for children, numerous schools have had to be closed in many coastal California communities, as families with children have been forced out by high housing costs. During Palo Alto's sharp increase in housing prices, school enrollment declined from 15,000 to 9,000, leading to a number of school closings in that community. People young enough to have school-age children have usually not yet reached their peak income earning years, when they might be able to afford high housing prices.

Whatever the vision or the accompanying rhetoric, what people say or even what they intend is far less important than what the actual consequences of their actions are, even if these consequences are ignored by the media and others when those consequences do not fit the prevailing vision. But, however irrelevant rhetoric may be to questions of fact, political rhetoric has played a major role in the creation of housing policies that have been disastrous.

"Protecting" and "Saving"

Some of the most powerful political rhetoric is based on undefined words— protecting what is called "our community" or the "fragile" environment, or bumper stickers that simply say "Save Pete's Harbor." Why a particular status quo should be protected or saved— or from whom— are questions seldom investigated and sometimes not even defined. Nor do those who speak constantly of "fragile" environments usually offer any empirically testable definition that would allow anyone to say that environment *A* is fragile and environment *B* is not, or provide any empirical test of whether one is more fragile than the other.

Since the fundamental problem of any economy— whether capitalist, socialist, feudal or whatever— is the allocation of scarce resources which have alternative uses, the fundamental policy issue is why the government should intervene to direct those resources to one citizen rather than another. This is especially so in the United States, where the Constitution decrees "equal protection" to all Americans. Saving Pete's Harbor means denying others the right to use that area for different purposes than those of the status quo. Mere assertions of the superiority of one set of uses over another cannot be decisive because each side can call its preferred uses superior. Nor is there any generally compelling reason why the issue should be settled by rhetorical skills, when the contending interests can put their money where their mouths are, bidding against each other for the use of the same resource, as is done all the time in a market economy. If there is some special reason for exempting Pete's Harbor from this process, then that specific reason is what needs to be heard, rather than rhetoric about "saving" Pete's Harbor.

Some of the most politically powerful rhetoric in defense of housing restrictions have taken the form of claims of saving or protecting "our community." Upscale communities like Loudoun County, Virginia, that keep moderate-income or low-income people from moving in, by such things as requiring several acres of land per house, would never gain public support by saying that they want to keep out the masses to insulate the elite. Instead, the argument by those in such places is that they are protecting "our community" and its "way of life" or perhaps its natural environment. What all this boils down to is that their desires are to be made legally preemptive over other people's desires, the 14th Amendment to the Constitution ("equal protection of the laws") notwithstanding.

Despite the rhetoric, what is called "our community" is in fact *not* their community. Each individual owns only that individual's private property and nobody owns the whole community. Obvious as this might seem, it is easily lost sight of in the rush of heady rhetoric. Sometimes all the land owned by everyone living in the community is only a fraction of the land in or near the community where people are forbidden to build anything.

For example, in Salinas, California, which has had the dubious distinction of having the most unaffordable housing in the nation— with housing costs taking 60 percent of the average income— the amount of land off-limits to building in Monterey County, where Salinas is located, is three times as much as the land actually owned by all the county inhabitants combined. In short, vast amounts of land for which the local inhabitants have paid nothing are nevertheless controlled by them politically for their own benefit, to provide a buffer zone between themselves and less affluent people.

"Nobody wants to give up this way of life," said a local resident with a 16-acre estate. What other people have to give up, in order for her way of life to continue unchanged does not matter, so long as such conflicts of interest are settled politically— in a process in which only those who are there already can vote. Her right to live as she pleases on her 16 acres of land is extended politically to her being able to prevent other people from living as they might choose on vastly more land in the same county, land for which she has paid nothing.

The idea of freezing current land use patterns by law is a radical departure from the history of housing and other land uses in the United States. Harlem was once farmland, far out in the country, and later became an urban middle class Jewish community, before becoming a working class black community. In Los Angeles, cows once grazed on land near what is today U.C.L.A.

The idea of freezing land use patterns in upscale communities, where people want to keep things the way they are, means denying other people the same rights as the existing inhabitants had when they decided where they wanted to live— that is, it denies others the "equal protection of the laws" promised by the 14th Amendment to the Constitution of the United States. To do all of this because the current inhabitants choose to call an area "our community," that does not in fact belong to them, is one sign of the power of political rhetoric. Moreover, this stopping other people from doing what they want to do, so that you can do what you want to do, is considered by many to be an expression of idealism, rather than consummate selfishness.

Sometimes an aura of far-sighted wisdom is projected by claims that things are being preserved for "posterity." But this simply means preserving the same privilege for the posterity of existing residents to keep out the posterity of other people. Often an image is invoked of trying to keep the last few patches of greenery from being paved over— in a country where trees alone cover more than six times the area of all the urban communities put together. Among the other jerry-built rationales for arbitrary restrictions is preserving farmland, without any coherent argument as to why farmland should be frozen in perpetuity, in a country with chronic agricultural surpluses for generations on end.

In short, most of the rhetoric of preservation cannot survive even a modest amount of scrutiny. But, politically, there is no reason why it must. The power of a vision is shown, not by the amount of hard evidence or logical analysis it has, but precisely by the fact that it needs neither of these things to succeed politically. The current economic crisis is just one of the fruits of the political success of rhetoric and visions.

"The Market" versus "Social Programs"

One of the most misleading terms used by people on both sides of many economic and social issues is "the market." This word creates the impression of some kind of impersonal mechanism, when it is as personal as the people in it. The market is nothing more and nothing less than many people competing with one another, and making voluntary transactions with each other, on such terms as are mutually agreeable. Equally misleading is the term "social programs," which has a much softer sound. Who, after all, could be against things that are "social," as distinct from "the dictates of the market"? But such rhetoric turns reality upside down. It is precisely "the market" that is voluntary and "social" programs that mean following government orders.

Decisions made in "the market"— that is, by voluntarily chosen transactions— differ from decisions made by government in fundamental ways that have much to do with how the housing boom was generated. Economic decisions and political decisions are made under very different incentives and constraints.

One of the biggest differences between economic decisions in the market and political decisions in government is that *costs* are an inescapable factor in economic decisions, while political decisions can often ignore costs— especially costs that fall on other people besides the advocates of particular policies or those government officials who impose those policies. That is nowhere more true than in housing markets, where even enormous costs can be— and have been— ignored completely.

A study of housing costs, for example, found that land-use restrictions in the name of "smart-growth" policies had added costs of more than $100,000 per home in 50 metropolitan areas of the United States. In a community of just 10,000 families, that adds up to more than a billion dollars' worth of extra housing costs loaded onto the people in such a small community, often on the basis of little more than some fashionable but unexamined phrases about "smart growth," "open space" and the like. That means a billion dollars *less* for maintaining the standard of living of those 10,000 families. In a city of a million families, that means $100 billion subtracted from the standard of living of those who live there. In places like coastal California, the artificial reduction of people's standard of living would be even more.

Crusades for land use restrictions, whether in the name of "open space," "smart growth" or other rationales, are never cast in terms of how many hundreds of thousands of dollars this will add to the price of an average home. Proposals of height restrictions on apartment buildings are never cast in terms of how much higher the rents will have to be when those seeking to build a ten-story building are forced to build two five-story buildings instead, especially in places where the cost of the land greatly exceeds the cost of what is built on the land. Neither the costs of particular requirements imposed by planning commissions nor the costs of the years-long delays that the planning commission approval process can take get calculated or considered. Advocates of such things as "open space" laws or planning commissions usually simply discuss the benefits they anticipate from having these things, as if there were no costs to be weighed in the balance.

In short, the weighing of benefits against costs, which is common and inescapable in the economic decisions of individuals, families or multinational corporations, is often completely absent in political decisions of government that do not involve any direct expenditures by the government itself, but which can entail billions of dollars in costs in local communities and trillions of dollars when nationwide policies are involved, especially in housing markets.

Many of the decisions made by government agencies overseeing the housing market involve no significant expenditures from the budgets of those agencies, but can entail vast costs and vast risks to others that are seldom even discussed. This is especially so when there is some political crusade for a desirable goal, such as wider home ownership, whose benefits are fervently proclaimed but whose costs and risks receive little or no attention, except for dismissing the arguments of others who try to warn about those costs and risks.

After lending quotas were imposed in the 1990s, the "affordable housing" crusade succeeded in raising the national home ownership rate from 64 percent— where it had been for roughly two decades— to 69 percent in 2005. Whether that was worth the price that the economy paid for the housing boom and bust is a question seldom addressed. Not only politicians, but social crusaders of various sorts as well, seldom count the costs or weigh the further repercussions of what they are advocating. Trade-offs do not make for rousing rhetoric, dramatic placards or catchy bumper stickers.

It is very doubtful if many in academic communities who have campaigned zealously for land use restrictions under any of the heady and lofty labels used for these restrictions, have any idea that they are in any way responsible for the dire financial conditions in the country today or for the millions of workers who have lost their jobs. Social crusaders are not forced to confront the consequences of their choices, even in their own minds or consciences, much less pay a tangible price for the havoc they leave in their wake while feeling noble.

Chapter 5

The Past and the Future

Clearly this was a crisis of regulated capitalism, but the pressing question is whether it was the capitalism or the regulations that were primarily responsible.

Jeffrey Friedman

A historian once said: "Bad ages to live through are good ages to learn from." The current economic crisis has certainly been a bad time to live through, so we can at least try to learn from it. Indeed, there are many things to *un*-learn from it.

Perhaps the first thing to question is the conclusion that many seem to be deriving from today's economic debacle— namely, that more government regulation of the housing and financial markets could have prevented the housing boom and bust, with its dire repercussions in the economy at large, and that more government regulation is the way to prevent a recurrence of today's crisis. This view was expressed succinctly in a *New York Times* editorial:

> Pretty much everyone agrees on the causes for the country's desperate financial mess: predatory lenders, weak regulations, even weaker regulators, and risky nigh unto incomprehensible financial instruments.

Among the many people not included in the *New York Times'* "pretty much everyone" is Peter Schweizer, a research fellow at the Hoover Institution, Stanford University, who said in his book *Architects of Ruin*:

> Without government intervention in the economy, the economic collapse would not have occurred. We would not have seen the explosion in subprime lending and the dramatic reduction of lending standards.

Fannie Mae would not have been allowed to inflate the housing bubble, and subprime lenders such as Countrywide would not have grown into the toxic behemoths they became. Without government intervention in the form of the Community Reinvestment Act, banks would not have been compelled to extend trillions of dollars in loans to people with horrible credit. Without government intervention the large investment houses would have learned fifteen years ago that taking foolish risks, such as investments in toxic mortgage-backed derivatives, would cost them dearly in the end.

At the very least, this is not quite the settled issue that the *New York Times* implies, though much of the media seems to prefer the *Times'* version of what happened.

Those who are saying today that *better* regulation could lead to better results are voicing an attractive truism that is very misleading in the real world. Similarly when Professor Richard A. Posner, in his book *A Failure of Capitalism*, says "we need a more active and intelligent government to keep our model of a capitalist economy from running off the rails." The desirability of such a government says nothing about its likelihood— and says nothing about the enormous damage that can be done by a government which is active and whose intelligence is devoted to serving its own political purposes, rather than the well-being of the economy. Conjuring up hypothetical governments to deal with real world problems can be a dangerous indulgence, especially in a world where so many are eager to cite "market failure" as a reason for government intervention, as if government is unfailing.

No doubt perfect government regulation could have solved the housing market problems and prevented them from turning into financial problems that engulfed the whole economy. But a perfect operation of the free market could have solved those problems as well. And perfect human beings could have prevented the problems from arising in the first place. But such truisms get us nowhere. Any serious attempt to deal with serious problems must begin with human beings, and human institutions, as they are— not as we wish or hope they are.

MARKETS: FREE AND UNFREE

Many things could have been done differently, in both the government sector and the private sector, that would have cushioned the economy against the housing boom and bust, or even prevented it. That is why specifying "the" cause of the deep recession that followed is not easy, and why highly regarded economists differ among themselves on what was the principal cause. A recapitulation of events may help. Perhaps it may also be useful to distinguish *enabling* causes from *impelling* causes from *precipitating* causes.

Enabling Factors

What enabled the housing boom to take off and soar to unprecedented heights of home prices was the availability of easy credit, created by the policies of the Federal Reserve System in lowering its interest rates to historically very low levels and keeping them at those levels for years. Given the sensitivity of housing prices to interest rates, this made high and rising home prices possible and real estate speculation virtually inevitable. But, although Federal Reserve policies applied nationwide, the housing boom and bust was highly localized in particular regions, such as coastal California and other places where local restrictions on building meant that a rising demand for houses met unresponsive supply, sending home prices skyrocketing.

By contrast, places like Houston and Dallas had very modest rises and falls of home prices during the boom and bust, even though the same enabling factor of easy credit was available in these places. The effect of an increased demand for housing, whether caused by Federal Reserve policies or by other things, does not automatically cause prices to rise, unless there are restrictions on the housing supply, as we have already seen in places and times where the building of homes and apartments has been relatively unfettered, so that rising demand for housing simply led to an increased supply of houses, rather than skyrocketing prices.

In short, more than one enabling cause, and some impelling and precipitating causes as well, were necessary to produce the "perfect storm" effect on the housing market and the economy. In other words, many people had to do the wrong things, in order for the economy to turn out as badly as it did.

Impelling Factors

Among the impelling factors were growing pressures from government regulatory agencies for mortgage lenders to reduce their lending requirements, so that people with lower incomes and lower credit ratings could become home buyers. Although these pressures were fueled politically by claims of racial discrimination and by crusades to create "affordable housing" that would enable less affluent people to become homeowners, the general lowering of mortgage lending standards allowed many people who were neither poor nor minorities to take out more risky loans, in order to lower their cash outlays through "creative" financing, even when many of those people could have qualified for conventional 30-year mortgages with a 20 percent down payment. Moreover, easy credit and "creative" financing enabled housing speculation to flourish and to become a major part of the increased demand for housing that sent home prices skyrocketing.

In short, there is no reason to believe that most of the people who went in for risky "creative" financing of their mortgages were either poor or minorities. At the height of the housing boom in 2005 and 2006, more subprime mortgage loans were made to middle-income and upper-income borrowers than to lower-income and moderate-income borrowers. In terms of the dollar volume of mortgage loans, the more affluent borrowers borrowed nearly twice as much as the less affluent borrowers, presumably reflecting the higher prices of the houses they were buying.

For these risky lending practices to persist, however, there had to be enabling factors as well as impelling factors. The normal pressures of a free market would have made increasingly risky mortgages increasingly difficult to sell and pass those risks on to others. But, thanks to government-sponsored enterprises like Fannie Mae and Freddie Mac, for whom the Department of Housing and Urban Development had set quotas for buying mortgages that banks and other lenders had made to people in the "underserved" population, the risks were of little concern to lenders who could get their profits immediately by reselling those mortgages, letting the risks become the problem of government-sponsored enterprises— and ultimately the taxpayers. However, Fannie Mae and Freddie Mac were by no means the only outlets for risky mortgages and, in fact, other kinds of institutions purchased more subprime loans than did these government-sponsored enterprises.

In a free market, the riskier mortgages constituting a growing share of the assets of Fannie Mae and Freddie Mac, as well as the assets of private firms like Bear Stearns, would make such securities less saleable to investors and so would constitute a brake on the practice of making risky mortgage loans in the first place. But the high ratings given to risky mortgage-based securities by the rating agencies Moody's, Standard & Poor's and Fitch enabled these risky securities to be accepted by investors across the United States and overseas. Although these rating agencies were and are private enterprises, they have by no means been operating in a free market.

While there are well over a hundred financial rating agencies, prior to 2003 only three— Moody's, Standard & Poor's, and Fitch— were officially recognized by the Securities and Exchange Commission as authorized agencies, whose ratings could be used to comply with the SEC's regulatory rules on the safety of financial assets. As Professor Lawrence J. White of New York University summarized the situation in 2002:

> Incumbent bond rating firms are protected, potential entrants are excluded, and new ideas and technologies for assessing the riskiness of debt (and therefore the allocation of capital) may well be stifled. This entry regulation is a perfect example of good intentions gone awry.

Securities and Exchange Commission regulation thus converted what would otherwise be a free market, with numerous rating agencies competing for customers on the basis of the relative reliability of their assessments of risk, into a captive market for a handful of rating agencies. Therefore, neither these few recognized agencies, nor others not recognized by the SEC, had the same incentives to develop new and better ways of assessing risk as they would have had if there were many agencies competing for the same business in a free market. The SEC-recognized rating agencies had this part of the market to themselves, and other rating agencies without the SEC imprimatur had no incentive to develop new ways of assessing the new securities whose business was by law off-limits to them. In the following years, and especially after federal legislation in 2006, more rating agencies were added to the SEC-approved list but much of this happened after the housing boom had peaked or after the boom had turned to bust.

For most of the period of the boom, only Moody's, Standard & Poor's and Fitch were recognized by the SEC. It was not the particular choices of rating-agencies selected by the SEC that is in question but the policy of giving those agencies a captive market. When rating agencies which had established enviable reputations over the years for the reliability of their risk assessments in a wider range of financial securities did not do as well in a narrower band of securities during a narrower band of time, during which the competitive pressures of a free market were not present, that is not a failure of a free market.

If anything, this situation might suggest that more competition from other rating agencies, using other methods of assessing risk, might have kept the big three on their toes and therefore created at least the possibility of more accurate ratings, even though the task of assigning *any* rating— high or low— to new and complex securities with very little track record was not an easy puzzle to solve nor one that necessarily had any solution. Although rating agencies had vast accumulations of data on many different kinds of securities, going back for generations, such data were no more reliable as a guide to the new and exotic securities than vast amounts of data on weather in Antarctica would be for predicting weather in Hawaii, as a former Moody's official put it.

Given the possibility that there may have been *no way* to accurately rate the new and esoteric securities, the difference between a free market and a government-controlled market is that such securities would have had a much harder time being sold in a free market, with the net result that the money that poured in from private investors to fuel the housing boom would have dried up long before it did. In other words, the false assurances of a government-mandated ratings cartel were an enabling factor that kept the boom in housing prices going, making the fall during the housing bust that much more drastic and with far wider repercussions in the financial markets.

Those who call for more or better regulation ignore the fact that the problem of determining the risk of new and exotic securities was no easier for government regulators, who had no special source of knowledge or wisdom denied to rating agencies that had been successful for years with their rating of other kinds of securities. Moreover, the immediate conditions in the housing market provided little logical or even political basis for the regulators to act very differently from the way that they did. As one financial expert put it:

> Mortgage credit conditions couldn't have seemed better in those years. By 2005, with unemployment declining and house prices surging, delinquencies and defaults had dropped to record lows. Hardly a borrower in San Diego or Miami was even late with a payment. Regulators would have had great difficulty making the case to lenders that their lending standards were out of whack: the regulators had no tangible evidence to point to, even if they had wanted some.

In short, one need not assume either stupidity or villainy to explain why some people acted as they did, even though economic disaster might have been averted if they had acted differently. The implicit assumption that sufficient knowledge is available beforehand— either to those in the market or those in government— is simply not true. As another study pointed out:

> Until well after the housing market bottoms out, nobody will know the final default rate of subprime mortgages; nor the final prices of mortgage-backed securities containing them; nor which banks made the wisest decisions; nor how unwise the other banks were.

Some experts in this field have said that most estimates of the value of the so-called "toxic assets" have been under-estimated, that they may not turn out to be toxic at all. But Secretary of the Treasury Timothy Geithner, after meeting with various corporate and banking executives, reached the opposite conclusion, namely that these executives regarded their assets as more valuable than they really were. A study of the housing and financial crisis concluded:

> Geithner may be right or he may be wrong. He, too, is human, as he demonstrated in his years at the New York Fed, when he did nothing to prevent the crisis. But as much as he may recognize his fallibility, his role as regulator compels him to act as if he were omniscient.

This is not a problem peculiar to Secretary Geithner but is common to government policy-makers and is one of the distinguishing factors between decisions made in the market and decisions made in government. Many complaints about decisions made in either the free market or in government are based on an implicit assumption that the required knowledge already existed when the decision was made, which may or may not be the case. But, whatever the initial knowledge or beliefs in either the market or the government, those in the market are forced to change their assessments when the responses of others in the market confront them with the choice of changing or facing financial losses. But, in government, not only are such incentives for change missing, the political incentives are just the opposite— that is, to continue to insist that existing policies are correct and that bad results are the fault of others.

In a complex story about intricate financial arrangements, it is possible to lose sight of a plain and fundamental fact— that behind all the esoteric securities and sophisticated financial arrangements are simple, monthly mortgage payments from millions of home buyers across the country. When many of those payments stop coming, no amount of financial expertise in Wall Street or government regulatory intervention from Washington can save the whole investment structure built up on the foundation of those mortgage payments.

The bedrock question then is: Why did so many monthly mortgage payments stop coming? And the bedrock answer is: Because mortgage loans were made to more people whose prospects of repaying them were less than in the past. Nor was this simply a matter of misjudgment by banks and other lenders. The political pressures to meet arbitrary lending quotas, set by officials with the power of economic life and death over banks and other mortgage lenders, as well as Fannie Mae and Freddie Mac, led to riskier lending practices than in the past. But the politicians of both parties who created those systemic dangers had few incentives to change what they were doing and, as events later showed, had little or no political price to pay when they could blame what happened on others.

Whatever the risks to the economy, the risks to the politicians who created these easier credit policies have been minimal, if not non-existent, considering how easily they have escaped blame for the housing boom and bust. According to the *New York Times*, in November 2009 Congressman Barney Frank "said in an interview that he planned to introduce legislation next year raising the maximum F.H.A. loan by another $100,000, to $839,750." Should this turn out as badly for the economy as Congressman Frank's previous "affordable housing" crusade when, in his own words, he chose to "roll the dice," there will always be someone else to summon before his committee to be denounced on nationwide television for being responsible for the calamity. And it will undoubtedly be someone in no position to answer back.

Precipitating Factors

Given the unstable and unsustainable situation created in housing and financial markets through the enabling and impelling factors at work, what was the precipitating factor that caused this house of cards to begin to fall?

The key was housing prices. So long as housing prices continued to rise, speculators, home buyers and lending institutions could all benefit, as could investors who bought mortgage-backed securities, whose incomes were based on monthly mortgage payments that were rolling in. But, once housing prices merely leveled off, speculators could find themselves in an untenable situation, owing money on multiple houses, bought with the expectation of being able to sell them soon and profitably in a rising market, before low "teaser" interest rates on adjustable-rate mortgages rose.

To some extent, many ordinary home buyers were in effect speculators as well, even if they were speculating only on a single house in which they lived— especially in very expensive housing markets where rising home prices were often necessary in order to keep refinancing the mortgage and thereby postponing the day when payments on the principal became due. Lending institutions were also speculating on rising home prices when they agreed to refinance houses, based on the increased market value of those houses. It was somewhat like a game of musical chairs, in which everything depended on what happened when the music stopped. In this case, the music stopped— the housing prices stopped rising— when the Federal Reserve stopped keeping its interest rate at historic lows. As interest rates rose, housing prices based on low interest rates stopped rising.

Once housing prices stopped rising, they needed to fall only a little bit— only 1.4 percent in a six-month period beginning in late 2006— to set off a wave of defaults and foreclosures. Speculators who had bought multiple homes, in the expectation of quickly and profitably reselling houses before the low initial monthly mortgage payments went up, defaulted on loans they could not repay when houses could no longer be sold quickly or even at as high a price as the speculators had paid.

Homeowners faced with rising monthly mortgage payments, as interest rates rose on adjustable-rate mortgages, often either could not afford the higher monthly mortgage payments or decided that they would not pay, especially after housing prices not only stopped rising but began falling, because their homes were now often worth less than the mortgages.

Just as home buyers could acquire equity in their homes without paying for it during a period of rising housing prices, so they could lose equity despite having paid for it, when housing prices fell. Where homeowners had borrowed against the equity in their homes, that too of course reduced the remaining equity and increased the chances of homeowners finding that they owed more than the house was worth— being "under water," as the saying goes. This too provided incentives for home buyers to stop making mortgage payments, even when they could have afforded to, leading to more delinquencies, defaults and foreclosures. The fact that laws in California and various other states gave lenders no recourse when home buyers defaulted made such defaults easier for the borrower than in states where lenders could seek through legal processes to seize other assets owned by those who still owed them money that was not covered by the value of the home they repossessed.

As falling prices lowered the value of homes, the process fed on itself, as the boom had. Banks that found themselves owning more foreclosed homes were quick to dump those houses on the market for whatever price they could get, since banks are not in the real estate business— and are likely to lose more money if they act as if they are, by trying to manage a growing inventory of foreclosed homes. In short, falling home prices led to more foreclosed houses being dumped onto the market, causing further falls in home prices.

Although unusually sharp and continuing declines in home prices tended to be heavily concentrated in particular housing markets, as were the delinquencies and defaults, the fact that the mortgages on those houses were sold nationwide, and the securities based on the monthly mortgage payments were sold internationally, spread the financial repercussions far beyond their source.

While the housing bust began in the latter half of 2006, mortgage payment delinquencies, defaults and foreclosures have continued in the years since then. As of November 2009, the *Wall Street Journal* reported:

The proportion of U.S. homeowners who owe more on their mortgages than the properties are worth has swelled to about 23%, threatening prospects for a sustained housing recovery.

More than 10 million American households were in this position, including more than 5 million who owed at least 20 percent more on their mortgages than the market value of their homes. Contrary to the impression created in politics and in the media, people often default under these conditions, not because they *cannot* afford to pay but because they *choose* not to pay. "About 588,000 borrowers defaulted on mortgages last year even though they could afford to pay," according to the *Wall Street Journal*. Moreover, this was more than double the number who did so the previous year. Over all, about 7.5 million people were at least 30 days late in their mortgage payments or in foreclosure. Nor were these all people who took out risky subprime mortgages. Once home prices began declining, even the prices of homes bought with conventional 30-year mortgages and a 20 percent down payment were driven down by the competition of foreclosed homes that were dumped on the market.

Like other aspects of the housing markets, these conditions tended to vary greatly by locality, being far more common in California, Nevada, Arizona and Florida than in the rest of the country. In Nevada, nearly 30 percent of mortgage borrowers owed at least 50 percent more than their homes were worth. These were not one-time events, but a continuation of the housing bust that began three years earlier. As throughout the boom and bust, these effects were highly localized. While home prices in Las Vegas were less than half of what they had been 37 months earlier, in Dallas they were down only 5 percent.

Financial Market Repercussions

Some of the history of housing markets may help explain some of the complacency in the financial markets handling securities based on mortgages, especially when this complacency was buttressed by high ratings given to these securities by the government-authorized securities-rating agencies. "Lending money to American homebuyers had been one of the least risky and most profitable businesses a bank could engage in for nearly a century," according to an economist at a leading financial firm. An official formerly in charge of collateralized debt obligations at Standard & Poor's likewise said, "the mortgage market had never, ever, had any problems, and nobody thought it ever would." It was the massive intervention of politicians which changed that market disastrously, not only for banks but for the entire economy.

The alternative explanation of what happened is that Wall Street "greed" was the cause. But those who use "greed" as an explanation offer not the slightest evidence that there was any less greed— however defined— during the many years when housing was among the safest investments than in the more recent years when it became one of the riskiest. Denouncing other people's shortcomings may provide both psychic and political benefits but these are not substitutes for either evidence or logic.

One of the theories behind the "greed" explanation of the financial market collapse is that the compensation system used by many financial companies encouraged excessive risk-taking by their executives, who bought risky mortgage-backed securities because of the higher rates of return that went with higher risks, even though this created financial dangers to their companies. But, where this compensation took the form of their own companies' securities, whose value depended on the safety of the investments the executives were making, it was these executives' own money that was at stake if the mortgage-backed securities they bought turned out to be worth less than expected.

Bear Stearns had more invested in securities based on subprime loans than any other investment bank. When those securities turned out to be worth far less than expected, Bear Stearns executives collectively lost billions of dollars on these securities that they held personally. At Lehman Brothers, the CEO alone lost a billion dollars. Yet Lehman Brothers CEO Richard Fuld was, as the *New York Times* put it, "raked over the coals in Congressional hearings about his huge compensation.

That most of it was in stock and options that he never cashed in seemed to be something most legislators could not comprehend." His compensation *would have been* huge if the stock had turned out to be worth what he thought it would be worth. But the idea that he benefitted at the expense of his company did not fit the actual facts.

Some top executives of various other financial institutions did collect large, *contractually* committed bonuses despite the losses their companies suffered. But the fact that this was not the case with some other major financial institutions suggests human error and the caprice of chance, rather than villainy.

A crucial error— as seen in hindsight— was in trusting the high ratings given by rating agencies to mortgage-backed securities whose actual risk proved to be greater than anticipated by the methods used by these agencies to make their risk assessments. The angry e-mails that flooded Moody's in 2007, when it belatedly downgraded some of the ratings it had given mortgage-backed securities after the housing bubble burst, suggest that many people in Wall Street— and in the government agencies regulating them— had put more trust in those ratings than the ratings turned out to deserve. "If you can't figure out the loss ahead of the fact, what's the use of your ratings?" one investment executive wrote to Moody's.

Villainy tends to be a more popular explanation of disasters than is human error or the inherent inadequacies of knowledge. Villainy at least provides someone to blame, while human error and incomplete knowledge are too widespread to provide the same emotional catharsis of denunciation. For politicians, someone to blame *outside of Washington* is especially welcome. But, while misjudgments in the financial markets made the housing boom and bust worse than it would have been otherwise, this was an *enabling* factor— one of the downstream levees that did not hold— but it was not an *impelling* factor behind the boom or a *precipitating* factor that caused the flood of mortgage delinquencies, defaults and foreclosures, without which the mortgage-backed securities in Wall Street could have lived up to their ratings.

POLITICAL INTERVENTIONS

Human beings make mistakes in both markets and government, despite the widespread notion that, when things go wrong in the market, that automatically means that the government should intervene— as if government makes no mistakes. But neither sainthood nor infallibility is the norm in Washington or in Wall Street. Any realistic assessment of the decision-making process in the market or in government must examine the incentives and constraints facing those who operate in these two venues. Above all, such an examination must be based on the hard facts about the actual consequences of decisions, regardless of the goals, hopes or rhetoric of those decisions.

Government actions cannot be discussed as if government is simply the public interest personified. Government actions are political actions, and nowhere more so than in a democracy. The time horizon of elected officials is all too often bounded by the next election. Quick fixes are one result. Nor is this something new or peculiar to American politics. Writing in Britain back in 1776, Adam Smith referred to "that insidious and crafty animal, vulgarly called a statesman or politician, whose councils are directed by the momentary fluctuations of affairs." In other words, quick fixes by politicians have been common on both sides of the Atlantic for centuries.

Many of the "problems" which politicians set out to "solve," are bad consequences of previous quick-fix "solutions" created by the same politicians or by other politicians. These include housing prices in some places that take half a family's income just to put a roof over their heads. Dealing with this problem by launching nationwide housing crusades to create "affordable housing" through mortgage lending quotas and riskier lending practices tried to solve one problem while creating another and bigger problem. This "solution" now confronts the country with a still bigger problem for which yet new "solutions" are being proposed, with the prospect of still bigger problems for this generation and for generations to come, who will have to pay off a national debt created by politicians who throw around the word "trillion" to the point where it has become familiar enough that its magnitude and dangers no longer evoke the alarm that it once would have.

However easy it may be for politicians to ignore the economic repercussions of their decisions, the costs of such repercussions are virtually inescapable in the marketplace, for they are reflected in prices, even if the individual decision-maker has no clue as to why those prices are what they are. For example, a photographer who wants to buy a telephoto lens, and is choosing between two lenses of the same quality and magnification, may prefer the one that lets in more light. While the photographer may have no idea what additional optical problems are created when a lens is built wider to let in more light, or the more complex lenses made of more expensive glass that may be required to handle those additional problems, nevertheless the huge price difference between the two lenses conveys all the information needed for decision-making. It is then up to the photographer to decide how much more light is worth how many hundreds more dollars, given the kinds of photographs that the particular photographer takes.

Facts have no such coercive power in politics as they have in markets. While a photographer who knows nothing about optical science is nevertheless forced to confront the fact that a particular lens that lets in more light can cost twice as much as a similar lens without this feature, the situation is completely different in politics, where what most voters believe, or can be induced to believe, is the ultimate reality for elected officials.

Economic Repercussions

Ironically, two Russian economists in the days of the Soviet Union saw a key fact about market economies that so many who live in market economies have missed: "Everything is interconnected in the world of prices, so that the smallest change in one element is passed along the chain to millions of others." In politics, however, a "good thing" can be advocated or enacted into law on the basis of the beneficial consequences anticipated, with little or no consideration of the many other repercussions that spread through the economy in all directions.

Setting an interest-rate ceiling, for example, may be intended to benefit borrowers but it creates incentives for lenders to lend only to people whose prospects of repayment are sufficiently high to make lending profitable at that imposed interest rate. Loan applicants are not "qualified" or "unqualified" absolutely. People whom it would be too risky to lend to at an interest rate of 5 percent may be worth lending to at an interest rate of 10 percent, with the extra interest covering higher rates of default. If an interest rate ceiling imposed by government is lowered enough, it would pay to lend only to millionaires— and, at a still lower interest rate ceiling, it would pay to lend only to billionaires. However politically attractive interest rate ceilings might be, they make it less likely that lower income people will get loans. And if different racial or ethnic groups are disproportionately represented in lower income brackets, then interest rate ceilings virtually guarantee that they will be disproportionately represented among those turned down for loans, including mortgage loans. For politicians, however, this differential in mortgage loan approvals can then become simply another isolated "problem" in the market for them to "solve"— with no awareness of how previous political "solutions" helped create this situation, much less any consideration of how the repercussions of their own new "solution" will spread through the economy.

Those with a taste for moral melodrama are all too willing to attribute different prices, differing interest rates or other differences to "greed," "racism" or other moral failings of other people. The many flaws and shortcomings of human beings virtually guarantee that there will be examples. But examples do not provide an over-all explanation. Moreover, wrong explanations are not just an intellectual problem, when they lead to laws and policies geared to a different situation from that actually existing in the real world.

Another crucial difference between markets and politics is that markets usually leave no choice between changing mistaken notions or paying big-time in lost money or even outright bankruptcy. Under the pressure of such alternatives, the market has already responded quickly to the housing crisis, with a drastic reduction in interest-only loans, no-down-payment loans and other such "creative" financing. But there is no such renunciation of pet notions in Washington. On the contrary, politicians who have played a major role in ruining the housing market are now eager to try their luck intervening in the automobile industry, in banking and in other sectors of the economy.

Survival in the market often requires recognizing mistakes and changing course, while survival in politics often requires denying mistakes, continuing the current policies and blaming the bad consequences on others. We have already seen in Chapter 4 how impervious to experience government decision-making can be, when the notion of improved housing's beneficial influence on social behavior has persisted for more than a century— and counting— despite such widespread and devastating evidence to the contrary as the degeneration of brand new public housing projects across the country into cesspools of crime, violence and vandalism when slum dwellers moved into these new homes and created new slums.

Despite such massive evidence, Section 8 housing vouchers continue the same notion in a different form, sending dysfunctional people to plague neighborhoods to which many other people have moved, often at some financial sacrifice over a period of years, precisely in order to escape such dysfunctional people. But those who make such government decisions, and those who applaud them from the sidelines, pay no price for persisting in empirically discredited assumptions. Perhaps if Section 8 vouchers were increased in value to the point where they would pay for living in Hollywood, or on Cape Cod, or in affluent gated communities where so many self-congratulatory believers in such social engineering live, then first-hand experience might have some hope of overcoming fashionable notions.

More generally, what is called a "solution" in politics is often simply a patch put over problems caused by previous political "solutions," which in turn were patches put over other political "solutions" before that.

What never seems to get through to many people is that policies have repercussions far beyond the particular goals of those policies.

In 2000, for example, Hillary Clinton called for tripling the number of Section 8 housing vouchers and building more public housing. In 2007, after the housing bubble burst, Senator Clinton proposed a plan "to preserve the American dream of home ownership" that would "curb unfair lending practices and hold brokers and lenders accountable, give families the support they need to avoid foreclosure and increase the supply of affordable housing." This was the same approach that had led to the housing crisis in the first place, now spiced up with depictions of victims and villains.

To single out home ownership or any other goal as the crusade of the day— as a "good thing"— ignores the fact that virtually nothing is a good thing categorically. We must have food to live but, beyond some point, an increasing intake of food is no longer a "good thing" because it makes us overweight and shortens our lives. Home ownership has undoubted benefits but it also has costs and risks, however much those costs and risks were ignored, downplayed or dismissed by politicians and social crusaders during the crusades for "affordable housing" that led to the boom and bust. Nor were homes made more affordable. As of 2006, a larger proportion of homeowners than of renters were paying more than 50 percent of their incomes for housing.

The disasters into which the heedless political pursuit of ever larger statistics on home ownership has led should at least make us aware of the dangers created by such heady and heedless adventures in the housing markets. An optimist might even hope that it would make us aware of the dangers of heady and heedless adventures in general.

Serial "Solutions"

We have seen how local political decisions that led to skyrocketing housing prices have been followed by national political "solutions" to make housing more affordable and how the resulting rise in foreclosure rates has led to a new round of political "solutions" to deal with that.

Politically, it is both harder and rarer to simply undo previous mistakes, because that means admitting those mistakes, either openly or tacitly, and that can jeopardize a whole career.

Instead, there tend to be a succession of political "solutions," each dealing with the negative effects of previous "solutions." These new policies are often based on the same kinds of assumptions that led to previously failed policies. But those who say that politicians never seem to learn overlook the fact that there is no reason for them to learn, when they pay no price for being wrong when they can simply blame others and continue on with policies that have been politically beneficial to themselves, however detrimental those policies may be for the country.

Against this background, it is perfectly understandable that the Federal Housing Administration (FHA) has not only greatly expanded its guarantees on low down payment mortgage loans but has also greatly raised the limit on the size of mortgage loan that it will guarantee. Although the FHA was created to help low-income home buyers get credit that they could not get in the private markets, and therefore FHA had a low limit on the size of the mortgage loan it would insure, that limit has been raised to more than $700,000 on single family homes and to more than $900,000 for a multiple-dwelling unit. One consequence is that, instead of cutting back on risky loans, FHA is now insuring far more homes in high-priced areas like California. While in 2007 the FHA insured less than 5,000 homes in California, in 2009 it insured more than 100,000 homes in the state before the end of November. Under the headline, "F.H.A. Extends Easy Loans to Wealthier Areas," the *New York Times* reported:

> In January, Mike Rowland was so broke that he had to raid his retirement savings to move here [San Francisco] from Boston.
> A week ago, he and a couple of buddies bought a two-unit apartment building for nearly a million dollars. They only had a little cash to bring to the table but, with the federal government insuring the transaction, a large down payment was not necessary.
> "It was kind of crazy we could get this big a loan," said Mr. Rowland, 27. "If a government official came out here, I would slap him a high-five."
> In its efforts to prop up a shattered housing market, the government is greatly extending its traditional support of real estate, including

guaranteeing the mortgages of middle-class and even upper-class buyers against default.

Since the Federal Housing Administration requires less than a 4 percent down payment, these three friends were able to buy a two-unit apartment building costing almost a million dollars with a total of only $33,000 between them for a down payment. In other words, the FHA was promoting exactly the kind of risky lending that had ruined private mortgage lenders, who had pulled back on such loans as a result. But the FHA was going further into such risky lending practices. In 2007, the FHA insured no loans at all on high-priced San Francisco real estate, but in 2009 they had insured 270 mortgage loans there before the end of November.

The mortgage loan on which the three friends made a total down payment of $33,000 would have required nearly a $200,000 down payment in the private market, which had learned its lesson about low down payment loans. But politicians have learned a very different lesson: That easy credit policies by the federal government are popular. As the *New York Times* reporter noted:

> Policy changes in [FHA] insurance, while introduced on a temporary basis, are becoming so popular that they could prove difficult to undo. With defaults rising, they pose new risks for taxpayers.

These risks were not hypothetical. In the same issue of the *New York Times* in which this story appeared, another news story appeared under the headline, "Mortgage Delinquencies Soar: One in 10 Borrowers Is at Least a Month Behind on Payments." For FHA loans, more than 14 percent of borrowers were at least a month behind on their payments. These problems, like many other housing problems during the boom and bust, were concentrated in four states: California, Florida, Arizona, and Nevada. In Florida, one-fourth of all people with mortgages were behind in their payments.

While the Federal Housing Administration insures other people's financial transactions, its own finances have reached the point where the *Wall Street Journal* reported in November 2009 that the FHA's own "capital reserves have fallen to razor-thin levels, increasing the likelihood the agency will eventually require a taxpayer bailout."

Something similar is happening at the Federal Deposit Insurance Corporation (FDIC), which insures bank accounts, but whose own financial resources have been depleted by numerous bank failures. In September 2009, the *Wall Street Journal* reported: "The evaporating deposit-insurance fund had $10.4 billion in June, the latest figure available, down from $45.2 billion in June 2008." This $10.4 billion is less than one-fifth of what the FDIC is supposed to have on hand to back the trillions of dollars' worth of bank accounts it insures. Meanwhile, government officials "estimated that bank failures from 2009 through 2013 will cost the FDIC $100 billion." However, in order to stay out of the red in 2009, the FDIC has, for the first time, required banks to prepay in 2009 their deposit insurance fees for 2009, 2010, 2011 and 2012. That puts off the problem for now, but leaves the question as to what the FDIC will do in the next four years, with so many banks no longer owing them insurance fees.

If there is any institution in America that is "too big to fail," it is the FDIC, whose failure would wipe out the life savings of millions of people— something that no politician of any party could allow to happen. What all this means, however, is that even the record-breaking official federal deficit *understates* the federal government's financial liabilities, since both FDIC and the FHA are expected to need huge infusions of cash to keep operating.

The financial markets that are at the center of our current economic problems have, over the generations, seen one government patch after another put on problems created by previous government patches. Perhaps the crown jewel of those who believe in government intervention in financial markets has been the Federal Deposit Insurance Corporation, because its guarantees of bank accounts have effectively put an end to runs on banks. There is no question that FDIC, by removing the incentives to start a run on a bank by those fearful of losing the money in their accounts, has reduced bank failures.

But why was such a law necessary in the first place? Because of massive bank failures during the Great Depression of the 1930s. Yet what has seldom been mentioned is that a wholly disproportionate share of those banks that failed then were in states with laws preventing a bank from having more than one location.

Whatever the rationale for preventing banks from having multiple branches, the economic consequence was increased risk. A bank located solely in a wheat-growing community is exposed to all the risks of a fluctuating wheat market, since both its depositors and those to whom it lends money are likely to include many people dependent on the price of wheat, which fluctuates in a world market beyond their control. However, a bank with branches not only in wheat-growing areas, but also in steel-producing areas, furniture-making areas, etc., has more diversified risks, and therefore lower risks overall, since all these markets are unlikely to fluctuate the same way at the same time.

It was precisely in states with laws forbidding multiple branches of banks that *state* deposit insurance arose, years before federal deposit insurance. In short, politicians were trying to solve a problem which politicians had created— namely, heightened risks of bank failures. Eventually, Washington politicians put a bigger patch over the patches of state politicians. That it was a good patch is undeniable. But it was solving a problem disproportionately created by other politicians, rather than by the market.

Even during the depths of the Great Depression, when thousands of American banks failed, larger banks with diversified risks, located in places where they were not constrained by state laws against multiple branches, had very low rates of failure. Ninety percent of the failing banks in that era were in small communities, and almost all were in states with laws against branch banking. Meanwhile, in Canada, which went through the same depression as the United States, there was *not one bank failure* during the years when thousands of American banks failed— and the Canadian government did not provide deposit insurance until 1967.

The Canadian Experience

Back during the Great Depression, Canada had 10 banks, with 3,000 branches across the country. The market can work— but only when politicians allow it to work. In our times as well, Canadian banks have not been toppling, or being bailed out, on a scale comparable to that of American banks. Among the differences between banks in the two countries are the following:

1. Subprime mortgages constitute only 7 percent of the mortgage portfolios of Canadian banks compared to 20 percent of the mortgage portfolios of American banks.
2. Canada has no institutions comparable to Fannie Mae and Freddie Mac, guaranteeing high-risk mortgage loans.
3. Canadian regulators concentrate on controlling risk, not pursuing home-ownership goals or imposing lending quotas.
4. Canadian laws require either a 20 percent down payment on mortgage loans or the purchase of mortgage insurance if the down payment is less than 20 percent.
5. Canadian home buyers cannot simply default and walk away from their mortgage debts because lenders can make legal claims against the borrowers' other assets to cover their unpaid debts.

Despite these differences, the home ownership rate in Canada is not too different from that in the United States, so the extra risks taken in the United States have not produced corresponding benefits. Moreover, the Canadian economy has been hit by the worldwide economic decline, just like the United States. The Canadian economy declined 7.3 percent in the first quarter of 2009, for example, compared to a 5.7 percent decline during the same period in the United States. Nevertheless, the Canadian housing and financial markets have not had to be bailed out on a scale comparable to that in the United States.

In short, Canada has had the advantage of operating under a different set of legal rules and policies that limit, rather than expand, risk. Moreover, Canadian banks got out of the risky mortgage-backed securities that have played a role in the American financial disasters.

Canadian regulators allowed banks to buy these securities and, at one time, a Canadian bank was among the world's top ten holders of such securities. But they got out of that market when the growing complexities and riskiness of such securities became apparent.

Since they did not have government-backed enterprises like Fannie Mae and Freddie Mac to relieve them of mortgage risk at the taxpayers' expense, ordinary market forces were enough to get Canadian financial institutions to abandon these esoteric and risky securities. If the purpose of all the frenzied activity in Washington was simply to make housing markets or financial markets less risky, an example of policies that have done that is not far away. But such mundane policies would not promote political melodrama nor— more important— the vast expansion of government power that benefits politicians, not least by allowing them to hand out vast sums of money to favored constituents, either from the public treasury or from private sources of capital directed by politicians and bureaucrats.

Policy Implications

No doubt there are things that American regulatory agencies could have done to keep financial institutions in Wall Street and elsewhere from adding to the risks in an already risky situation by the way they marketed securities based on mortgages. But what an ideal regulatory agency *could* do is no clue whatever to what actual regulatory agencies are *likely* to do, especially with members of Congress like Barney Frank and Christopher Dodd breathing down their necks. What banks could have done ideally in the past or can do ideally in the future is likewise no clue to what they have done or will do when government agencies from the Federal Reserve System to the Justice Department are telling banks that they had better meet arbitrary quotas in their lending if they want to avoid big trouble from the government.

In housing markets, there have been an abundance of theories and of fervently believed doctrines, but not nearly such an abundance of willingness to subject those theories and doctrines to the test of evidence. Politicians would be gambling their entire careers on a roll of the dice, if they were to publicly subject the policies and programs that they have been advocating for years to empirical tests of their consequences. For others outside of politics, their only stake might be ego or ideology, but some people have been known to risk their lives for such things.

Most members of the general public have no such vested interests at risk when deciding whether belief *A* proves to be more consistent with the facts than belief *B*. That is one of the few hopeful aspects of the financial crisis we are in— that there are many people who just want to know what the truth is, so that we can all avoid a repetition of the disaster that has overtaken us, regardless of what theory, doctrine, political party or editorial position is vindicated or discredited in the process.

Consequences

Let us go back to square one to consider the empirical consequences of policies in the housing market. Politicians in Washington set out to solve a national problem *that did not exist*— a nationwide shortage of "affordable housing"— and have now left us with a problem whose existence is as undeniable as it is painful. When the political crusade for affordable housing took off and built up steam during the 1990s, the share of their incomes that Americans were spending on housing in 1998 was 17 percent, compared to 30 percent in the early 1980s. Even during the housing boom of 2005, the median-priced home nationwide took just 22 percent of the median American income.

What created the illusion of a nationwide problem was that, in particular localities around the country, housing prices had sky-rocketed to the point where people had to pay half their income to buy a modest-sized home and often resorted to very risky ways of financing the purchase. In Tucson, for example, "roughly 60% of first-time home buyers make no down payment and instead now use 100% financing to get into the market," according to the *Wall Street Journal* in 2005.

Almost invariably, these locally extreme housing prices have been a result of local political crusades in the name of locally attractive slogans about the environment, open space, "smart growth" or whatever other phrases had political resonance at the particular time and place.

Where housing markets have been more or less left alone— in places like Houston or Dallas, for example— housing did not take even half as big a share of family incomes as did comparable housing in places like the San Francisco Bay Area, where heavily hyped political crusades had led to severe restrictions on building. It was in precisely these extremely high housing cost enclaves that the kind of people for whom the national housing crusade expressed much concern— minorities, low-income people and families with children— were forced *out* disproportionately.

Political Crusades

Few things blind human beings to the actual consequences of what they are doing like a heady feeling of self-righteousness during a crusade to smite the wicked and rescue the downtrodden. Statistical studies about disparities between blacks and whites in mortgage loan approval rates might be said to have "jump-started" the housing crusades that took off in the 1990s. Politicians and the media led this crusade, with many community activists following in their wake, much like scavengers, able to extract large sums of money from banks and other institutions by raising claims of discrimination, whose power to delay government approval of bank mergers and other business decisions made pay-offs to these activists the only prudent course for those accused.

Even where loudly proclaimed concern for the poor and minorities gave impetus to the drive for over-riding traditional mortgage lending standards, this is not to say that the poor and minorities were the sole beneficiaries or even the main beneficiaries. When you open the floodgates, you cannot tell the water where to go. Housing speculators— especially "flippers"— found the new and looser home mortgage rules a bonanza. So did many others. It is by no means clear that the poor or minorities came out ahead at all, after the housing boom turned to bust and many were left with mortgage payments they couldn't meet on homes they couldn't afford.

With rich rewards available— politically, ideologically and financially— from the "affordable housing" crusade, there were ample incentives to keep this crusade going for years. Meanwhile, various special interests found ways to benefit themselves from all this, whether as home builders, real estate investors or others, and therefore added their voices in support of the open-ended goal of more home ownership through various ways of achieving, or seeming to achieve, affordable housing. Supporters of such policies and programs easily drowned out the voices of those economists and others who increasingly warned of the risky financial arrangements that were behind the statistics on the growing numbers of home buyers that were so triumphantly being paraded as fruits of the crusade for affordable housing and the stamping out of mortgage lending discrimination.

In short, this was a crusade that was feeding on its own successes by its own criteria, and was not likely to stop unless it got stopped.

The housing market collapse dealt a blow to some of the devices that fed the crusade— "creative" financing and lax lending standards, for example— but even the ensuing national crisis did nothing to end the political attractiveness of the goal of making housing affordable by government fiat, rather than by individuals buying or renting housing that was within their own income range. Just as the utter discrediting of public housing projects did not discredit the underlying beliefs that caused such projects to be built, so in this case even the more widely disastrous consequences of the affordable housing crusade have led only to seeking other ways of carrying on that same crusade, based on the same discredited assumptions and the same disregard of repercussions.

While some Congressional Democrats have proposed a moratorium on mortgage foreclosures or allowing judges to change the terms of mortgage contracts, Senate Republicans have proposed "providing government-backed, 4% fixed mortgages to any credit-worthy borrower." What these proposals from politicians of both parties all have in common is an utter absence of any serious consideration of the repercussions in multiple directions of arbitrary government fiats.

Anyone who expected any such consideration of repercussions by most members of either political party would have little chance of avoiding painful disappointments. Certainly few politicians of either party have questioned whether the track record of politicians in the housing market justified more of the same in other markets. Many are in fact eager to extend political intervention into other industries receiving the government "stimulus" or bailout money.

THE NEW DEAL IDEAL

Whatever the long-run prospects for more rational government policies in the future, the current disaster is already upon us, and how it is dealt with by those in power is the pressing issue of the day.

Many of the policies for dealing with the current financial crisis are reminiscent of the policies of Franklin D. Roosevelt's New Deal administration for dealing with the Great Depression of the 1930s. Indeed, many of the advocates of such policies today cite the New Deal as a model for government intervention to bring the economy out of an economic crisis. Congressman Barney Frank, for example, said, "This is equivalent to what FDR had to do . . . to save capitalism from its own excesses." A front-page *Los Angeles Times* column was titled "A Time for Boldness Beyond the New Deal," and claimed that the New Deal "wasn't stimulative enough." But, before using the New Deal as a model, we should examine that history more carefully than many have done.

The Stock Market Crash

The huge stock market crash of 1929 has long been regarded as the cause of the massive unemployment that marked the decade of the 1930s. The tragedy of that decade is undeniable. Not only did unemployment soar as high as 25 percent for 1933, the annual unemployment rate remained above 20 percent for four consecutive years, 1932 through 1935. Literally thousands of banks failed across the country. Stock prices fell to a fraction of their 1929 peaks, as American corporations as a whole operated in the red for two consecutive years. Mass foreclosures of homes and farms drove families into makeshift housing, including shanty towns christened "Hoovervilles" for President Herbert Hoover, who was widely blamed for this catastrophe that struck while he was in the White House.

The view that Hoover's successor, Franklin D. Roosevelt, was responsible for getting the country out of the Great Depression was once widespread and still has enough support among opinion-makers today that a new administration in Washington in 2009 invokes FDR and his policies as a precedent to follow in dealing with today's financial crises. More fundamentally, the Great Depression has been seen— then and now— as a failure of the free market that required massive government intervention to save the economy. FDR has been credited with being the first President of the United States to understand the need for federal intervention to deal with a depression.

This picture, however, has been increasingly challenged in recent years by scholars, especially economists, but by some historians as well.

While federal intervention in the economy during the Great Depression was indeed on an unprecedented scale, it is now increasingly recognized that this intervention was begun by President Herbert Hoover, and that Franklin D. Roosevelt's New Deal was largely a further expansion of what Hoover had already begun. Even at the time, Walter Lippmann pointed this out in a 1935 newspaper column:

> The policy initiated by President Hoover in the autumn of 1929 was something utterly unprecedented in American history. The national government undertook to make the whole economic order operate prosperously. . . the Roosevelt measures are a continuous evolution of the Hoover measures.

President Hoover was himself well aware that he was doing something unprecedented by intervening in the economy to try to get the country out of a depression. "No President before had ever believed there was a government responsibility in such cases," he said in his memoirs. Even former members of President Franklin D. Roosevelt's own administration admitted in later years that many of Hoover's initiatives were taken over and expanded under FDR, though the political and media image of Hoover invoked in many election years thereafter was that Hoover had been a "do nothing president."

The real question, however, is not who should be credited with first taking on the responsibility for initiating federal intervention, but whether that intervention itself deserves credit, in the first place. Today it is so widely accepted that the federal government must "do something" to cope with recessions and depressions that the actual consequences of government interventions tend to receive relatively little scrutiny in the media or in politics.

Job Creation

Since mass unemployment was the most visibly painful aspect of the Great Depression, one of the main thrusts of the Roosevelt administration then, like that of the Obama administration today, was to create jobs.

During the Great Depression of the 1930s, the government created vast numbers of jobs— there were more young men in the Civilian Conservation Corps than in the Army— but unemployment never fell below double digits during the first seven years under President Franklin D. Roosevelt. For the first 21 consecutive months of FDR's administration, unemployment never fell below 20 percent. The fallacy of those who see government-created jobs as an answer to unemployment is in regarding such jobs as a *net increase* in employment. But the money that pays for government-created jobs is taken from the private sector, leaving less demand and less employment there. Huge increases in government-created jobs may make little or no net difference in mass unemployment.

There are ways in which government policies can, theoretically, create a net increase in employment. But this is a little like saying that better regulation can prevent crises in financial markets. It is true in the abstract but the real question in the real world is whether what government is likely to do is likely to increase employment on net balance. The track record of the New Deal offers little support to that conclusion.

Whatever its shortcomings economically, what government job creation programs can do politically is create a large class of people beholden to the government, and likely to vote for those who gave them jobs in hard times. The *political* success of the New Deal is beyond dispute. That FDR could be re-elected in a landslide in 1936 and re-elected again to an unprecedented third term in 1940, despite never having gotten unemployment down into single digits during his first two terms, is an indication that President Obama may also be able to succeed politically, even if his policies turn out to be an economic disaster for the country as a whole.

One of the policies that the current administration shares with both the Hoover and Roosevelt administrations in the 1930s is the notion that government needs to keep prices from falling to the level they would reach under supply and demand in a free market. Today the emphasis is on trying to maintain housing prices with government subsidies, while Presidents Hoover and FDR sought to maintain both industrial and agricultural prices, as well as the price of labor. But in 1934 Walter Lippmann pointed out the problem with that approach when he said, "in a depression men cannot sell their goods or their service at pre-depression prices. If they insist on pre-depression prices for goods, they do not sell them. If they insist on pre-depression wages, they become unemployed."

Today, in the current recession, the banks and other financial institutions have already recognized that economic reality by selling foreclosed houses at large discounts over the prices at which those houses sold just a few years ago. But politicians have no incentive to follow suit and every incentive to try to maintain housing prices, instead of letting those prices fall through supply and demand. That is because rescuing existing homeowners and lenders gains their political support without offsetting losses of support from taxpayers and voters who do not follow the economics of what is happening.

Market versus Government

The larger question that remains as relevant as ever today is: Was it the failure of the free market that led to the massive unemployment which persisted throughout the decade of the 1930s or was the Great Depression prolonged by the government interventions that were intended to shorten it?

Two facts are clear from the outset: (1) the stock market crash in October 1929 marked a major downturn in the economy as a whole and a rise in unemployment; and (2) during all the previous history of the United States, when the federal government let the economy recover from downturns on its own, no depression ever turned out to be as deep or as long-lasting as the Great Depression of the 1930s. In short, a plausible case can be made that either the market or the government was responsible for the severity and duration of the Great Depression. What must be done is to go beyond plausibility and scrutinize the facts more closely.

Because the stock market crash occurred first and the government began to intervene on a large scale some time later, we can trace what happened before and after the federal interventions, which began under Herbert Hoover and continued under Franklin D. Roosevelt. Month by month statistics on unemployment, compiled in the late twentieth century by economists Richard Vedder and Lowell Gallaway, enable us to follow events in some detail.

Two months after the stock market crash in October 1929, unemployment rose and peaked at 9 percent, after which it began a generally downward movement over the next several months and subsided to a level of 6.3 percent by June 1930. Although these levels of unemployment were higher than those before the stock market crash, and were a legitimate cause for concern, they were not even half of the unemployment rate that would begin, and persist for years, after major federal interventions in the economy.

The first of these major interventions began in June 1930, when Congress passed the Smoot-Hawley tariffs, the highest in more than a century, in an effort to reduce imports and thus preserve American jobs by having the formerly imported goods produced in the United States instead. A public appeal signed by a thousand economists from leading universities warned against the consequences of the Smoot-Hawley tariffs, but these warnings were ignored, just as the many warnings about the risky housing markets were ignored in our times. As already noted, unemployment stood at 6.3 percent at this time. In November of 1930— five months after the Smoot-Hawley tariffs— unemployment reached double digits for the first time in the decade, at 11.6 percent.

In other words, unemployment had not yet reached double digits until more than a year after the stock market crash. In the meantime, there were the Smoot-Hawley tariffs and unemployment rose to double digits just five months after those tariffs that were supposed to reduce unemployment. Moreover, while the initial rise in unemployment after the stock market crash began to subside after peaking two months later, the double digit unemployment that began after the Smoot-Hawley tariffs continued for every month throughout the entire remainder of the decade of the 1930s.

Not all of this was due to the Smoot-Hawley tariffs alone. These tariffs, passed during the Hoover administration, were only the first in a series of major federal interventions in the market that continued under FDR throughout the remainder of the decade. The biggest of the New Deal interventions was the National Industrial Recovery Act of 1933, which controlled prices and wages in industry. The Agricultural Adjustment Act of 1933 established federal control over prices and output in agriculture. The National Labor Relations Act of 1935 made it mandatory for employers to negotiate wages and working conditions with labor unions. FDR also took the country off the gold standard and issued thousands of executive orders— more than all the subsequent Presidents of the United States in the twentieth century combined.

The New Deal administration not only set up *policies* to deal with existing economic problems of the 1930s, it set up enduring *institutions* to change the way the American economy operated. Thus we are, in the twenty-first century, paying agricultural subsidies to millionaires and billionaires because of a program created during the Great Depression to help small farmers who were having a hard time. Again, once you have opened the floodgates you cannot tell the water where to go. Programs set up to help one constituency deal with a current problem acquire new constituencies and take new directions. Even if the original problem gets solved, that does not mean that the program will end, or even that it will not continue to expand.

The Roosevelt administration's rapid succession of sweeping and unpredictable interventions in the economy, interspersed with anti-business rhetoric, caused even a liberal like John Maynard Keynes to question whether some of the New Deal reforms, including some he regarded as "wise and necessary," might "impede" economic recovery because they could "upset the confidence of the business world and weaken their existing motives to action."

Business investments in fact remained unusually low during the uncertainties of the New Deal era, as investments have tended to remain low during other periods of uncertainty, such as today. According to a financial historian, throughout the 1930s "the amount banks lent for each dollar of reserves remained at about half the level of the 1920s." Meanwhile, the unemployment rate never fell below the double-digit level for any year in either of FDR's first two terms in office. Whatever the vision, that is the record. An economic and statistical analysis in a leading scholarly journal in 2004 concluded that government policies in the 1930s prolonged the depression by several years.

Ending the Depression

What brought the Great Depression of the 1930s to an end? Over the years, fewer and fewer people have accepted the once common belief that it was the New Deal policies of President Roosevelt that ended the Great Depression. A competing explanation is that World War II ended the Great Depression. It is certainly true that unemployment virtually disappeared during the war and production increased. But to say that the war ended the depression still leaves unanswered the real question: What specifically about the war caused unemployment to fall and output to rise?

Advocates of a massive government spending program today— the so-called "stimulus package"— argue that it was the rise of federal spending during the war which supplied the demand for output and for the labor which produced that output. This explanation certainly sounds plausible. But the question is: Are we prepared to bet literally trillions of dollars in government expenditures today on plausibility, without bothering to scrutinize that plausible explanation of what happened when similar policies were tried before?

The mere existence of World War II, which began in September 1939, did not greatly change output or employment in the United States, which did not enter the war until December of 1941. Although the war started in 1939, the unemployment rate in the United States was 14.6 percent in 1940, compared to 14.3 percent three years earlier. So the existence of the war, as such, was clearly not sufficient to end the Great Depression. The first year after 1930 for which the unemployment rate was no longer in double digits was 1941, when unemployment fell to 9.9 percent. High as that might seem in later times, more than a decade had passed before the unemployment rate dropped even slightly below 10 percent for even a single month. The next year— the first full year when the United States was at war— the unemployment rate fell below 5 percent, and for the next three years it was below two percent.

Clearly the war seems to have had a dramatic effect in reducing unemployment. But the real question still remains: Was that because of federal spending?

As already noted, the unemployment rate in 1940 was 14.6 percent. But the federal deficit was higher in 1936, when the unemployment rate was also higher, at 17 percent. If federal deficit spending is considered to be the crucial factor, then the question must be faced: Why did a bigger deficit not produce a lower unemployment rate at the earlier time (1936) compared to the later time (1940)?

President Franklin D. Roosevelt himself put his finger on a change that is today often overlooked by those who attribute the end of the Great Depression to increased government spending during wartime. In his whimsical way that some found charming, FDR said that "Dr. New Deal" was replaced by "Dr. Win-the-War." The Roosevelt administration abandoned much of its anti-business stance and replaced New Deal zealots in high places with people from the private business and financial sectors, who could deal with the industrialists needed for war production. Far from generating uncertainty in the business community, the pendulum swung to the other side, with cost-plus government contracts that *guaranteed* business profits to producers of war materiel. Taking 12 million men out of the workforce to serve in the military forces also greatly reduced the potential for unemployment, though that aspect is often overlooked by those eager to credit federal spending for ending mass unemployment.

In short, the war ended the New Deal— and the end of the New Deal saw the economy recover, as it had recovered from depressions on its own throughout the history of the country prior to the 1930s.

The Lessons of the New Deal

If there is a lesson in the New Deal experience, it seems to be the opposite of the one drawn by those who have advocated massive government spending and massive government interventions in the economy. The lesson that seems more consistent with the evidence is that massive and unpredictable government interventions in the economy create uncertainties as to what government is going to do next— in addition to uncertainties as to what the actual economic consequences of government policies will turn out to be.

In that atmosphere of uncertainty generated by unpredictable government policy experiments, people tend to hold on to their money. The velocity of circulation of money slowed down during the Great Depression, just as it has today. Massive government deficit spending did not stimulate private spending then, any more than it is stimulating it now.

It is of course not possible to conduct laboratory experiments to determine what would have happened without government intervention after the stock market crash of 1929. The closest thing to such an experiment might be the experience after the stock market crash of 1987, a decline very similar to that in 1929. The 1987 stock market crash is not remembered as vividly today as the earlier stock market crash because its aftermath was so different. Unlike what had been done by Presidents Hoover and Roosevelt, President Ronald Reagan did *not* intervene in 1987, despite media criticisms of his inaction. The net result of leaving the stock market and the economy to recover on their own was what the distinguished British magazine *The Economist* later called 20 years of "an enviable combination of steady growth and low inflation."

This was not the only time when doing nothing produced a better track record than massive government interventions. A sharp economic downturn in the early 1920s was allowed to recover on its own and quickly did so. There have been similar results in other countries. J.A. Schumpeter, writing in the 1930s about an economic downturn in England back in the 1820s, said, "the inaction of government, however reprehensible on humanitarian grounds, contributed to recovery at least by not hampering it."

Conservatives have no monopoly on skepticism about government intervention during an economic downturn. It was none other than Karl Marx who referred to "crackbrained meddling by the authorities" that can "aggravate an existing crisis."

In January 2009, before taking office, president-elect Barack Obama declared: "There is no disagreement that we need action by our government, a recovery plan that will help to jumpstart the economy." In response, hundreds of economists, including some with Nobel Prizes, put a full-page advertisement in the *New York Times* and other publications with the headline: "With all due respect Mr. President, that is not true." It continued:

> Notwithstanding reports that all economists are now Keynesians and that we all support a big increase in the burden of government, we the undersigned do not believe that more government spending is a way to improve economic performance. More government spending by Hoover and Roosevelt did not pull the United States economy out of the Great Depression in the 1930s. More government spending did not solve Japan's "lost decade" in the 1990s. As such, it is a triumph of hope over experience to believe that more government spending will help the U.S. today.

The actual track record of government interventions supports these economists' conclusions. As Alan Reynolds of the Cato Institute pointed out:

> In the late 19th and early 20th centuries, nobody thought the government could or should do anything except stand aside and let the mistakes of business and banking be fixed by those who made them. There were no Keynesian plans to borrow and spend our way out of recessions. And bankers had no Federal Reserve to bail them out until 1913. Yet recessions after the Fed was created soon turned out to be much deeper than before (1920–21, 1929–33, 1937–38) and often more persistent.

However, those who say that the government must "do something" during a recession or depression seldom, if ever, compare what actually happens when the government does something with what happens when it does nothing.

Purpose and Success

No one can pronounce the New Deal administration— or today's administration in Washington— either a success or a failure, without knowing what it has been trying to do. What we may wish any administration would be trying to do is no clue to what its actual goals and priorities are. Nor can we assume that any administration's rhetoric is a reliable guide to its purposes, much less its actual consequences.

Our assessment of the success or failure of the New Deal will be quite different if we assume that its efforts were directed primarily toward getting the country out of the Great Depression as quickly and as fully as possible, rather than some other goal. Walter Lippmann, perhaps the leading journalist of that era, saw the New Deal's primary goal as entirely different from economic recovery. According to Lippmann, the New Dealers would "rather not have recovery if the revival of private initiative means a resumption of private control in the management of corporate business." He saw their goal as fundamental and enduring changes in the institutions of American society, rather than the most expeditious ending of the current economic crisis. To Lippmann "the essence of the New Deal is the reduction of private corporate control by collective bargaining and labor legislation, on the one side, and by restrictive, competitive and deterrent government action on the other side."

It is a matter of record that many of the leading decision-makers of the New Deal administration in the 1930s were advocates of government intervention in the economy and of a fundamental restructuring of the economy— a New Deal— years *before* the stock market crash of 1929 and the Great Depression that followed, which put them in a position to carry out ideas to which they were dedicated, long before there was any economic crisis to deal with. The New Deal succeeded in using a transient crisis to create enduring institutions, including among others the Federal National Mortgage Association or "Fannie Mae," which FDR created in 1938, and which has been at the heart of the housing boom and bust that led to today's financial crises.

What of the new administration of our time? Do its early initiatives indicate that their primary goal is to put the current economic crisis behind us, as quickly and as fully as possible, or *to use that crisis to impose new and enduring changes in the American economy and society*? The answer to that question depends far more on what this administration has actually done, rather than on what it has said.

Within a month after the Obama administration took office in January 2009, a spending bill involving hundreds of billions of dollars was passed in just two days, even though the legislation was more than a thousand pages long and it was virtually impossible that members of Congress could have read it all in the time available, much less weighed its consequences.

As noted at the end of Chapter 3, both the Congressional Budget Office in the United States and *The Economist* magazine in Britain have pointed out that most of the money in the "stimulus" bill would not be spent in 2009 nor all of it before the end of 2010. Even a supporter of the "stimulus" bill like Professor Alan Blinder of Princeton said, "it's still too slow."

If the purpose was to get the current economic crisis behind us, then the slow-moving policies passed in haste make no sense. But if the purpose is to use the current crisis to create enduring changes in the institutions of the American economy and society, then the haste makes perfect sense. In this latter case, it doesn't matter how slowly the spending gets underway; what matters is how fast the law gets passed, while the public is panicked, and before any opposition can get organized. The massive spending already provided by the Bush administration bailout of 2008 has provided a basis on which Washington politicians can tell General Motors how to make cars and other companies what their CEOs' salaries should be.

The argument that government officials have a right to protect the taxpayers' money through intervention into the decisions made by companies that spend bailout money is politically effective, however logically deficient. *Rights are not the issue.* Anyone who owns a home has a right to take a hammer and smash every window in that house. But no one believes that the right to do so says anything about the wisdom of doing so. All of us have rights to do all sorts of things that would be counterproductive and even disastrous. The purpose of government is not to exercise every conceivable right it has but to exercise whatever wisdom it has for the benefit of the country.

It is hardly wisdom to say that the taxpayers' money will be safeguarded by making it harder for companies receiving that money to compete for top executives against other companies that are not restricted by pay caps. If Wal-Mart is free to offer five times what General Motors can offer to a top executive, how likely is that executive to go to work for General Motors? Similarly, how do other politically determined restrictions safeguard the taxpayers' money when the companies subject to those restrictions have to compete with companies not subject to such restrictions and such uncertainty as to additional future restrictions? The fact that the administration's pay "czar" has also taken it upon himself to *raise* the pay of some other executives of businesses with government bailouts suggests that the idea of safeguarding the taxpayers' money may be simply a rationale for expanded government power.

The current economic crisis itself grew out of politicians intervening in businesses and markets, making decisions for which they have neither experience nor expertise, much less a stake. To extend the same principle to other sectors of the economy is to invite a wider disaster, rather than an end to the current crisis. Asserting a right to do so is completely beside the point— which is whether the country will be better off or worse off if politicians continue the pattern of interventions that brought on the current economic problems in the first place.

Shortly before the Obama administration took office, the man who would become President Obama's chief of staff, Rahm Emanuel, said, "You never want a serious crisis to go to waste." He added: "What I mean by that is that it's an opportunity to do things you could not do before." In other words, both this statement and the deeds of the new administration point toward their using the current crisis to forward their long-run agenda of a politically guided economy. Rushing through legislation toward that end, in the name of ending the crisis, and doing so during the early "honeymoon" period of a new administration, when both the public and the media are uncritical, makes perfect sense in pursuit of such a goal, though it makes little or no sense on an assumption that they are trying to get the economic crisis over as quickly as possible.

Instead, what we are talking about is *using* a crisis to fundamentally and enduringly change the institutions of American society. However confident or enthusiastic the new administration may be about remaking the institutions of America to fit their vision, those institutions have had a remarkably successful track record over a period of more than two centuries. What is now being proposed is to jettison all that for the sake of untried theories, because of an economic situation that has arisen in a relatively few years, as a result of government interventions with a terrible track record that have led to a crisis which now provides an opportunity for more of the same— in the name of "change."

Many of the very same politicians whose interventions pushed bankers and other lenders into riskier lending practices that backfired are now seeking to do an encore in other industries, such as automobile manufacturing. Meanwhile, a growing list of government directives are being imposed on banks receiving bailout money:

> Financial institutions that are getting government bailout funds have been told to put off evictions and modify mortgages for distressed homeowners. They must let shareholders vote on executive pay packages. They must slash dividends, cancel employee training and morale-building exercises, and withdraw job offers to foreign citizens.

Whatever the merits or demerits of any of these directives individually, all of them represent things which the Constitution of the United States never authorized the government to do. Moreover, all are things imposed *after* the bailout, not as a precondition for receiving the bailout, and so leave open the question of how many additional arbitrary directives will follow. This adds to the uncertainties that inhibit economic activity.

Against this background, it is possible to understand why some banks have sought to return the money that the federal government lent them under the Troubled Asset Relief Program (TARP)— and why the

Obama administration has *refused* some offers of repayment, which would mean relinquishing the power that goes with TARP loans.

The market has already demonstrated how fast it can adjust to the housing market collapse, when no-down-payment mortgages, interest-only mortgages and other "creative" ways of financing home purchases declined drastically in California, in just a couple of years. But the political arena still abounds with the same vision of government micro-management— and even the same personalities— that put the housing market, and ultimately the economy, on the road to ruin.

Despite differences of personalities and of the times, the underlying vision of the New Deal and that of the current administration are fundamentally similar. However that vision is conceived or articulated by those who believe in it, it is a vision of the federal government exercising vastly more power over the economy and the society than was ever granted to it by the Constitution of the United States. What the government buys with the enormous sums of money it dispenses is the power to give orders to the recipients that the Constitution never authorized them to give. Politicians are, in effect, buying up our freedom with our own tax money.

SUMMARY AND IMPLICATIONS

Before we go forward as a nation, it is well to look at where we have been, despite being urged to take drastic actions immediately— and, in fact, *especially* when being urged to take drastic actions immediately.

Whether we look at the American economy in general or the housing market in particular, we see a history of remarkable progress for generation after generation— and a few recent years when things turned very bad, very quickly.

It has been almost axiomatic, for at least a century, that the American economy produces more output than any other economy in the world. All this is so much taken for granted that no one considers it worth commenting on the fact that 300 million Americans today produce more output than more than a billion people in India or an even larger population in China— indeed, more than these two countries combined, even though their combined population is more than eight times the population of the United States. We also produce more than Japan, Germany, Britain and France combined.

The housing market has, of course, changed drastically in the past few years, as have other things in the economy. But does all this suggest that (1) we need to change some recent bad policies or that (2) we need to restructure a whole economic system that has worked well for centuries? More specifically, does it mean that we need to allow politicians a bigger say in how American businesses are run?

Lenders did not spontaneously begin to lend to people who would not have qualified for loans under the traditional criteria that had evolved out of years of experience in the market. Such risky loans were made under growing pressures from government regulatory agencies and politicians, and even threats of prosecution from the Justice Department, if the statistical profiles of borrowers whose loan applications were approved did not match the government's preconceptions.

The growth in subprime loans was one way of meeting arbitrary quotas for lending to people who did not meet the criteria for loan approval that had prevailed for years. Quota lending was one of many political patches put over problems caused by previous political "solutions." Often these interventions have focussed on some limited goal, with no real concern about, or even awareness of, the wider ramifications of what they were doing. It is doubtful whether most of the state politicians of the past who enacted laws to prevent branch banking had anything in mind more far-reaching than enabling local banks to avoid having to compete with branches of much bigger and better-known banks. It seems even less likely that these local politicians felt any responsibility for the thousands of bank failures during the Great Depression of the 1930s.

Nor is it likely that the national politicians of our own times, who for years made "home ownership" the touchstone of housing policy, will acknowledge any responsibility for the financial disasters and widespread unemployment today. What that means is that the voting public must at a minimum be skeptical of political spin, no matter how often it is echoed in the media. What would be even better would be to develop some sense of awareness that everything "is interconnected in the world of prices, so that the smallest change in one element is passed along the chain to millions of others." It is a caution especially apt when someone is pushing the political crusade of the day as an overriding "good thing," whether home ownership, mortgage foreclosure mitigation or a restructuring of the whole economy.

The very idea that the current economic crisis will go to "waste" if it is not used by politicians to rush through a fundamental restructuring of the economy, while the public is too panicked to object, should at the very least give us pause, if not set off alarm bells.

Writing in the **Wall Street Journal** in September 2009, Professor Allan Meltzer of Carnegie Mellon University, a leading authority on the monetary history of the United States said: "Most economists now believe that the recession is expected to end before much of the government spending takes hold." However welcome that might be, from the standpoint of the public, if it turns out to be true, letting the economy recover on its own was never a viable option politically, for it would have meant letting a crisis "go to waste" when politicians want to "do something."

From the standpoint of those who seek to remake the economic institutions of America, the worst case scenario would have been to have the economy begin visibly recovering on its own before they could get their blueprint for salvation enacted into law. The urgency behind the hasty passage of the "stimulus" legislation was real, even if the reason for that haste was not a swift spending of the money to speed economic recovery. The similar urgency behind the administration's attempt to get a massive medical care bill passed before the August 2009 Congressional recess— *even though the bill would not have taken effect until 2013*— was another repetition of the pattern of seeking fast passage of legislation that would be slow to go into operation.

Will the history of the New Deal and the Great Depression repeat itself? Or will the economy soon begin recovering from the current recession, as some economists believe? There is, of course, no way to know in advance. What we can know is what kinds of policies have led to what kinds of consequences in the past and what the repetition of such policies is likely to produce today. If history teaches us anything, it is that past mistakes have often been repeated, even in the name of doing something new and different— that is, in the name of "change." Comments made years ago by distinguished British historian Paul Johnson remain very apt in our times:

> The study of history is a powerful antidote to contemporary arrogance. It is humbling to discover how many of our glib assumptions, which seem to us novel and plausible, have been tested before, not once but many times and in innumerable guises; and discovered to be, at great human cost, wholly false.

SOURCES

PREFACE

The opening comment from the *New York Times'* financial reporters is from page B1 of the November 25, 2009 issue, in an article titled "An Upturn in Housing May Be Reversing." Justice Oliver Wendell Holmes' advice about thinking is quoted from pages 738 and 1162 of *Holmes-Laski Letters*, Volumes I and II respectively.

CHAPTER 1: THE ECONOMICS OF THE HOUSING BOOM

The epigraph is from page 95 of *Financial Shock* by Mark Zandi. The increase in the median price of American single-family homes from 2000 to 2005 is shown on page 162 of the *Financial Services Fact Book, 2007*, published by the Insurance Information Institute. The sharp home price increases in New York, Los Angeles and San Diego are from page 40 of the October 16, 2006 issue of *Newsweek,* in a column titled "The Worrying Housing Bust." That more than two-thirds of mortgage loans originated in 2004 were sold to the secondary market, and that Fannie Mae and Freddie Mac purchased more than a third of such loans was reported on page 355 of the Summer 2005 issue of the *Federal Reserve Bulletin*, under the title "New Information Reported under HMDA and Its Application in Fair Lending Enforcement." The quote about the profits and risks of government-sponsored enterprises is from page A10 of the July 12–13, 2008 issue of the *Wall Street Journal*, under the headline "Fannie Mae Ugly." The fact that home equity accounts for 42 percent of a household's net worth is from page 4 of "Net Worth and the Assets of Households: 2002," *Current Population Reports*, P70–115, published by the U.S. Census Bureau in April 2008. The statement that mortgage debt represents 82 percent of a homeowner's liabilities is from page 423 of the October 2003 issue of the *Federal Reserve Bulletin*, under the title "Recent Changes to a Measure of U.S. Household Debt Service." That 60 percent of a homeowner's income was required to pay the monthly mortgage in Salinas, California, was shown on a graph on page A6 of the August 26–27, 2006 issue of the *Wall Street Journal*, in a front-page story titled "In Tony Monterey County, Slums and a Land War." Changes in the interest rate on a conventional 30-year mortgage from 1973 to 2005 were shown on page 7 of the October 2006 issue of the *Monthly Labor Review*, in an article titled "Recent Employment Trends in Residential and Nonresidential Construction." That borrowers with higher interest rates tend to have higher rates of payment delinquency and foreclosure was shown on page 368 of the Summer 2005 issue of the *Federal Reserve Bulletin*, under the title "New Information Reported under HMDA and Its Application in Fair Lending Enforcement." The decline in the Federal Reserve's interest rate from 2001 to 2003 is from page 69 of *Financial Shock* by Mark Zandi. The fact that the Federal Reserve reduced the federal funds rate to its lowest level in decades during the early years of the 21st century was mentioned on pages 276 and 277 of an article titled "Monetary Policy, Credit Extension, and Housing Bubbles: 2008 and 1929" in *Critical Review*, Vol. 21, combined numbers 2 and 3 (2009). The increased reliance on savings as the primary source of a down payment on a home among California home buyers after the housing bust is from page 24 of the report *State of the California Housing Market 2008–2009*, published by the California Association of Realtors. The decreasing proportion of first-time home buyers in California in the early years of the twenty-first century is from page 13 of the same study, while the disparity in the size of down payments between first-time home buyers and repeat home buyers in California is from page 39. The fact that the top ten areas with the highest rates of home price appreciation were in California is from page 4 of the study "California's Newest Homeowners: Affording the Unaffordable," *California Counts: Population Trends and Profiles*, published by the Public Policy Institute of California in August 2005. The increase in home prices in California after the decade of the 1970s is discussed on pages 232 to 234 of *Regulatory Takings: Law, Economics, and Politics*, by William A. Fischel. The statement that in 2005 the median-priced San Francisco Bay Area home cost more than three times the national average is from page A11 of a front-page story from the October 16, 2005 issue of the *San Francisco Chronicle*, under the headline "Making Ends Meet: Struggling in Middle Class." The fact that the median sales price of a home in San Francisco reached $765,000 in 2005 was reported on page 3 of the study "California's Newest Homeowners: Affording the Unaffordable," *California Counts: Population Trends and Profiles*, published by the Public Policy Institute of California. The $2,000 per day increase in the value of homes in San Mateo County, California, during March 2005 is from page 1 of the April 15, 2005 issue of the *San Mateo County Times*, under the headline "County's

Home Prices Bust Record." The statement that the median price for homes in San Mateo County, California, soared to over one million dollars in 2007 is from page 1 of the August 16, 2007 issue of the *San Mateo County Times*, in an article titled "Median Home Cost over $1M," while the relatively small size of these homes is mentioned on page 6 of the same article. That the median sales price for homes in the state of California reached $561,000 in 2006 was shown on page 63 of the study *State of the California Housing Market 2008–2009*, published by the California Association of Realtors. The 13 percent increase nationwide in home price appreciation from 2004 to 2005, and the rates of appreciation for Arizona and Michigan were reported on pages 1, 2 and 15, 16 of the report "House Price Appreciation Continues at Robust Pace," published by the Office of Federal Housing Enterprise Oversight on March 1, 2006. The quote about a graduate student in San Francisco "visiting one exorbitantly priced hovel after another" is from page F1 of the September 16, 2007 issue of the *San Francisco Chronicle*, under the headline "Squeeze Hits Landlords." The fact that incomes were rising less rapidly in California than in the rest of the nation at the same time that the state's home prices were soaring is from page 238 of *Regulatory Takings: Law, Economics, and Politics*, by William A. Fischel. The rate of population increase in the San Francisco Bay Area during the 1970s compared with the national rate is from page 9 of a 1982 study by the Stanford Environmental Law Society titled *Land Use and Housing on the San Francisco Peninsula*, edited by Thomas M. Hagler, while the nearly four-fold rise of home prices in Palo Alto, California, during the 1970s when the city's population declined by 8 percent was mentioned on pages 85 and 89. The wide range in the cost of a quarter-acre lot in Chicago, San Diego, New York and San Francisco was noted on pages 15 and 16 of the study "The Impact of Zoning on Housing Affordability," Working Paper 8835, written by Edward L. Glaeser and Joseph Gyourko and published by the National Bureau of Economic Research in March 2002. The amount of open space in San Mateo County, California, is noted on page 2 of the December 10, 2003 issue of the *San Mateo County Times*, under the headline "Open Space." The connection between home price increases and restrictive land use laws is quoted from page 35 of the study "The Planning Penalty: How Smart Growth Makes Housing Unaffordable," written by Randal O'Toole and published by the Independent Institute in 2006. The fact that 23 of the 26 "severely unaffordable" international urban areas follow "smart-growth" policies is from page 38 of the same study. The quote from the former governor of the Reserve Bank of New Zealand is from the "Introduction" to the study *4th Annual Demographia International Housing Affordability Survey: 2008*. The minimum lot size restrictions enacted in Loudoun County, Virginia, were described on pages B1 and B4 of the July 24, 2001 issue of the *Washington Post*, in an article titled "Loudoun Adopts Strict Controls on Development," while similar restrictions enacted in Fayette County, Kentucky, were mentioned on page 33 of the study, "The Planning Penalty: How Smart Growth Makes Housing Unaffordable," written by Randal O'Toole and published by the Independent Institute in 2006. The wide range in home prices between communities with and without growth-management policies is quoted from page 6 of the same study. The comparison of home prices between Houston and San Jose is from page 8 of the October 17, 2007 issue of *Policy Analysis*, No. 602, in a study titled "Do You Know the Way to L.A.?: San Jose Shows How to Turn an Urban Area into Los Angeles in Three Stressful Decades." The real estate advertisement from the *St. Louis Post-Dispatch* is from page G7 of the March 1, 2009 issue, and that from the *San Francisco Chronicle* of the same date is from page P6 of its Real Estate section. The fact that the city of Houston experienced rising income during the 1970s while still maintaining housing affordability is noted on page 32 of "The Planning Penalty: How Smart Growth Makes Housing Unaffordable," written by Randal O'Toole and published by the Independent Institute in 2006, while the high income and low housing costs in Dallas are mentioned on page 33. The "skyrocketing prices" in Manhattan and the less than 10 percent increase in the housing stock there from 1980 to 2005 were noted on pages 332 and 333 of the October 2005 issue of the *Journal of Law and Economics*, under the title "Why Is Manhattan So Expensive?: Regulation and the Rise in Housing Prices." The almost tripling of the population of the city of Las Vegas between 1980 to 2000 at a time when the real median home price remained unchanged was mentioned on page 332 of the same study. The rise in Las Vegas home prices in recent years as a result of the increased resistance of environmental groups to land development was discussed on page 125 of *The Best-Laid Plans* by Randal O'Toole. Information on the extent of development of the land area of the United States is from page 143 of *Sprawl: A Compact History* by Robert Bruegmann and pages 56 and 57 of *The Road More Traveled* by Ted Balaker and Sam Staley. Congressman Dick Armey's quote is from page 183 of his book *Armey's Axioms*. The increased affordability of housing in most of the nation in 2005 was reported on page A1 of the December 29, 2005 issue of the *New York Times*, under the headline "Twenty Years Later, Buying a House Is Less of a Bite." The fact that more than 90 percent of homes in San Diego and San Francisco were selling for at least 140 percent of construction costs was shown on page 26 of the Fall 2002 issue of *Regulation*, in an article titled "Zoning's Steep Price." That housing costs in the ten most expensive metropolitan areas were more than twice the national average in 2004 is from page A1 of the September 22, 2004 issue of the *Wall Street Journal*, in an article titled "After Big Run-Up in Real Estate, Some on Coasts Are Cashing Out." The disparity in the share of income required to pay housing costs in high-priced cities like New York and Los Angeles compared to affordable communities such as Tampa and Dallas was reported on pages A1 and C9 of the December 29, 2005 issue of the *New York Times*, under the headline "Twenty Years Later, Buying a House Is Less of a Bite." The fact that adjustable rate mortgages made up 90 percent of subprime loans by 2006 was noted on page 139 of an article titled "A Crisis of Politics, Not Economics: Complexity, Ignorance, and Policy Failure" in *Critical Review*, Vol. 21, combined numbers 2 and 3 (2009). That the average subprime borrower made only a 5 percent down payment on a home in 2006 is from page 131 of that same article. That "stated income" loans or "liar loans" made up over half of subprime loans by 2006 is from page 40 of *Financial Shock*, by Mark Zandi. The fact that subprime borrowers were committing more than 40 percent of their incomes to their mortgages in 2006 is from the same page. The statement that nearly 15 percent of adjustable rate mortgages had initial interest rates below 2 percent in 2005 and 2006 is from page 56 of the Winter 2009 issue of the *University of Colorado Law Review*, under the title "The Law & Economics of Subprime Lending." That creative mortgage products such as interest-only loans and adjustable-rate mortgages kept initial monthly mortgage payments down in the early years of the twenty-first century was reported on page D1 of the July 14, 2005 issue of the *Wall Street Journal*, under the headline "Housing Gets Even Less Affordable." Data on the growth of interest-only mortgage loans from 2002 to 2005 are from page A16 of the May 20, 2005 issue of the *San Francisco Chronicle*, in a front-page story titled "High Interest in Interest-Only Home Loans," and also from pages C1 and C6 of the July 15, 2006 issue of the *New York Times*, in an article titled "Keep Eyes Fixed on Variable Mortgages." The Chicago man who took out a home equity loan on his home, which had vastly appreciated in price, was mentioned on page 18 of the June 13, 2005 issue of *Time*, under the headline "America's House Party." The story of the Oakland family who refinanced and ultimately lost their home to foreclosure was told on pages A1 and A21 of the August 10, 2008 issue of the *San Francisco Chronicle*, under the headline "Foreclosed Family's Last Goodbye to Home." The soaring value of home equity loans from 2003 to 2007 was noted on page 165 of the *Financial Services Fact Book, 2009*, published by the Insurance Information Institute. The increase in the use of "cash-out refinancing" by homeowners during the housing boom was reported on page 167 of the same study and also page 26 of the February 2009 issue of *The American Spectator*, in an article titled "The True Origins of This Financial Crisis." The statement that over a five-year period, Americans extracted $2.3 trillion of equity from their homes is from page 6 of a special section of the May 30, 2009 issue of *The Economist*, titled "Surviving the Slump." The rise in reverse mortgages from 2001 to 2005 was shown on page 156 of the *Financial Services Fact Book, 2007*, published by the Insurance Information Institute. The decrease in homeowners' equity as a share of home value from 1945 to 2003 is from page 55 of the April 19, 2004 issue of *Newsweek*, in a column titled "Is Housing a New Bubble?" Accounts of speculators making large profits by "flipping" houses are from page 83 of the April 2005 issue of *Money*, under the headline "They Call Them Flippers," and also from page 71 of the October 3, 2005 issue of *Forbes*, in an article titled "Diamonds in the Rough." The rapid pace of home sales in California in 2004 and 2005 is from page 60 of the study *State of the California Housing Market 2008–2009*, published by the California Association of Realtors, while the fact that more than half of the homes sold during these two years received multiple offers from prospective buyers is from page 33. The high percentage of homes purchased as investments in 2005 and 2006 was mentioned on page 33 of the Winter 2009 issue of the *University of Colorado Law Review*, under the title "The Law & Economics of Subprime Lending." The description of the general characteristics of subprime borrowers is from pages 55 and 56 of the same article, while the statement that the great majority of adjustable rate subprime mortgages entered foreclosure before a rise in interest rates occurred is from page 28. The description of mortgage-backed securities as a "blizzard of increasingly complex new securities" is from page 11 of *Financial Shock* by Mark Zandi. The comments from the officials at Moody's on the difficulties of rating mortgage-backed securities during the housing boom are from pages 38 and 41 of an article titled "Triple-A Failure" in the April 27, 2008 issue of *New York Times Magazine*. The statement that the Federal Reserve does not have a specific definition for "predatory lending" is from page 345, note 2 of the Summer 2005 issue of the *Federal Reserve Bulletin*, under the title "New Information Reported under HMDA and Its Application in Fair Lending Enforcement."

CHAPTER 2: THE POLITICS OF THE HOUSING BOOM

The epigraph is from page 126 of the December 20, 2008 issue of *The Economist*, in an article titled "The Battle of Smoot-Hawley." Pressures on Fannie Mae from the Clinton Administration to expand lending to low and moderate income borrowers were mentioned on page C2 of the September 30, 1999 issue of the *New York Times*, under the headline "Fannie Mae Eases Credit to Aid Mortgage Lending." The Department of Housing and Urban Development's setting of numerical goals for Fannie Mae and Freddie Mac to buy more mortgages that were made to less qualified applicants was discussed on pages 16 and 17 of *Civil Rights and the Mortgage Crisis*, published by the U.S. Commission on Civil Rights in September 2009. Data on the increase in the levels of these lending goals from 1996 to 2006 are from page 18 of *Civil Rights and the Mortgage Crisis* and the HUD publication urging "creativity" to overcome "financial barriers to homeownership" is mentioned on page 9 of the same report. The "voluntary" agreement of the Mortgage Bankers Association to expand mortgage lending to minority and low-income borrowers was described on page D1 of the September 13, 1994 issue of the *Washington Post* in an article titled, "Lenders Agree to Anti-Bias Pledge"; on page A17 of the September 20, 1994 issue of the *Washington Times* in an article titled "Robin HUD and Mortgage Lending"; and on page 1 of the September 19, 1994 issue of *National Mortgage News* in an article titled, "MBA Fair Lending Pact." Data on the affordability of homes as measured by comparing home prices to income in Youngstown, Ohio, Las Vegas and San Diego are from pages 30, 33, and 34 of the study *4th Annual Demographia International Housing Affordability Survey: 2008*. Newspaper accounts depicting the lack of affordable housing as a nationwide problem are from page A18 of the July 5, 2002 issue of the *New York Times*, under the headline "Facing Up to the Housing Crisis," and also page B7 of the June 9, 2002 issue of the *Washington Post*, in a column titled "Housing on the Back Burner." J.A. Schumpeter's quote is from page 529 of his *History of Economic Analysis*. The news report highlighting the increased affordability of housing in most of the nation is from page A1 of the December 29, 2005 issue of the *New York Times*, under the headline "Twenty Years Later, Buying a House Is Less of a Bite." The findings of the Heritage Foundation study can be found on page 9 of the August 22, 1990 *Backgrounder*, No. 783, titled "Washington's Continuing Fiction: A National Housing Shortage." Information on the affordability of housing in the United States is from pages 24 to 30 of the Fall 2002 issue of *Regulation*, in an article titled "Zoning's Steep Price," and also pages 117 and 118 of *The Best-Laid Plans* by Randal O'Toole. Data showing that for the United States as a whole, home costs have not exceeded 25 percent of a home buyer's income since 1985 can be found on page 33 of the report *The State of the Nation's Housing 2008*, published by the Joint Center for Housing Studies of Harvard University in 2008. That the median home price in America is 3.6 times the median income of Americans, while the median home prices in Britain, Australia and New Zealand take a much higher share of these countries' median income, was shown on page 11 of *4th Annual Demographia International Housing Affordability Survey: 2008*. Data on housing's share of American consumer spending in 1901 and in 2002 to 2003 are from pages 6 and 63 of *100 Years of U.S. Consumer Spending: Data for the Nation, New York City, and Boston*, Report 991 of the U.S. Department of Labor. The statement that until 1970, median home prices in the United States were about twice as much as the median family income is from page 117 of *The Best-Laid Plans* by Randal O'Toole, while the affordability of housing in San Francisco in 1969 is discussed on page 118. The increase in the ratio between home prices and income in San Jose, California, from 1969 to 2005 is from page 8 of the October 17, 2007 issue of *Policy Analysis*, No. 602, in an article titled "Do You Know the Way to L.A.?: San Jose Shows How to Turn an Urban Area into Los Angeles in Three Stressful Decades." The fact that 23 of the 26 "severely unaffordable" international urban areas follow "smart-growth" policies is from page 38 of the study "The Planning Penalty: How Smart Growth Makes Housing Unaffordable," written by Randal O'Toole and published by the Independent Institute in 2006. The purpose of the Community Reinvestment Act of 1977 is quoted from Section 802 of Title VIII of the Act of October 12, 1977

(Public Law 95–128; 91 Stat. 1147), *United States Statutes at Large, 1977,* Volume 91, published by the United States Government Printing Office in 1980. The fact that the Community Reinvestment Act of 1977 was passed after only one day of debate in the Senate and no debate in the House of Representatives was mentioned on page 19 of *Architects of Ruin* by Peter Schweizer. The 1989 inquiry by the Department of Justice into the lending practices of banks and savings and loans in Atlanta was described on page 26 of the April 30, 1989 issue of the *New York Times*, in an article titled "U.S. Investigates Possible Bias by Atlanta Lenders." The law establishing annual goals for the purchase of mortgages by Fannie Mae and Freddie Mac was Section 1334 of the Housing and Community Development Act of 1992. Attorney General Janet Reno's warnings to banks whose lending patterns were believed to be racially biased based on statistical disparities are from page B7 of the December 14, 1993 issue of the *Washington Times*, in an article titled "Bank to Pay $960,000 in Loan-Bias Settlement," and page A2 of the December 14, 1993 issue of the *Wall Street Journal*, under the headline "Shawmut Settles Charges of Bias in Its Lending." The fact that black-owned banks reject black mortgage loan applicants at a higher rate than white-owned banks do is from an article in the February 1997 issue of the *Journal of Financial Services Research*, titled "Do Black-Owned Banks Discriminate Against Black Borrowers?" The high rate of default and foreclosure among minority homeowners during the housing bust is discussed on page 15 of the study "Subprime Mortgages, Foreclosures, and Urban Neighborhoods," Working Paper 2009–1, published by the Federal Reserve Bank of Atlanta in February 2009; page A12 of the January 8, 2008 issue of the *New York Times*, under the headline "Baltimore Is Suing Bank Over Foreclosure Crisis"; page B3 of the May 4, 2008 issue of the *Orlando Sentinel*, in an article titled "Foreclosure Crisis Hits Hard in Black Communities"; pages A1 and A10 of the January 5, 2009 issue of the *Wall Street Journal*, in a story titled "Housing Push for Hispanics Spawns Wave of Foreclosures"; and page A1 of the November 4, 2007 issue of the *Atlanta Journal-Constitution*, under the headline "Black Atlantans Frequently Snared by Subprime Loans." The increased pressures imposed by the Department of Housing and Urban Development upon lenders during the 1990s are mentioned on page 6 of "How Did We Get into This Financial Mess?" *Cato Institute Briefing Papers*, No. 110, November 18, 2008. Information about the manual on nondiscriminatory lending issued by the Federal Reserve Bank of Boston is from page 18 of *Meltdown,* by Thomas E. Woods, Jr. The insistence of the Clinton Administration that banks with unsatisfactory ratings under the 1977 Community Reinvestment Act be prohibited from diversifying their business is from page A3 of the October 22, 1999 issue of the *Wall Street Journal*, under the headline "Glass-Steagall Overhaul Remains on Hold." That a satisfactory record of meeting community credit needs was required of banks seeking to diversify their business is quoted from the Gramm-Leach-Bliley Act of November 12, 1999 (Public Law 106–102; 113 Stat. 1350). The tactics employed by ACORN against banks are described on page 21 of *Meltdown*, by Thomas E. Woods, Jr. The concessions made by banks to community activist groups were discussed in the *Wall Street Journal*, September 10, 1987, section 2, page 35, under the headline "Public Service or Blackmail? Banks Pressed to Finance Local Projects." The pledge by Sumitomo Bank of California to give 20 percent to 25 percent of its contracts to minority-owned businesses was reported on page A22 of the January 6, 1999 issue of the *Wall Street Journal*, under the headline "Gramm's Glass-Steagall Beef." President George W. Bush's efforts to increase home ownership were discussed on page 31 of the August 23, 2004 issue of *Barron's*, under the headline "Nothing Down." The decline in the proportion of 30-year fixed-rate mortgages from 2001 to 2006 and the increase in subprime loans are from page 4 of the November 2008 *Financial Services Outlook*, published by the American Enterprise Institute, and the extent of subprime and non-traditional loans purchased by Fannie Mae and Freddie Mac from 2005 to 2007 is noted on page 5. The Department of Housing and Urban Development's impact on Fannie Mae and Freddie Mac was described on pages A1 and A2 of the June 10, 2008 issue of the *Washington Post*, in an article titled "How HUD Mortgage Policy Fed the Crisis." The magnitude of the mortgage guarantees of Fannie Mae and Freddie Mac was reported on page 1 of the May 2005 *Financial Services Outlook*, published by the American Enterprise Institute. Information on the rankings of Gross Domestic Product by nation is from page 26 of the *Pocket World in Figures*, 2009 Edition, published by *The Economist*. Warnings of an impending decline in American home prices were issued on page 68 of the September 13, 2003 issue of *The Economist*, in an article titled "Hot Property." Concerns about the high costs of American homes and the risks to investors at large should those prices fall are from page 13 of the June 18, 2005 issue of *The Economist*, under the headline "After the Fall." The testimony of Treasury Secretary John W. Snow can be found on page 11 of *Hearing*

Before the Committee on Financial Services: U.S. House of Representatives, One Hundred Eighth Congress, first session, September 10, 2003 and also page 33 of *Hearing Before the Committee on Financial Services: U.S. House of Representatives*, One Hundred Ninth Congress, first session, April 13, 2005. The quote from Josh Rosner about the risks posed by pushing homeownership on people that were financially unqualified is from section 3, pages 1 and 9 of the October 3, 2004 issue of the *New York Times*, in an article titled "A Coming Nightmare of Homeownership?" Gregory Mankiw's warnings on the systemic risk posed by the implicit government guarantee of Fannie Mae and Freddie Mac are from page 110 of *Architects of Ruin* by Peter Schweizer. The statement that the housing market was "losing touch with reality" and concerns that a downturn in housing prices posed significant risks to the economy are from pages 92 and 93 of the September 20, 2004 issue of *Fortune*, in an article titled "Is the Housing Boom Over?" Concerns over massive defaults and costs to taxpayers if Fannie Mae and Freddie Mac were not reined in are from page 8 of the May 2005 *Financial Services Outlook*, published by the American Enterprise Institute. President George W. Bush's calls for millions more homeowners were quoted on page 10 of *Civil Rights and the Mortgage Crisis*. The criticisms of President George W. Bush's efforts to increase home ownership can be found on page 31 of the August 23, 2004 issue of *Barron's*, under the title "Nothing Down." The concerns expressed by the Chair of the Federal Deposit Insurance Corporation (FDIC) about problem loans and higher-risk loans are from page 13 of *Hearing Before the Committee on Banking, Housing, and Urban Affairs: United States Senate*, One Hundred Seventh Congress, first session, June 20, 2001. Federal Reserve Chairman Alan Greenspan's testimony about the housing market is quoted from pages 5 and 6 of *Hearing Before the Joint Economic Committee: Congress of the United States*, One Hundred Ninth Congress, first session, June 9, 2005. Greenspan's concerns about the risks posed by the growth of Fannie Mae and Freddie Mac were reported on pages 19 and 31 of *Hearing Before the Committee on Financial Services: U.S. House of Representatives*, One Hundred Ninth Congress, first session, February 17, 2005. His comment about turmoil in the financial markets is from page 1 of the September 17, 2007 issue of the *Financial Times* (London), in an article titled "Greenspan Alert on Homes," and his statements about the prevalence of subprime loans are from page B1 of the September 14, 2007 issue of *USA Today*, under the headline "Greenspan Slow to See Subprime Danger." Congressman Barney Frank's comments about the role played by Fannie Mae and Freddie Mac in creating affordable housing are from page 3 of *Hearing Before the Committee on Financial Services: U.S. House of Representatives*, One Hundred Eighth Congress, first session, September 10, 2003. His comments about subsidized housing are from pages 97 and 98 of *Hearing Before the Committee on Financial Services: U.S. House of Representatives*, One Hundred Eighth Congress, first session, September 25, 2003. Congressman Barney Frank's fears that concerns about the soundness of Fannie Mae and Freddie Mac might reduce affordable housing can be found on page 3 of *Hearing Before the Committee on Financial Services: U.S. House of Representatives*, One Hundred Eighth Congress, first session, September 10, 2003. His statements that there was no government bailout guaranteed if Fannie Mae and Freddie Mac failed are from the same page. Details on the costs of the bailout of Fannie Mae and Freddie Mac can be found on page A14 of the January 29, 2009 issue of the *Wall Street Journal*, under the headline "Fan and Fred's Lunch Tab," and also page 11 of *The Budget and Economic Outlook: Fiscal Years 2009 to 2019*, released by the Congressional Budget Office on January 8, 2009. Senator Christopher Dodd's comments on Fannie Mae and Freddie Mac are from page 454 of *Hearing Before the Committee on Banking, Housing, and Urban Affairs: United States Senate*, One Hundred Eighth Congress, first and second sessions, February 25, 2004. Senator Dodd's characterization of President Bush's calls for Fannie Mae and Freddie Mac to undergo reform as "ill-advised" is from pages C1 and C4 of the August 11, 2007 issue of the *New York Times*, under the headline "Fannie Mae's Offer to Help Ease Credit Squeeze Is Rejected, as Critics Complain of Opportunism." Senator Dodd's remarks from July 2008, that Fannie Mae and Freddie Mac were on "a sound footing" are from page S6594 of the July 11, 2008 *Congressional Record: Senate*. Details of the government takeover of Fannie Mae and Freddie Mac are from pages A1 and A15 of the September 8, 2008 issue of the *Wall Street Journal*, under the headline "U.S. Seizes Mortgage Giants." The remarks of Congresswoman Maxine Waters are from page 9 of *Hearing Before the Committee on Financial Services: U.S. House of Representatives*, One Hundred Eighth Congress, first session, September 25, 2003. Congressman Joe Baca's statement that debates on the regulation of Fannie Mae and Freddie Mac could restrict access to minority homeownership is from page 86 of *Hearing Before the Committee on Financial Services: U.S. House of Representatives*, One Hundred Eighth Congress, first session, September 10, 2003.

The letter from 76 House Democrats dated June 28, 2004, to President Bush urging his Administration to abandon its criticisms of the government-sponsored enterprises can be accessed from the web site of the House Committee on Financial Services at http://financialservices.house.gov/LtrBushGSEs.pdf. Testimony from the representative of the National Association of Homebuilders is from pages 83 and 84 of *Hearing Before the Committee on Financial Services: U.S. House of Representatives*, One Hundred Eighth Congress, first session, September 25, 2003. Testimony from an official of the National Urban League calling for increased affordable housing for minorities is from pages 90 and 91 of the same hearing. The testimony from the Director of Freddie Mac is from pages 42 and 44, while the comments of Fannie Mae's CEO Franklin Raines are from pages 45 and 46 of the same hearing. Details of the accounting irregularities uncovered at Fannie Mae in 2004 by the Office of Federal Housing Enterprise Oversight (OFHEO) and the subsequent investigation of OFHEO at the request of Republican Senator Kit Bond are from pages 13 and 14 of the September 27, 2004 issue of *Barron's*, under the title "Fannie Whacked"; pages E1 and E2 of the November 20, 2004 issue of the *Washington Post*, under the headline "Freddie Mac Problems Led to Tougher OFHEO"; and page C2 of the November 23, 2004 issue of the *New York Times*, in an article titled "Congress Urges Ouster of 2 Regulators." Congressman Frank's statement calling for a change of leadership at OFHEO was quoted on page E2 of the November 20, 2004 issue of the *Washington Post*, in the previously mentioned article "Freddie Mac Problems Led to Tougher OFHEO." The donations made to members of Congress by the employees and political action committees of Fannie Mae and Freddie Mac were reported on page A10 of a story beginning on the front page of the October 5, 2008 issue of the *St. Louis Post-Dispatch*, under the headline "Bond's Tough Talk on Fannie, Freddie Rings Hollow to Some." The statement by Rep. Chris Shays on the power and influence wielded by Fannie Mae was quoted on page A2 of the November 22, 2004 issue of the *Wall Street Journal*, in an article titled "Fannie, Freddie Regulator Is Split Over Moves to Toughen Oversight." The political protection enjoyed by Fannie Mae and Freddie Mac, including the limitations imposed on their regulator, the Office of Federal Housing Enterprise Oversight (OFHEO), and the less strict capital requirements placed on these government-sponsored enterprises were discussed on pages A1 and A12 of the September 14, 2008 issue of the *Washington Post*, under the headline "How

Washington Failed to Rein In Fannie, Freddie." Warnings about Fannie Mae and
Freddie Mac from Congressmen Jim Leach, Richard Baker and Christopher Shays
were mentioned on pages 108, 109 and 116 of *Architects of Ruin* by Peter Schweizer.
The favorable terms on loans that Senator Christopher Dodd received from
Countrywide Financial Corporation were mentioned on page A11 of the June 13,
2008 issue of the *Wall Street Journal*, under the title "Dodd Tied to Countrywide
Loans," and page A14 of the February 3, 2009 issue of the *Wall Street Journal*, under
the title "Dodd's Peek-A-Boo Disclosure." The relationship of Countrywide
Financial Corporation and politically well-connected individuals was mentioned on
page 99 of *Architects of Ruin* by Peter Schweizer. Senator Bob Bennett's ties to
Fannie Mae and Freddie Mac were reported in the Politics section of the September
12, 2008 issue of the *Salt Lake Tribune*, under the headline "Background on Big
Mortgage Takeover Targets." The statement that Fannie Mae and Freddie Mac
hired ex-politicians is from page 80 of the July 19, 2008 issue of *The Economist*, in
an article titled "A Brief Family History: Toxic Fudge." The many prominent
political figures from both parties appointed to lucrative positions at Fannie Mae
and Freddie Mac are mentioned on pages 106 and 114 of *Architects of Ruin* by Peter
Schweizer. The granting of $12 million of TARP funds to Boston's OneUnited
Bank after Congressman Barney Frank's intervention was reported on page A1 of
the January 22, 2009 issue of the *Wall Street Journal*, under the headline "Political
Interference Seen in Bank Bailout Decisions." Congresswoman Maxine Waters' ties
to OneUnited Bank were reported on the front page of the March 13, 2009 issue of
the *New York Times*, under the headline "A Representative, Her Ties and a Bank
Meeting." Congressman Barney Frank's intervention to prevent the closure of a
GM distribution center in his home state of Massachusetts was reported on page
A14 of the June 5, 2009 issue of the *Wall Street Journal*, under the title "Barney
Frank, Car Czar." Gerald P. O'Driscoll's comments on Fannie Mae and Freddie
Mac are from the September 9, 2008 issue of the *New York Post*, under the headline
"Fannie/Freddie Bailout Baloney."

CHAPTER 3: THE HOUSING BUST

The epigraph is from page 166 of *Architects of Ruin* by Peter Schweizer. Robert J. Samuelson's quote is from page 37 of the February 25, 2002 issue of *Newsweek*, under the headline "The Last Great Bull Market." Details on the Federal Reserve System and the rise in interest rates between 2004 to 2006 are from pages A1 and C8 of the June 30, 2006 issue of the *New York Times*, in an article titled "Fed Raises Rates, But Scales Back Talk of Inflation." The rise in mortgage interest rates following the increase of the Federal Reserve's interest rates was noted on page 35 of the Winter 2009 issue of the *University of Colorado Law Review*, in an article titled "The Law & Economics of Subprime Lending." That home prices declined for the first time in more than a decade in 2006 was reported on page D1 of the October 26, 2006 issue of the *Wall Street Journal*, under the headline "Home Prices Keep Sliding; Buyers Sit Tight." The high rates of foreclosure among counties in California in 2006 were reported on page C1 of the October 14, 2006 issue of the *San Francisco Chronicle*, under the headline "Foreclosure Activity Skyrockets in East Bay." The 87 percent increase in foreclosures filed nationally in June 2007, as well as the near tripling of foreclosures in the Bay Area were reported on pages C1 and C2 of the July 12, 2007 issue of the *San Francisco Chronicle*, in an article titled "Foreclosure Activity Rises Dramatically." The 800 percent increase in the number of California homes reverting to bank ownership in 2007 was reported on pages C1 and C2 of the July 25, 2007 issue of the *San Francisco Chronicle*, under the headline "Foreclosures Go Through the Roof." The $40,000 cost to banks to foreclose on a loan was reported on pages C1 and C6 of the March 31, 2007 issue of the *New York Times*, in an article titled "Lenders May Prove Adjustable." That half of all existing homes sold in the San Francisco Bay Area in December 2008 were homes that had been foreclosed was reported on the front page of the January 22, 2009 issue of the *San Francisco Chronicle*, under the headline "Foreclosures Fuel Home Sales Surge," while the near 47 percent decline in home prices in the Bay Area was reported on page A12 of the same article. The contrast between the boom and bust years in Phoenix, Arizona, was reported in a front-page story in the November 7, 2006 issue of the *New York Times*, under the headline "After Arizona's Housing Boom, 'For Sale' Is a Sign of the Times." The record-setting decline in the Standard & Poor's home-price index was reported on page A2 of the December 31, 2008 issue of the

Wall Street Journal, under the headline "Home Prices Declined at Record Pace in October." The steep declines in home prices in coastal California, as well as in Las Vegas, Miami, and Phoenix during 2008 were reported in a December 30, 2008 press release issued by Standard & Poor's titled "Home Price Declines Worsen as We Enter the Fourth Quarter of 2008 According to the S&P/Case-Shiller Home Price Indices." That California was home to 16 of the 25 metropolitan areas with the steepest home-price declines was reported on page A13 of a story beginning on the front page of the October 22, 2008 issue of the *Wall Street Journal*, under the headline "California Home Sales Revive, But Not Without Intense Pain." The $100,000 price decline in California homes from 2007 to 2008 was reported on page 63 of *State of the California Housing Market 2008–2009*, published by the California Association of Realtors. The dramatic home price increases in San Diego from 2000 to 2005 were reported on page 40 of the October 16, 2006 issue of *Newsweek*, under the headline "The Worrying Housing Bust," while the home price declines from 2006 to 2008 were reported on page C1 of the December 31, 2008 issue of the *San Diego Union-Tribune*, under the headline "Home Prices Down 26.7% from Year Ago." The extent of home price declines in the United States as measured by various indices was shown on pages 8 and 9 of *The State of the Nation's Housing 2008*, published by the Joint Center for Housing Studies of Harvard University in 2008. That there were great disparities in the severity of home price declines among different metropolitan areas was shown on page 8 of the same report. The low rate of decline of home prices in Dallas during the housing bust, and its affordability during the boom years, were reported on page A2 of the December 31, 2008 issue of the *Wall Street Journal*, under the headline "Home Prices Declined at Record Pace in October," and pages A1 and C9 of the December 29, 2005 issue of the *New York Times*, in an article titled "Twenty Years Later, Buying a House Is Less of a Bite." The quote from Alan Greenspan about "local bubbles" in housing markets in the United States is from a front-page story in the May 23, 2005 issue of the *Wall Street Journal*, under the headline "As Prices Rise, Homeowners Go Deep in Debt to Buy Real Estate." That 55 percent of borrowers who financed a home purchase with an option ARM owed more than the value of their home, and that 28 percent of such mortgages were delinquent or in foreclosure was reported on page C1 of the January 30, 2009 issue of the *Wall Street Journal*, in an article titled "Option ARMs See Rising Defaults." The decline in the proportion of 30-year fixed-rate mortgages to just one-third of all mortgages was reported on page 4 of the November 2008 *Financial Services Outlook*, published by the American Enterprise Institute. The high rate of delinquency among borrowers with adjustable-rate loans, interest-only loans, and payment-option loans was shown on page 19 of *The State of the Nation's Housing 2008*, published by the Joint Center for Housing Studies of Harvard University in 2008. Federal Reserve Board Chairman Ben Bernanke's testimony is from page 12 of *Hearing Before the Committee on Financial Services: U.S. House of Representatives*, One Hundred Tenth Congress, first session, September 20, 2007. The statement that minority homeowners took out a disproportionate share of subprime loans is from page C4 of the December 20, 2006 issue of the *New York Times*, under the headline "Study Predicts Foreclosure for 1 in 5 Subprime Loans." The high rate of foreclosures among minority homeowners during the housing bust was reported on page 15 of "Subprime Mortgages, Foreclosures, and Urban Neighborhoods," Working Paper 2009–1, published by the Federal Reserve Bank of Atlanta in February 2009; page A12 of the January 8, 2008 issue of the *New York Times*, under the headline "Baltimore Is Suing Bank Over Foreclosure Crisis"; page B3 of the May 4, 2008 issue of the *Orlando Sentinel*, in an article titled "Foreclosure Crisis Hits Hard in Black Communities"; pages A1 and A10 of the January 5, 2009 issue of the *Wall Street Journal*, in a story titled "Housing Push for Hispanics Spawns Wave of Foreclosures"; page A1 of the November 4, 2007 issue of the *Atlanta Journal-Constitution*, under the title "Black Atlantans Frequently Snared by Subprime Loans"; and page B1 of the April 26, 2007 issue of *USA Today*, under the headline "In 2005, Half of Minorities Purchased Their Homes with Subprime Loans." The high number of foreclosed properties owned by speculators in the San Francisco Bay Area, Las Vegas, Arizona, and Florida was reported on pages A1 and A10 of the December 16, 2007 issue of the *San Francisco Chronicle*, in an article titled "Foreclosures: How Megaflipping Flopped." The remarks of Holman Jenkins are from page A15 of the February 18, 2009 issue of the *Wall Street Journal*, under the headline "How Democracy Ruined the Bailout." The fact that five states— California, Florida, Arizona, Nevada and Illinois— accounted for nearly 60 percent of foreclosures in the first quarter of 2009 was reported on page B1 in an article titled "Foreclosures Take a Big Jump" in the April 16, 2009 issue of *USA Today*. The German bank that had to be bailed out by regulators due to losses on U.S. subprime mortgages was mentioned on page A18 of the October

31, 2007 issue of the *Wall Street Journal* in a news story that began on the front page under the headline "Bernanke, In First Crisis, Rewrites Fed Playbook." The impact of the subprime crisis on Wall Street was discussed on page 52 of the Winter 2009 issue of the *University of Colorado Law Review*, in an article titled "The Law & Economics of Subprime Lending." The more than five-fold increase in the value of subprime mortgages from 1995 to 2003 was shown on page 20 of the same article. The stability of the mortgage credit market in the early years of the twenty-first century was noted on page 154 of *Financial Shock*, by Mark Zandi. The foreclosure rates of subprime mortgages from 2005 to 2008 are shown on page 64 of *Civil Rights and the Mortgage Crisis*, published by the U.S. Commission on Civil Rights in September 2009. Collateralized debt obligations were described on page 39 of an article titled "Triple-A Failure" in the April 27, 2008 issue of *New York Times Magazine*. The statement that the purchase of mortgage-backed securities was "a leap in the dark" is from page 13 of a special report (with its own separate page numbers) titled "Greed— and Fear" within the January 24, 2009 issue of *The Economist*. The decision by Moody's to revise its model for evaluating subprime mortgages is quoted from page 41 of an article titled "Triple-A Failure" in the April 27, 2008 issue of *New York Times Magazine*. The process of gaining the highest rating for mortgage-backed securities by "shopping" them to the three major rating agencies was mentioned on page 54 of the Winter 2009 issue of the *University of Colorado Law Review*, in an article titled "The Law & Economics of Subprime Lending." The quote from Professor Stanley Liebowitz is from page 24 of the February 2009 issue of *The American Spectator*, under the headline "The True Origins of This Financial Crisis." The increase in the ratio of homes sold in California costing less than half a million dollars from 2007 to 2008 was reported on page 4 of *State of the California Housing Market 2008–2009*, published by the California Association of Realtors. The amount of a down payment as a percentage of the sales price of California homes in 2006 compared with 2008 was reported on page 14 of the same report. The decline of zero down payment mortgages in California from 2007 to 2008 was reported on page 15 of the same report. The declining share of interest-only adjustable rate mortgages in California from 2007 to 2008 was shown on page 16 of the same report. That fixed-rate mortgages rose from 55 percent of all mortgages in California in 2005 to more than 90 percent of the state's mortgages in 2008 was shown on page 61 of the same report. The dramatic decrease in the share of first-time California home buyers resorting to second mortgages to finance a home purchase from 2006 to 2008 was shown on page 18 of that same report. The steep drop in the share of adjustable rate mortgages nationally from 2004 to 2007 is from page 161 of the *Financial Services Fact Book, 2009*, published by the Insurance Information Institute. The dramatic decline in the value of subprime mortgages from 2006 to 2007 is shown on page 19 of the report *The State of the Nation's Housing 2008*, published by the Joint Center for Housing Studies of Harvard University in 2008. The declining use of subprime mortgages by various American racial and ethnic groups after 2006 is shown on page 61 of *Civil Rights and the Mortgage Crisis*. The increased selectivity of lenders and mortgage insurers in the wake of the housing bust is discussed on pages B1 and B5 of the January 24, 2009 issue of the *New York Times*, under the title "Costs and Tighter Rules Thwart Refinancings." That half of all banks tightened lending standards on prime mortgages in 2009 was discussed on page A4 of a story beginning on the front page of the May 5, 2009 issue of the *New York Times*, under the headline "Where Housing Crashed Early, Glimmers of Recovery Emerge." The fact that in May 2009, the personal saving rate rose to 6.9 percent, its highest level since December 1993, was noted on page B7 of the June 27, 2009 issue of the *New York Times*, in an article titled "As Incomes Rebound, Savings Hits Highest Rate in 15 Years." That holders of subprime mortgage bonds in Atlanta began dumping foreclosed homes on the market in 2009 was discussed on page C1 of the July 9, 2009 issue of the *Wall Street Journal*, under the headline "Subprime Resurfaces as Housing-Market Woe." The fact that these foreclosed homes were selling for a fraction of the value of their original loan amount is from the same page. The high volume of mortgage loans insured by the Federal Housing Administration (FHA) and the high rate of delinquency of its loans were discussed on page A16 of the May 4, 2009 issue of the *Wall Street Journal*, under the title "The Next Housing Bust." The near doubling of the FHA's loan ceiling in 2008 to $719,000, its low down payment requirements, and other risks in its underwriting standards were described on the same page. Continuing government pressures on banks to continue to make risky loans to meet the requirements of the Community Reinvestment Act, even after the financial crisis, are mentioned on pages 172 and 173 of *Architects of Ruin* by Peter Schweizer. Accusations by members of the Senate Banking Committee of greed on Wall Street, and their criticisms of lax regulatory oversight were reported on page A24 of the September 24, 2008 issue of the *New York Times*, under the headline "In a Crisis, Senatorial Rhetoric Bursts Forth." The hearing before the House Financial Services Committee in which leaders of the country's largest banks were "hectored" by lawmakers was reported on page C1 of the February 12, 2009 issue of the *Los Angeles Times*, in an article titled "Economic Crisis: Lawmakers Give Banks a Scolding." Senator Christopher Dodd's criticism of the Bush Administration is quoted from page A15 of the September 12, 2008 issue of the *Washington Post*, under the headline "Where Was Sen. Dodd?" Senator Dodd's remarks about Alan Greenspan can be found on page 124 of the September 17, 2007 issue of *Fortune*, in an article titled "Oh, the People You'll Blame!" Senator Christopher Dodd's favorable comments about Fannie Mae and Freddie Mac are from his opening statement from the February 7, 2008 hearing "Reforming the Regulation of the Government Sponsored Enterprises." (Senator Dodd's remarks as prepared were released in a press release by the U.S. Senate Banking Committee.) Republican Senator Robert Bennett of Utah likewise depicted Fannie Mae and Freddie Mac as enterprises that "emerge as the heroes because they're the only ones with money left." Senator Bennett's remarks are from page 3 of the Washington section of the March 7, 2008 issue of the *American Banker*, under the title "GSE Reform Hearing Turns to Broader Debate Over Bailout." Details on the costs of the bailout of Fannie Mae and Freddie Mac can be found on page A14 of the January 29, 2009 issue of the *Wall Street Journal*, under the title "Fan and Fred's Lunch Tab." Data on the costs of the bailouts of Bank of America, Citigroup, J.P. Morgan Chase, and Wells Fargo are from pages 78 and 79 of the February 16, 2009 issue of *Fortune*, in an article titled "The World According to TARP." Senator Christopher Dodd's statements that Fannie Mae and Freddie Mac were "fundamentally strong" are quoted from page A10 of the July 12–13, 2008 issue of the *Wall Street Journal*, under the headline "Fannie Mae Ugly." The editorial critical of Senator Christopher Dodd appears on page A12 of the July 21, 2008 issue of the *Wall Street Journal*, under the title "Fannie and Freddie's Enablers." Congressman Barney Frank's claim that the subprime crisis resulted from too little regulation is from page 11 of the August 20, 2007 issue of the *Financial Times* of London, under the title "A (Sub)Prime Argument for More Regulation." Congressman Frank's statements that bad decisions in the private sector and a conservative philosophy are what led to the financial crisis are from page D9 of the September 28, 2008 issue of the *Boston*

Globe, under the title "Frank's Fingerprints Are All Over the Financial Fiasco." Congressman Frank's further statements that excessive deregulation caused the financial crisis can be found on page A17 of the July 11, 2008 issue of the *Washington Post*, under the title "Capitalism's Reality Check," and page A11 of the September 14, 2007 issue of the *Boston Globe*, under the title "Lessons of the Subprime Crisis." Senator Charles Schumer's statement that deregulation led to the financial crisis is from page S8991 of the September 18, 2008 *Congressional Record: Senate*. The exchange between Maria Bartiromo and Congressman Barney Frank is from page 20 of the December 22, 2008 issue of *BusinessWeek*, under the title "Facetime: Barney Frank on Detroit, Housing, and Executive Pay." Congressman Barney Frank's assertion that he opposed giving mortgages to unqualified borrowers was quoted from his op-ed statement, "Is There an Antidote to the Republican Amnesia?" posted to the Huffington Post on March 18, 2009. The remark from Congressman Barney Frank's letter to the heads of Fannie Mae and Freddie Mac criticizing the companies' lending standards to condominium buyers as "too onerous" is quoted from an editorial titled "Barney the Underwriter" on page A14 of the June 24, 2009 issue of the *Wall Street Journal*. Senator Kit Bond's comments are from page S8970 of the September 18, 2008 *Congressional Record: Senate*. The newspaper account detailing Senator Kit Bond's past efforts to obstruct the OFHEO can be found on the front page of the October 5, 2008 issue of the *St. Louis Post-Dispatch*, under the headline "Bond's Tough Talk on Fannie, Freddie Rings Hollow to Some." Senator Barbara Boxer's statement about judges modifying the loans on principal residences is from page S2259 of the April 1, 2008 *Congressional Record: Senate*. The legislation introduced by Congressman John Conyers and Senator Richard Durbin which would allow bankruptcy judges to modify home mortgages is mentioned on page A13 of the February 13, 2009 issue of the *Wall Street Journal*, under the title "Don't Let Judges Tear Up Mortgage Contracts." Senator Harry Reid's remarks about amending the Bankruptcy Code to allow judges to modify mortgage terms are from page S1218 of the February 27, 2008 *Congressional Record: Senate*. Republican Senator Mitch McConnell's proposal of granting "government-backed, 4% fixed mortgages" to credit-worthy borrowers, and Professor Edward Glaeser's criticisms of that proposal are from page A13 of the February 5, 2009 issue of the *Wall Street Journal*, under the title "The GOP Has a Dumb Mortgage Idea." Senator Christopher Dodd's discussions of foreclosure mitigation can be found on pages S1812, S1815, S1816, and S1831 of the February 6, 2009 *Congressional Record: Senate*. Senator Christopher Dodd's proposed legislation to improve the regulation of Fannie Mae and Freddie Mac and encourage more funding for affordable housing is from page A2 of the May 13, 2008 issue of the *Washington Post*, in an article titled "Senate Talks Collapse on a Housing Bill." Congressman Barney Frank's housing-rescue proposal is discussed on page 8 of the May 2008 issue of *Mortgage Banking*, in an article titled "Congress, Administration Each Propose FHA Mortgage Relief." That 43 percent of modified loans were again delinquent within eight months was reported on page 32 of the February 21, 2009 issue of *The Economist*, under the title "Can't Pay or Won't Pay?" The information about the various government programs to increase homeownership rates in the United States since 1922, and the increased rates of foreclosures that followed those government interventions, is from pages 15 to 18 of an article titled "Obsessive Housing Disorder" in the Spring 2009 issue of *City Journal*. That there were 30 state examiners to watch over thousands of consumer finance companies in California, and that as a result mortgage companies were inspected only about once every four years, is from pages 154 and 155 of *Financial Shock* by Mark Zandi. The political pressures imposed on these regulators were mentioned on page 155 of the same book. Federal Reserve Chairman Alan Greenspan's comments about the level of bank capital/asset ratios in the era before the Civil War are quoted from page 6 of an article titled "Harnessing Market Discipline" in the September 2001 issue of *The Region*, published by the Federal Reserve Bank of Minneapolis. Information on the $700 billion economic bailout package (TARP) signed by President Bush in 2008 can be found on pages A1 and A12 of the October 4, 2008 issue of the *New York Times*, under the headline "Bush Signs Bill," while information on the $787 billion stimulus package signed by President Obama in 2009 is from page A11 of the February 14, 2009 issue of the *New York Times*, in an article titled "A Smaller, Faster Stimulus Plan, but Still with a Lot of Money." Data on the costs of the bailouts of J.P. Morgan Chase, Wells Fargo, AIG, Bank of America, and Citigroup are from pages 78 and 79 of the February 16, 2009 issue of *Fortune*, in an article titled "The World According to TARP." Adam Smith's remarks on the misapplication of money set aside by government for a particular purpose can be found on page 873 of his *The Wealth of Nations*, Modern Library edition. David Ricardo's remarks on the same subject are from page 248 of Volume I and pages 194 and 195 of Volume IV of *The Works and Correspondence of David Ricardo*, edited by Piero Sraffa and published by Cambridge University Press. The Congressional Budget Office's estimate that the federal deficit would reach $1.4 trillion in 2009 is from page A4 of the October 8, 2009 issue of the *Wall Street Journal*, in a news story titled "Deficit Complicates Push on Jobs," and the CBO's estimate that the deficit would continue to run at over a trillion dollars a year as late as 2019 is from page 33 of the June 13, 2009 issue of *The Economist*, under the headline "Seeing Red." Data on the share of the American national debt that is foreign owned are from pages 240 and 241 of *Analytical Perspectives, Budget of the United States Government, Fiscal Year 2009*, published in 2008 by the U.S. Government Printing Office. The drop in business spending on equipment and software in the last quarter of 2008 was reported on page A10 of the January 31, 2009 issue of the *Wall Street Journal*, under the title "A Capital Strike." The fact that distressed-debt deals in 2009 were taking place at nearly double the rate of 2008 is from a front-page story titled "Distressed Takeovers Soar," from the August 11, 2009 issue of the *Wall Street Journal*. That banks were reluctant to lend money to borrowers after the Bush administration's bailout was noted on page B5 of the January 27, 2009 issue of the *New York Times*, from an article beginning on page B1 titled "Something to Fear, After All." The fact that banks which had received funding from the Troubled Asset Relief Program (TARP) were lending 23 percent less in new loans in February 2009 compared to the previous October when the TARP was launched was reported on page A1 of the April 20, 2009 issue of the *Wall Street Journal*, under the headline "Bank Lending Keeps Dropping." The fact that bank lending in the United States declined in 2009 from $7.14 trillion in May to $6.78 trillion in September is from page 83 of the October 17, 2009 issue of *The Economist*, in an article titled "Slim Pickings, No Appetite." The historic fall in monetary velocity is reported on page A10 of the January 31, 2009 issue of the *Wall Street Journal*, under the title "A Capital Strike." The continued decline of jobs in the private sector, the less than 1 percent increase in jobs in state and local governments, and a view of the performance of jobs in the public and private sectors during recessions over the past 40 years were shown in a graphic on page A15 of the August 20, 2009 issue of the *New York Times*, under the headline "Government Jobs Have Grown Since Recession's Start, Study Finds." The 247,000 jobs lost in July 2009— down from a peak of 741,000 jobs lost in January 2009— were reported on the front page of the August 8, 2009 issue of the *New York Times*, in an article titled "Job Losses Slow, Signaling Momentum for a Recovery." The fact that the unemployment rate reached 9.7 percent in August 2009 and 25.5 percent among teenagers was reported on page A1 of the September 5–6, 2009 issue of the *Wall Street Journal*, under the headline "Job Losses Weigh on Recovery." The comment that job losses "continued to moderate from their worst numbers of the year" was quoted from a front-page story titled "Unemployment Hits 9.7% Despite Slower Job Losses," from the September 5, 2009 issue of the *New York Times*. The fact that the unemployment rate in October 2009 exceeded 10 percent for the first time in more than a quarter of a century was reported on the front page of the *Wall Street Journal* of November 7–8, 2009, under the headline "Grim Milestone as Jobless Rate Tops 10%." The decline in February 2009 of the Dow Jones Industrial Average to one-half of where it had been 16 months earlier was reported on page A1 of the February 24, 2009 issue of the *Wall Street Journal*, under the headline "Stocks Drop to 50% of Peak." The fact that business investment fell 38 percent in the first quarter of 2009 was reported on page A14 of the April 30, 2009 issue of the *Wall Street Journal*, under the headline "Better Bad News." The fact that the stock markets of Asian nations such as Indonesia, China, Singapore, and South Korea experienced greater percentage increases than the United States in the first half of 2009 was reported on page 70 of the August 15, 2009 issue of *The Economist*, in an article titled "On the Rebound." The growth in industrial production in Asian nations in the second quarter of 2009, at a time when industrial production was falling in the United States, was noted on page 69 of the same article. The growth in GDP in France and Germany in the second quarter of 2009, and the continued decline in GDP in the United States were reported on the front page of the August 14, 2009 issue of the *Wall Street Journal*, under the headline "Europe Recovers as U.S. Lags." That the economies of Europe and Asia were experiencing recovery while consumer spending in the United States fell, and the caution by Federal Reserve officials that economic activity in the United States would remain "weak for a time" were reported on the same page. The fact that industrial production in the United States increased by one-half of one percent in July 2009 was reported on page A2 of the August 15–16, 2009 issue of the *Wall Street Journal*, in an article titled "Industrial Output Climbs, While Prices Stay Steady." Discussion of the lack of clarity of the TARP legislation was from pages 28 and 29 of *Getting Off Track*, by John B. Taylor.

President Obama's remarks leading up to Treasury Secretary Geithner's presentation of the Administration's bank stabilization plan are from the President's February 9, 2009 press conference. The lack of details in Treasury Secretary Geithner's plan was noted on page B8 of the February 11, 2009 issue of the *St. Louis Post-Dispatch*, under the headline "Son of TARP." The critical remarks from the *New York Times* are from page A26 of the February 11, 2009 issue, under the title "The Bailout's Next Chapter." Other critical assessments of Treasury Secretary Geithner's presentation can be found on page A17 of the February 13, 2009 issue of the *Washington Post*, under the title "Treasury's Salesman-in-Training," and also page D1 of the February 11, 2009 issue of the *Washington Post*, in an article titled "Geithner Plan Lacks Freshness and Clarity." The estimate by the Congressional Budget Office that it would be September 2010 before 74 percent of the stimulus funds were spent was reported on page A11 of the February 14, 2009 issue of the *New York Times*, under the headline "A Smaller, Faster Stimulus Plan, but Still with a Lot of Money." The comments from *The Economist* magazine about the stimulus plan are from page 13 of the February 14, 2009 issue, under the title "The Obama Rescue." The fact that, as of May 29, 2009, only 6 percent of the funds of the $787 billion stimulus package had been spent was reported on page A1 of the June 9, 2009 issue of the *Los Angeles Times*, under the headline "Obama Faces Stimulus Doubts." That only a little more than 10 percent of the stimulus funds had been spent by August 2009 was reported on page A12 of the August 8–9, 2009 issue of the *Wall Street Journal*, under the title "A Jobs Bottom." The statement by then President-elect Obama about "shovel-ready projects" was reported on page 11 of an article titled "Don't Know Much About Economics" in the January 5–12, 2009 issue of the *Weekly Standard*. The slow rate of stimulus spending on infrastructure was reported on page A2 of the August 5, 2009 issue of the *Wall Street Journal*, under the headline "Stimulus Slow to Flow to Infrastructure."

CHAPTER 4: HOUSING MYSTIQUES AND HOUSING MISTAKES

The epigraph is from page 594 of "Considerations on Representative Government" in *The Collected Works of John Stuart Mill*, Vol. XIX, published by the University of Toronto Press. The need for more affordable housing in the United

States was stated on page 12 of the July 2002 issue of the *National Real Estate Investor*, in an article titled "Need for Affordable Housing Is Rising." The benefits of decent and affordable housing were described on page 1 of *Meeting Our Nation's Housing Challenges*, a report by the Bipartisan Millennial Housing Commission published in 2002. Jacob Riis' descriptions of the tenements of New York's Lower East Side as "nurseries of crime" are from pages 3 and 5 of his *How the Other Half Lives*, Harvard University Press edition. The fact that many of those living in tenements that were to be closed down had to be forcibly removed by the police was noted on page 14. Jacob Riis' observation that some people "carry their slums with them wherever they go" is from page 21 of the same book. That many middle-class blacks are opposed to housing voucher programs was noted on pages 84 to 91 of the Autumn 2000 issue of *City Journal*, under the title "Let's End Housing Vouchers." The Boston neighborhood described as "the worst slum in the city," but which also had low rates of delinquency, disease, and infant mortality was discussed on page 10 of *The Death and Life of Great American Cities* by Jane Jacobs. President George W. Bush's statements about encouraging home ownership are from a front-page story in the December 21, 2008 issue of the *New York Times*, under the headline "White House Philosophy Stoked Mortgage Bonfire." Criticisms of studies that claimed discrimination in lending can be found in Chapter 15 of *Backfire: A Reporter's Look at Affirmative Action*, written by Bob Zelnick, and pages 178 to 183 of my *Economic Facts and Fallacies*. See also a study titled "The Role of Race in Mortgage Lending: Revisiting the Boston Fed Study," a Working Paper published in December 1996 by the Division of Research and Statistics, Federal Reserve Board of Governors; "Mortgage Lending, Race, and Model Specification," *Journal of Financial Services Research*, February 1997, pages 43 to 68; "A Study That Deserves No Credit," on page A14 of the September 1, 1993 issue of the *Wall Street Journal*; page 13 of the Mortgage section of the August 19, 1993 issue of *The American Banker*, under the title "Boston Fed's Bias Study Was Deeply Flawed"; "Mortgage Lending to Minorities: Where's the Bias?" *Economic Inquiry*, January 1998, pages 3 to 28; and "The Community Reinvestment Act: Looking for Discrimination That Isn't There," *Policy Analysis*, No. 354, October 6, 1999, published by the Cato Institute. Approval rates for black and white borrowers seeking government-backed, conventional, and refinancing loans can be found on pages 870 and 871 of the November 1991 issue of the *Federal Reserve Bulletin*, in an article titled "Home

Mortgage Disclosure Act: Expanded Data on Residential Lending." The limitations of the data in the Federal Reserve System's mortgage study are described on page 859 of the same article. Newspaper editorials claiming discrimination in lending based on the findings of the Federal Reserve's study can be found on page A12 of the October 23, 1991 issue of *USA Today*, under the title "Discrimination and Loans," and also page C2 of the October 25, 1991 issue of the *St. Louis Post-Dispatch*, under the title "Racial Gap Persists in Mortgage Lending." News accounts claiming discrimination in mortgage lending include a front-page story from the March 31, 1992 issue of the *Wall Street Journal*, under the headline "Behind the Figures: Federal Data Detail Pervasive Racial Gap In Mortgage Lending," and also a story from page D1 of the October 22, 1991 issue of the *New York Times*, under the title "Racial Gap Detailed on Mortgages." That income was the only financial characteristic of loan applicants in the Federal Reserve's study was noted on page 867 of the November 1991 issue of the *Federal Reserve Bulletin*, in an article titled "Home Mortgage Disclosure Act: Expanded Data on Residential Lending," while the factors that lenders must evaluate in considering a loan applicant's ability to repay a loan are discussed on page 875. Data on disparities in net worth between blacks and whites in the highest income quintile are shown on page 14 of "Net Worth and the Assets of Households: 2002," *Current Population Reports*, P70–115, published by the U.S. Census Bureau in April 2008. The differences between blacks and whites in inherited wealth are reported on page 1334 of the March 2002 issue of the *American Journal of Sociology*, under the title "Lifetime Inheritances of Three Generations of Whites and Blacks." The comparison of the net worths of white and minority mortgage loan applicants in Boston is from page 8 of the January 1998 issue of *Economic Inquiry*, in an article titled "Mortgage Lending to Minorities: Where's the Bias?" That whites were denied conventional mortgage loans more often than Asian Americans was shown on page 870 of the November 1991 issue of the *Federal Reserve Bulletin*, under the title "Home Mortgage Disclosure Act: Expanded Data on Residential Lending"; on page 808 of the November 1992 issue of the *Federal Reserve Bulletin*, under the title "Expanded HMDA Data on Residential Lending: One Year Later"; and on page 53 of *Civil Rights and the Mortgage Crisis*, published by the U.S. Commission on Civil Rights in September 2009. Data on conventional mortgage loan denial rates for whites and various minorities are reported on page 53 of *Civil Rights and the Mortgage Crisis*. Data showing that white borrowers resorted to subprime loans more often than Asian American borrowers are from page 61 of *Civil Rights and the Mortgage Crisis*; page 379 of the Summer 2005 issue of the *Federal Reserve Bulletin*, under the title "New Information Reported under HMDA and Its Application in Fair Lending Enforcement"; and also page 5 of the November 2007 - Brief #2 published by the Joint Center for Political and Economic Studies under the title "African Americans and Homeownership: The Subprime Lending Experience, 1995 to 2007." The higher credit scores of Asian Americans compared to whites were reported on page 80 of a report by the Board of Governors of the Federal Reserve System titled *Report to the Congress on Credit Scoring and Its Effects on the Availability and Affordability of Credit*, submitted to the Congress pursuant to section 215 of the Fair and Accurate Credit Transactions Act of 2003, published in August 2007. The frequency with which blacks, whites, Hispanics, and Asians resorted to subprime loans in the metro Atlanta area was reported on page A12 of the November 6, 2007 issue of the *Atlanta Journal-Constitution*, under the title "Answers to Credit Woes Are Not In Black and White." Comparisons of credit ratings between whites with lower incomes and blacks with higher incomes are from the front page of the September 21, 1999 issue of the *Washington Post*, under the headline "Racial Disparity Found in Credit Rating." The fact that black-owned banks reject black mortgage loan applicants at a higher rate than white-owned banks do is from an article in the February 1997 issue of the *Journal of Financial Services Research*, titled "Do Black-Owned Banks Discriminate Against Black Borrowers?" The news story comparing the frequency with which black and white borrowers used subprime loans is from page A2 of the April 11, 2005 issue of the *Washington Post*, in an article titled "Disparities Found in Sub-Prime Lending." The conclusions of the 2002 study that included credit history among its variables in studying mortgage default can be found on page 18 of "New Evidence on the Relationship Between Race and Mortgage Default: The Importance of Credit History Data," prepared by Unicon Research Corporation and published on May 23, 2002. That many factors considered in credit underwriting and pricing are absent from HMDA data was noted on page A158 of the September 2006 issue of the *Federal Reserve Bulletin*, in an article titled "Higher-Priced Home Lending and the 2005 HMDA Data." The greater incidence of higher priced loans among black and Hispanic borrowers as compared to whites, and data showing that Asian Americans were the group who resorted to such loans least of all appeared on page A159 of the same article. The findings of the study of mortgage lending in Boston can be found on page 2 of "Mortgage Lending in Boston: Interpreting HMDA Data," Working Paper No. 92–7, October 1992, published by the Federal Reserve Bank of Boston. News stories claiming discrimination in lending following the release of the Boston Fed's study can be found on page 1 of the Economy section of the October 9, 1992 issue of the *Boston Globe*, in an article titled "Study Shows Racial Bias in Lending," and also page A3 of the October 9, 1992 issue of the *Wall Street Journal*, under the title "Boston Fed Finds Racial Discrimination in Mortgage Lending Is Still Widespread." The *BusinessWeek* article that declared the Boston Federal Reserve Bank's study "definitive" was on page 78 of the October 26, 1992 issue, under the headline "There's No 'Whites Only' Sign, But…" The remarks by the head of the Federal Reserve Bank of Boston can be found on page 48 of the January 4, 1993 issue of *Forbes*, in an article titled "The Hidden Clue." The conclusion by the Federal Reserve in Washington that the claims of discrimination in the 1992 Boston Fed study were "difficult to justify" was stated on page 1 of the study "The Role of Race in Mortgage Lending: Revisiting the Boston Fed Study," a Working Paper published in December 1996 by the Division of Research and Statistics, Federal Reserve Board of Governors. The fact that blacks and Hispanics in Boston were more likely to buy lower-priced homes than whites at a time when banks were concerned about home prices declining especially sharply in such houses was reported on page 13 of the Mortgage section of the August 19, 1993 issue of *The American Banker*, under the title "Boston Fed's Bias Study Was Deeply Flawed." Nobel-Prizewinning economist Gary Becker's assessment of the Boston Federal Reserve study can be found on page 18 of the April 19, 1993 issue of *BusinessWeek*, under the title "The Evidence Against Banks Doesn't Prove Bias." Stan J. Liebowitz's criticisms of the 1992 Boston Federal Reserve Bank study are in an article titled "Anatomy of a Train Wreck" in the October 20, 2008 issue of *National Review*. The manual issued by the Boston Federal Reserve Bank, calling for less stringent lending standards, is cited on pages 293, 294 and 295 of an article titled "Anatomy of a Train Wreck: Causes of the Mortgage Meltdown" by Stan J. Liebowitz in *Housing America*, edited by Holcombe and Powell. Information on the sex discrimination case brought by the EEOC against Sears can be found on page 77 of the May 25, 1992 issue of *Forbes*, under the title "Spiral of Silence," and also

E.E.O.C. v. Sears, Roebuck & Co., 839 F.2d 302 at 360. The Justice Department's discrimination case against Decatur Federal Savings & Loan was discussed on page C18 of the September 18, 1992 issue of the *Wall Street Journal*, in an article titled "Decatur Federal Settles U.S. Charge of Racial Bias in Mortgage Lending." The Federal Reserve Board's refusal to grant permission to Shawmut National Corporation to acquire New Dartmouth Bank was reported in section 3, page 4 of the November 28, 1993 issue of the *New York Times*, in an article titled "Lending-Bias Rules Create Quandary for Banks." The $960,000 settlement paid by the mortgage subsidiary of Shawmut National Corporation, and the warnings issued by Attorney General Janet Reno to lenders are from page B7 of the December 14, 1993 issue of the *Washington Times*, in an article titled "Bank to Pay $960,000 in Loan-Bias Settlement." That the Federal Reserve withdrew its opposition to Shawmut's acquisition of the New Dartmouth Bank following Shawmut's near million dollar settlement with the Justice Department was reported on page A24 of the December 20, 1993 issue of the *Washington Times*, under the headline "How to Rob a Bank Legally," while the fact that no individual complaints were filed by minorities claiming they had been discriminated against was also noted in the same column. The Justice Department's settlement with Chevy Chase Federal Savings Bank requiring the bank to open new branches in minority neighborhoods was discussed on page D1 of the August 23, 1994 issue of the *New York Times*, under the title "Wider Attack on Loan Bias Seen in Accord with S.& L." Senator William Proxmire's definition of "redlining" is quoted from page 17630 of the *Congressional Record: Senate*, for June 6, 1977. Senator William Proxmire's suggestion that the level of a bank's investment in its local community be a determining factor in regulators' decisions to approve or disapprove that bank's expansion of its business was made in a speech recorded on page 17603 in the *Congressional Record: Senate*, for June 6, 1977. The Clinton administration's statements about breaking down "racial and ethnic barriers" to home ownership are quoted on page 9 of *Civil Rights and the Mortgage Crisis*, published by the U.S. Commission on Civil Rights in 2009. Gale Cincotta's claim that redlining causes urban decline was quoted on page 15 of the August 25, 1975 issue of the *Wall Street Journal*, in a front-page story titled "To Fight 'Redlining', Citizens Groups Turn To, Yes, 'Greenlining.'" That the FDIC considers a bank's CRA performance when assessing a bank's application for permission to have mergers and make other business decisions was reported on page

16 of *Civil Rights and the Mortgage Crisis*. The Federal Reserve's denial of a merger application on CRA grounds for the first time in 1989 was reported on page 11, note 20, of the same publication. Chicago banks' commitment of $173 million to causes designated by community organizing groups was reported on page B11 of the May 5, 1986 issue of the *New York Times*, in an article titled "Local Pressure Bringing More Lending in Inner Cities." Information on the millions of dollars that Jesse Jackson's organizations have received from financial institutions over the years can be found on pages A1 and A11 of the March 27, 2001 issue of the *Washington Post*, in an article titled "Jackson's Fundraising Methods Spur Questions"; page A16 of the July 29, 2008 issue of the *Wall Street Journal*, under the title "Fannie Mae's Political Immunity"; pages 20 and 21 of the May 27, 2002 issue of *Insight*, in an article titled "Freddie Mac, Verizon Made Jesse's Hit List"; and page 14 of *Architects of Ruin* by Peter Schweizer. Congressman Barney Frank's defense of community activists who challenge banks on their lending standards is from page H11541 of the November 4, 1999 *Congressional Record: House*. The favorable view of community activist organizations presented by the Joint Center for Housing Studies at Harvard University is quoted from page 134 of "The 25th Anniversary of the Community Reinvestment Act: Access to Capital in an Evolving Financial Services System," published in March 2002. Gale Cincotta's statement— "We want it. They've got it. Let's go get it."— was quoted from her obituary on page B9 of the August 17, 2001 issue of the *New York Times*. Efforts by the group ACORN to compel banks to extend more loans to low- and moderate-income families under the Community Reinvestment Act are mentioned on page A22 of the October 25, 2008 issue of the *Los Angeles Times*, under the title "Don't Blame the Victims." Congressman Paul Broun's criticism of ACORN is from page H1018 of the February 4, 2009 *Congressional Record: House*. The harassment against bankers and the mayor of Baltimore by ACORN activists was described on page 52 of an article titled "ACORN's Nutty Regime for Cities" in the Spring 2003 issue of *City Journal*. The account of hundreds of protesters at Senator Phil Gramm's home is from page A24 of the April 19, 1999 issue of the *Wall Street Journal*, under the headline "Gramm Crusades to Overturn Community Lending Act." That community activist groups have used the Community Reinvestment Act to induce banks to make billions of dollars in loans and cash payments was reported on page A18 of the October 22, 1999 issue of the *Wall Street Journal*, in a column titled "A

Transparent Ploy to Hide a Liberal Racket." The fact that community activists have extracted over $1 trillion from banks and other financial institutions since 1977 was reported on page 125 of "The 25th Anniversary of the Community Reinvestment Act: Access to Capital in an Evolving Financial Services System," published in March 2002 by the Joint Center for Housing Studies at Harvard University. The empirical study by Professor George J. Benston that found little evidence of redlining was titled "The Community Reinvestment Act: Looking for Discrimination That Isn't There," *Policy Analysis*, No. 354, published by the Cato Institute. The statement by a community activist in Chicago that banks should make loans in all neighborhoods, even if some prove to be unprofitable, appeared on page 143 of the March 22, 1976 issue of *Business Week*, in an articled titled "The Law Closes in on Mortgage Discrimination." The quote by a banker about being pressured to make unsound loans appeared on page B3 of the May 12, 1975 issue of the *Washington Post*, in a column titled "Hemming, Hawing and Redlining," which began on page B1. Senator Jake Garn's concerns about the rights of depositors, in the wake of legislation to curb to redlining, were cited on page 32 of the September 5, 1975 issue of the *New York Times*, in an article titled "Senate Votes a 'Redlining' Curb Ordering Loan Data from Banks." Gale Cincotta's claim that owning a home is a "right" was quoted on the front page of the February 17, 1981 issue of the *Wall Street Journal*, under the headline "Costly Credit, Energy Viewed as Death Knell for Easy Homeowning." Senator Paul Sarbanes' statement that the Community Reinvestment Act would not require lenders to depart from safe and sound practices appeared on page 17633 of the June 6, 1977 *Congressional Record: Senate*. The *Washington Post* editorial about the role of prejudice in mortgage lending is from page A16 of the March 9, 1976 issue under the headline "'Redlining.'" Professor Richard A. Posner's claim that Fannie Mae and Freddie Mac engaged in risky business practices because they were private enterprises appeared on page 241 of his book *A Failure of Capitalism*. Professor Posner's statements that government inaction was what led to an economic crisis are from page 243 of the same book. The statement that "a philosophical distaste for regulation" contributed to the financial collapse is from page 18 of *Financial Shock* by Mark Zandi. Professor Posner's argument that neither the Community Reinvestment Act of 1977 nor subsequent legislation *required* banks to make risky loans is from pages 241 and 242 of his book *A Failure of Capitalism*. Assertions from officials of various bank regulators that the Community Reinvestment Act was not responsible for the mortgage crisis are from pages 29 to 31 of *Civil Rights and the Mortgage Crisis*, published by the U.S. Commission on Civil Rights in 2009. The new regulatory amendments to the Community Reinvestment Act, requiring banks to use "innovative or flexible" lending practices in order to meet their lending obligations under the Act, were discussed on page 368 of *Critical Review*, Vol. 21, Nos. 2 and 3 (2009), in an article titled "Cause and Effect: Government Policies and the Financial Crisis." The fact that a lender with a policy of not issuing mortgages on homes valued below $60,000 could be charged with discrimination was mentioned on page 6C of the March 9, 1994 issue of the *Arizona Daily Star*, in an article titled "U.S. Expands Lending Discrimination Definition." That loans made under the Community Reinvestment Act had been as profitable as non-CRA loans back in 1995 is from page 1507 of the May 1995 *University of Pennsylvania Law Review*, in an article titled "The Community Reinvestment Act Reconsidered." The statement that "Hardly a borrower in San Diego or Miami was even late with a payment" during the peak of the housing boom was made on page 154 of *Financial Shock* by Mark Zandi. The statement that "even a bad loan is a good loan" during a boom was quoted on page 38 of *Civil Rights and the Mortgage Crisis*, published by the U.S. Commission on Civil Rights in 2009. The widening gap between the foreclosure rates of prime and subprime loans after housing prices began to decline in 2006 is shown on page 64 of the same publication. Differences between Fannie Mae/Freddie Mac and competing private companies were described on pages 265 and 266 of *Housing America*, edited by Holcombe and Powell, in an article by Lawrence J. White titled "Fannie Mae, Freddie Mac, and Housing: Good Intentions Gone Awry." The fact that only three securities-rating firms were recognized by the Securities and Exchange Commission for purposes of certifying the investments made by financial institutions regulated by the SEC was noted on page 300 of the same book, in an article titled "Anatomy of a Train Wreck: Causes of the Mortgage Meltdown." The decline of the black population in San Francisco since 1970 was discussed on the front page of the April 9, 2007 issue of the *San Francisco Chronicle*, under the headline "S.F. Moves to Stem African American Exodus." Data on declining black population by at least 10,000 in each of four counties between the 1990 and the 2000 censuses are shown in the following Census publications: *1990 Census of Population: General Population Characteristics*

California, 1990 CP–1–6, Section 1 of 3, pages 27, 28, 30, and 31; *Profiles of General Demographic Characteristics 2000* (2000 Census of Population and Housing: California), Table DP–1, pages 2, 20, 39, and 42. The fact that between 2002 and 2006 San Francisco lost more than 16,000 households with incomes of less than $150,000, while at the same time the city gained more than 17,000 households with incomes of more than $150,000 is shown on the front page of the June 22, 2008 issue of the *San Francisco Chronicle*, in an article titled "Exodus of S.F.'s Middle Class." The decline in school enrollment in the city of Palo Alto during the 1970s and the subsequent closing of several schools in that community were reported on page 90 of a 1982 study by the Stanford Environmental Law Society titled *Land Use and Housing on the San Francisco Peninsula*, edited by Thomas M. Hagler. Details on land use restrictions in Monterey County, California, are from pages A1 and A6 of the August 26–27, 2006 issue of the *Wall Street Journal*, under the headline "In Tony Monterey County, Slums and a Land War." The statement that trees take up more than six times as much space as all of the urban communities in the United States is from page 57 of *The Road More Traveled* by Ted Balaker and Sam Staley. The additional $100,000 or more in costs added to the price of homes in communities with "smart-growth" policies was noted on page 2 of "The Planning Penalty: How Smart Growth Makes Housing Unaffordable," written by Randal O'Toole and published by the Independent Institute in 2006. The fact that homeownership rates in the United States rose from a two-decades'-long level of 64 percent to 69 percent in 2005 was noted on page 366 of an article titled "Cause and Effect: Government Policies and the Financial Crisis" in *Critical Review*, Vol. 21, combined numbers 2 and 3 (2009).

CHAPTER 5: THE PAST AND THE FUTURE

The epigraph is from page 129 of an article titled "A Crisis of Politics, Not Economics: Complexity, Ignorance, and Policy Failure" in *Critical Review*, Vol. 21, combined numbers 2 and 3 (2009). The quote "Bad ages to live through are good ages to learn from" is from page 5 of *The Hollow Years: France in the 1930s* by Eugen Weber. The claim that there was consensus on the causes of the financial crisis is from an editorial titled "That Promised Financial Reform," from page A26 of the

October 14, 2009 issue of the *New York Times*. Peter Schweizer's argument that it was government intervention which led to the financial crisis is from pages 167 and 168 of his book *Architects of Ruin*. The comment by Professor Richard A. Posner about the need for a more active and intelligent government is on page xii of his book *A Failure of Capitalism*. Data showing that in 2005 and 2006 more subprime mortgage loans were made to middle and upper income borrowers than to lower and moderate income borrowers are from page 71 of *Civil Rights and the Mortgage Crisis*, published by the U.S. Commission on Civil Rights in 2009. The fact that the dollar volume of subprime loans made to more affluent borrowers was nearly double that of less affluent borrowers is from page 72 of the same publication. The fact that other institutions purchased more subprime loans than Fannie Mae and Freddie Mac is shown on pages 102 and 103 of *Civil Rights and the Mortgage Crisis*. Professor Lawrence J. White's remarks about the protected status of Moody's, Fitch, and Standard & Poor's are from page 2 of the January 2005 *Financial Services Outlook*, published by the American Enterprise Institute. The proposition that regulators did not have evidence of potential problems in the housing market in 2005 was discussed on page 154 of *Financial Shock*, by Mark Zandi. The conclusion that the full extent of the housing market collapse cannot be determined until some time after the housing market bottoms out was on page 160 of an article titled "A Crisis of Politics, Not Economics: Complexity, Ignorance, and Policy Failure" in *Critical Review*, Vol. 21, combined numbers 2 and 3 (2009). Disagreements among experts as to the value of "toxic" assets, including Treasury secretary Timothy Geithner's claim that many banks believe their assets to be more valuable than they really are, were noted on pages 160 and 161 of the same article. Barney Frank's proposed legislation to further increase the FHA's loan limits was reported on page B6 of the November 20, 2009 issue of the *New York Times*, in an article titled "F.H.A. Extends Easy Loans to Wealthier Areas," which began on page A1. The fact that a 1.4 percent decline in home prices beginning in 2006 led to a wave of foreclosures was noted on page 23 of *Meltdown*, by Thomas E. Woods, Jr. The fact that about 23 percent of American homeowners owe more on their mortgages than their properties are worth was reported on the front page of the November 24, 2009 issue of the *Wall Street Journal*, under the headline "1 in 4 Borrowers Under Water." The fact that about 588,000 borrowers defaulted on their mortgages in 2008, even though they could afford the payments, was reported on the same page. The fact that nearly 30 percent of borrowers in Nevada owe 50 percent or more on their mortgage than the value of their home is mentioned on page A4 of the same article. Information on home price declines in Las Vegas and Dallas is from page B4 of a *New York Times* article that began on page B1 of the November 25, 2009 issue, under the title "An Upturn in Housing May Be Reversing." That lending money to home buyers had been a highly profitable and low risk endeavor for banks for nearly a century was stated on page 1 of *Financial Shock* by Mark Zandi. The comment from the official at Standard & Poor's about the historic stability of the mortgage market is quoted from page 171 of an article titled "A Crisis of Politics, Not Economics: Complexity, Ignorance, and Policy Failure" in *Critical Review*, Vol. 21, combined numbers 2 and 3 (2009). The billion dollar losses suffered by executives at Lehman Brothers and at Bear Stearns as a result of receiving compensation in the form of their banks' stock, which became devalued due to the banks' subprime investments, were noted on page 150 of that same article. The account of Lehman Brothers CEO Richard Fuld being "raked over the coals" in Congressional hearings is from page B6 of the July 31, 2009 issue of the *New York Times*, in a story beginning on page B1 under the headline "It May Be Outrageous, but Wall Street Pay Didn't Cause This Crisis." The angry e-mails that were sent to Moody's after it downgraded some of its ratings on subprime investment vehicles were discussed on page 136 of an article titled "A Crisis of Politics, Not Economics: Complexity, Ignorance, and Policy Failure" in the journal *Critical Review*, Vol. 21, combined numbers 2 and 3 (2009). Adam Smith's remarks about politicians can be found on page 435 of his *The Wealth of Nations*, Modern Library edition. The quote from the Soviet economists about the interconnected nature of prices is from page 172 of *The Turning Point*, by Nikolai Shmelev and Vladimir Popov. Hillary Clinton's calls for a tripling of the number of Section 8 housing vouchers and more public housing were reported on page B5 of the October 31, 2000 issue of the *New York Times*, under the title "Lazio Sought to Make a Legislative Mark in Housing." Senator Hillary Clinton's proposal to assist homeowners facing foreclosure was reported in an article from the August 18, 2007 *New York Times on the Web*, under the headline "Waking Up to the Real Estate Nightmare." That a higher share of homeowners than renters had housing costs exceeding 50 percent of household income in 2006 was shown on page 28 of *The State of the Nation's Housing 2008*, published by the Joint Center for Housing Studies of Harvard University in 2008. Information about policy changes by the Federal Housing Administration, including the raising of the FHA's loan limit and its increasing presence in the risky and high-cost California housing market, is from pages A1 and B6 of the November 20, 2009 issue of the *New York Times*, in an article titled "F.H.A. Extends Easy Loans to Wealthier Areas." The fact that more than 14 percent of FHA-insured loans were at least one month past due in the third quarter of 2009 was reported on page B6 of the November 20, 2009 issue of the *New York Times*, in an article beginning on page B1 with the headline "Mortgage Delinquencies Soar." The fact that one in four people with mortgages in Florida is behind in payments is from page B6 of the same article. The declining capital reserves of the FHA were reported on page A6 of the November 13, 2009 issue of the *Wall Street Journal*, under the headline "Housing Agency Reserves Fall Far Below Minimum." The decline in the FDIC's deposit-insurance fund was reported on page A2 of the September 30, 2009 issue of the *Wall Street Journal*, in an article titled "Bank-Bailout Fund Faces Years in Red as Failures Jolt System." The fact that the FDIC's deposit-insurance fund had fallen to below one-fifth of its statutory minimum is from page 89 of the September 26, 2009 issue of *The Economist*, in an article titled "Fiscal Iceberg." The fact that the FDIC in 2009 planned to raise $45 billion by requiring banks to prepay their deposit premiums through 2012 was reported on page A2 of the September 30, 2009 issue of the *Wall Street Journal*, in an article titled "Bank-Bailout Fund Faces Years in Red as Failures Jolt System," and also on page 8 of the Business section of the November 13, 2009 issue of the *Boston Globe*, in an article titled "Banks to Prepay $45B for Insurance Fees." That a disproportionate share of the banks that failed during the Great Depression of the 1930s were in states with laws against branch banking was noted on pages 31, 55, and 58 of *FDR's Folly*, written by Jim Powell, while the statement that about 90 percent of these unit banks failed during the Great Depression can be found on the same pages. The fact that Canada experienced no bank failures during the Great Depression is from page 352 of *A Monetary History of the United States: 1867–1960*, written by Milton Friedman and Anna Jacobson Schwartz. Information about the differences between banks in Canada and the United States is from page A17 of the May 7, 2009 issue of the *Wall Street Journal*, under the headline "Regulation Didn't Save Canada's Banks." The decline in GDP for the first quarter of 2009 in the United States is noted on page B3 of the May 30, 2009 issue of the *New York Times*, in an article titled "Revising Report, U.S. Says 1st Quarter Was

Not So Bad." The share of income required by American families to cover mortgage costs during the early 1980s, 1998 and 2005 was reported on page A1 of the December 29, 2005 issue of the *New York Times*, under the headline "Twenty Years Later, Buying a House Is Less of a Bite." That roughly 60 percent of first-time home buyers in Tucson relied on 100 percent financing to purchase a home in 2005 was reported on page D2 of the December 22, 2005 issue of the *Wall Street Journal*, in an article beginning on page D1 under the headline "Housing Affordability Hits 14-Year Low." The Republican proposal of granting "government-backed, 4% fixed mortgages" to credit-worthy borrowers was mentioned on page A13 of the February 5, 2009 issue of the *Wall Street Journal*, under the headline "The GOP Has a Dumb Mortgage Idea." Congressman Barney Frank's reference to Franklin D. Roosevelt is quoted from page A3 of the October 15, 2008 issue of the *Wall Street Journal*, in an article titled "Democrats Mull $300 Billion Stimulus." The claim that the New Deal "wasn't stimulative enough" is from the front page of the February 11, 2009 issue of the *Los Angeles Times*, under the headline "A Time for Boldness Beyond the New Deal." Data showing that the annual unemployment rate exceeded 20 percent in the United States from 1932 through 1935 is shown on page 126 of Part 1 of *Historical Statistics of the United States: Colonial Times to 1970*, a publication of the U.S. Bureau of the Census published in 1975. Ways in which Franklin D. Roosevelt's New Deal policies were a further extension of the approach used by his predecessor, Herbert Hoover, are discussed on pages 148 and 149 of *The Forgotten Man*, written by Amity Shlaes and in Chapter 3 of *FDR's Folly* by Jim Powell. Walter Lippmann's remark that Roosevelt's New Deal was a "continuous evolution" of Hoover's measures is from page 757 of *A History of the American People*, written by Paul Johnson. President Hoover's recognition that his interventions in the economy were unprecedented is from page 29 of *The Memoirs of Herbert Hoover: The Great Depression, 1929–1941*. Data on page 77 of *Out of Work* by Richard Vedder and Lowell Gallaway show that the unemployment rate never fell below 20 percent during the first 21 months of FDR's administration. Walter Lippmann's comments about how maintaining pre-depression prices and wages during a depression leads to unsold goods and unemployed workers are quoted from page 92 of *FDR's Folly*, by Jim Powell. Information about unemployment rates in the wake of the October 1929 stock market crash and after the signing of the Smoot-Hawley tariffs are from page 77 of *Out of Work* by Richard Vedder and Lowell Gallaway. That FDR issued more executive orders during his administration than the combined total of all of his twentieth-century successors was reported on page xiii of *FDR's Folly* by Jim Powell. The concerns expressed by John Maynard Keynes about some of the New Deal reforms can be found on page xiv of the same book. That business investment remained low throughout the Great Depression is from page 161 of the same book. The statement that lending by banks during the 1930s was at about half the level of the 1920s is from page B5 of the January 27, 2009 issue of the *New York Times*, from an article beginning on page B1 under the headline "Something to Fear, After All." The fact that the unemployment rate never fell below the double-digit level for any year during FDR's first two terms in office is shown on page 77 of *Out of Work* by Richard Vedder and Lowell Gallaway. The study which concluded that the New Deal policies prevented a normal recovery in the economy and prolonged the Great Depression was published in the August 2004 issue of the *Journal of Political Economy*, in an article titled "New Deal Policies and the Persistence of the Great Depression: A General Equilibrium Analysis." Unemployment rates in the United States for the years 1937, 1940, 1941, 1942, and 1943 to 1945 are shown on page 126 of Part 1 of *Historical Statistics of the United States: Colonial Times to 1970*, a publication of the U.S. Bureau of the Census published in 1975. The federal deficit for the years 1936 and 1940 can be found on page 1105 of Part 2 of the same publication. FDR's discussion of "Dr. New Deal" and "Dr. Win-the-War" can be found on pages 569 to 571 of *The Public Papers and Addresses of Franklin D. Roosevelt: 1943 Volume*, published by Harper & Brothers. The fact that FDR enlisted the leadership of individuals from the business and financial sectors when mobilizing the United States for World War II is discussed on pages 22, 23, and 24 of *Depression, War, and Cold War: Challenging the Myths of Conflict and Prosperity* by Robert Higgs. The decline in the velocity of the circulation of money during the Great Depression was discussed on pages 301 to 303 of *A Monetary History of the United States: 1867–1960* by Milton Friedman and Anna Jacobson Schwartz. Media criticisms of President Ronald Reagan for not intervening in the economy in the aftermath of the stock market crash of October 1987 can be found on page A35 of the October 22, 1987 issue of the *New York Times*, under the headline "Abroad at Home: It's Morning Again"; on page A2 of the October 29, 1987 issue of the *Washington Post*, in an article titled "Fiddling While Wall St. Burns"; and section 4, page 27 of the November 22, 1987 issue of the *New York Times*, in a column titled

"Abroad at Home: Nobody at Home." The comments on 20 years of prosperity after 1987 from *The Economist* magazine are from page 35 of the September 22, 2007 issue, in an article titled "The Turning Point." The downturn in the economy during the 1920s that was left to recover on its own is mentioned on page 745 of the essay "Banking and Finance in the Twentieth Century," written by Eugene N. White and published in *The Cambridge Economic History of the United States, Volume 3: The Twentieth Century*, edited by Stanley L. Engerman and Robert E. Gallman. The comments from J.A. Schumpeter on non-intervention in an economy during a downturn are from page 110 of his essay "Depressions: Can We Learn from Past Experience?" in *Essays of J.A. Schumpeter*, edited by Richard V. Clemence. Karl Marx's remark about "crackbrained meddling by the authorities" is from his letter to Friedrich Engels dated February 3, 1851 and reprinted on page 275 of Volume 38 of their *Collected Works* in the edition published in Moscow in 1982. The advertisement signed by hundreds of economists in January 2009 stating that increased government spending had not succeeded in pulling the United States out of the Great Depression and would not succeed in alleviating the current economic crisis appeared on page A11 of the January 28, 2009 issue of the *New York Times*, under the headline, "With all due respect Mr. President, that is not true." The comments of Alan Reynolds about the severity of recessions after the creation of the Federal Reserve appeared on page A13 of the August 21, 2009 issue of the *Wall Street Journal*, under the headline "Big Government, Big Recession." Walter Lippmann's comments about the goals of the New Deal were quoted on page xv of *FDR's Folly* by Jim Powell. That many of the decision makers of the New Deal administration were advocates of government intervention and in favor of restructuring the economy, even before the stock market crash of 1929 and the Great Depression, is discussed on pages 3, 10, and 15 of *FDR's Folly* by Jim Powell, and also pages 53 to 56 and 64 to 69 of *The Forgotten Man* by Amity Shlaes. Professor Alan Blinder's comments on the stimulus bill of 2009 are from page A13 of the February 4, 2009 issue of the *Wall Street Journal*, under the headline "My Economic Wish List." The fact that the Obama administration's pay czar increased the base salaries of some of the employees under his review is from page C1 of the October 28, 2009 issue of the *Wall Street Journal*, in an article titled "Pay Czar Increased Base Pay at Firms." Rahm Emanuel's remarks about crisis as an opportunity not to be "wasted" were quoted on page 25 of the February 1, 2009 issue of *New York Times Magazine*, in an article titled "The Big Fix." The growing demands placed on banks receiving government bailout money were described on the front page of the March 11, 2009 issue of the *New York Times*, under the headline "Some Banks, Feeling Chained, Want to Return Bailout Money." The statement that most economists believe the current recession will end before much of the stimulus spending takes hold is quoted from page A17 of the September 1, 2009 issue of the *Wall Street Journal*, under the title "What Happened to the 'Depression'?" Paul Johnson's quote can be found on page 138 of *The Quotable Paul Johnson* edited by George J. Marlin, et al.

INDEX

INDEX